WALKING THE LAND

Perspectives on Israel Studies

S. Ilan Troen, Natan Aridan, Donna Divine, David Ellenson,
Arieh Saposnik, and Jonathan Sarna, *editors*

Sponsored by the Ben-Gurion Research Institute for the Study of Israel and Zionism of the Ben-Gurion University of the Negev and the Schusterman Center for Israel Studies of Brandeis University

WALKING THE LAND

A HISTORY OF ISRAELI HIKING TRAILS

SHAY RABINEAU

INDIANA UNIVERSITY PRESS

This book is a publication of

Indiana University Press
Office of Scholarly Publishing
Herman B Wells Library 350
1320 East 10th Street
Bloomington, Indiana 47405 USA

iupress.org

Manufactured in the United States of America

First printing 2023

Library of Congress Cataloging-in-Publication Data

Names: Rabineau, Shay, author.
Title: Walking the land : a history of Israeli hiking trails / Shay Rabineau.
Description: Bloomington, Indiana : Indiana University Press, 2023. | Series: Perspectives on Israel studies | Includes bibliographical references and index.
Identifiers: LCCN 2022019722 (print) | LCCN 2022019723 (ebook) | ISBN 9780253064530 (hardback) | ISBN 9780253064547 (paperback) | ISBN 9780253064554 (ebook)
Subjects: LCSH: Trails—Israel—History. | Hiking—Israel—History.
Classification: LCC GV199.44.I75 R33 2023 (print) | LCC GV199.44.I75 (ebook) | DDC 796.51095694—dc23/eng/20220708
LC record available at https://lccn.loc.gov/2022019722
LC ebook record available at https://lccn.loc.gov/2022019723

CONTENTS

ACKNOWLEDGMENTS

ILAN TROEN AND MAOZ AZARYAHU helped me set the initial boundaries of this study and provided a great deal of assistance in the United States and Israel. Ruth Kark supported my postdoctoral research year in the Department of Geography at the Hebrew University of Jerusalem.

Other help came from the Israel Trails Committee; the Society for the Protection of Nature in Israel; the Israel Institute; the Palmach Museum; the Haganah Archive; the National Library of Israel; the Yad Tabenkin Archive; the Abraham Path Initiative; the Center for Israel Studies at Binghamton University; and my colleagues in the Center: Randy Friedman and Lior Libman.

Shai Yagel merits special mention as an invaluable field contact in Israel. As Coordinator of Waymarking for the Israel Trails Committee, he allowed me to observe the process of defining and blazing trails; later, as someone involved in every aspect of trail development in Israel, he provided important insights and practical help as I completed the book manuscript.

Julian Bender, who has walked thousands of miles of trails across Israel, Palestine, Jordan, and Sinai, made the maps for this book. I am grateful for his excellent work.

Many others provided material assistance, moral support, and intellectual input, and while some will inevitably be forgotten, here is at least a partial list: Allan Arkush, Aviv Ben-Or, Moti Ben-Shitrit, Greg Bercaw, Yoram Bilu, Franklin Bodine, Evan Bryant, Christa Case Bryant, Piers Burdekin, Noga Collins-Kreiner, Talia Ditkoff, Carmel Dvir-Edri and the whole Dvir family, Yossi Feldman (of blessed memory), Rachel Fish, Sylvia Fuks-Fried, Emir Galilee, Dany Gaspar, Randall Geller, Gili Greenbaum, Iris Han, Assaf Harel, Sara Hirschhorn, Ben Hoffler, Maoz Inon, Jonathan Karp, Michael Koplow, David Landis, Kanan Makiya, Anisa Mehdi, Arly Mintz, Mark Petrie, Chase Rabineau, Jehuda Reinharz, George Rishmawi, Adam Rosenfeld,

Ari Roth, Shai Rozen, Raed Saadeh, Jacob Saar, Jonathan Sarna, Martina Sedlakova, Avraham Shaked, Eugene Sheppard, Noam Stillman, Tzion Sheetrug, Heba Taha, Alon Tal, William Ury, Josh Weiss, and Yael Zerubavel.

Finally, I'm grateful to my wife and children, who moved to Jerusalem with me for two separate yearlong stints and infused our experiences there with excitement and wonder. This book is dedicated to Amanda, Ariella, Talia, Lev, and Jedidiah.

NOTE ON TRANSLITERATION, TRANSLATION, AND LANGUAGE USE

WHEN USING HEBREW AND ARABIC terms, this book uses generally accepted rules of transliteration. Rather than use complex diacritical marks that make little sense to most readers, this book uses standard combinations of English letters to represent certain Hebrew and Arabic sounds; for example, "ch," as in the name of the composer Bach, is used for the Hebrew letter *chet*. The careful reader, however, will notice that transliteration methods are not always consistent. Words, phrases, and names that are commonly written differently follow alternate schemes. The word *halutzim*, which means "pioneers" in Hebrew, appears frequently in this book and begins with the letter *chet* but is spelled here with an H, in the same way that the holiday of *Chanukah* is often rendered in English as "Hanukkah." Incidentally, in this book, the holiday happens to take the latter spelling as well. Such exceptions abound. Mea culpa.

Hebrew-language sources are listed as such in the bibliography. Translations are mine unless otherwise noted. Throughout the text of this book, I leave certain frequently used terms untranslated, or I use the transliterated Hebrew terms interchangeably with English terms. Examples of this include *simun shvilim*, which literally means "marking of trails" but technically corresponds with what trail developers describe as "waymarking" and yet, in the end, has its own specific connotations when used in Israel. When I write "waymarking," I refer to common practices of marking trails in Israel and elsewhere. When I write *simun shvilim*, or translate it as "Israeli waymarking," I refer specifically to the larger Israeli waymarking project, bearing in mind the ways it diverges from European waymarking.

"Land of Israel" is a term I use interchangeably throughout the book with the Hebrew term *Eretz Israel*. As noted in the book, it simply means "land of Israel," but it carries a mythological and metahistorical weight in Hebrew that necessitates capitalization in English. "Land of Israel," or "the Land," is used to signal the existential meaning with which Jewish Israelis burden such terms. When land in Israel is discussed simply as a space or a commodity, "land" is not capitalized.

WALKING THE LAND

Introduction

Israeli Hiking Trails and Their Spatial, National, and Existential Dimensions

Beginnings

On the morning of November 22, 1947, as Jewish leaders in Tel Aviv and Jerusalem discussed the impending United Nations (UN) vote on the partition of Palestine, a group of young men and women began walking across the rocky plains near the Dead Sea. They were scouts from the Palmach, the strike force of the underground Haganah militia, and they were on a clandestine assignment approved by the organization's highest leadership. Their destination loomed ahead, lit by the rising sun and silhouetted against the southwestern sky: a headland called Ras Feshkha, which lay deep inside territory where the ruling British had forbidden Jews from traveling and which the UN Partition Plan had designated as part of a future Arab state. Upon reaching a narrow footpath at the base of the mountain, the scouts unloaded their gear and prepared to climb.

Many of them had ascended the Ras Feshkha path before. It was part of the route to Masada, the mountain fortress where, in ancient times, Jewish rebels had been besieged by the Roman army, and that, in modern times, had become a Zionist civil-religious pilgrimage destination. Over the previous several years, the Palmach had sent its recruits to places like Masada in order to physically condition them, deepen their camaraderie, and increase their knowledge of the country they saw as the Jewish homeland. On many of those treks, undercover as hikers, Palmach fighters had evaded British policemen, fought Bedouin Arabs, and trained with illegal weapons in remote valleys and isolated canyons. But Ras Feshkha, with its sheer cliffs, was a danger to everyone who walked along the Dead Sea shore. The narrow footpath the Palmach scouts were climbing was the only safe path that ascended the headland. It was also the objective of their mission.

Armed not with guns and grenades, but with paintbrushes, ladders, compasses, and paint, the Palmach scouts began transforming the hard-to-follow footpath into a marked hiking trail. Using the ladders, they placed red-and-white markings high on boulders and cliff faces, where erasure would be nearly impossible. Using the compasses, they recorded the location of each blaze before moving to the next and so made their way up the mountain, creating a chain of striped markings from the bottom to the top. By the time they were done, they had created a three-kilometer trail: one small section of what they envisioned as a much longer trail that would ensure Jewish access to Masada, regardless of the outcome of the partition plan. The marked route was not just a trail but a claim on territory. It was the first marked hiking trail in the Middle East and the prototype for all of the Israeli hiking trails that would follow.

Today, Israel has one of the most extensive and highly developed hiking trail systems of any country in the world. More than ten thousand kilometers of trails, marked with hundreds of thousands of colored blazes, crisscross Israeli-controlled territory, from the country's farthest borders to its densest metropolitan areas. The thousand-kilometer Israel National Trail crosses the country from north to south. Millions of hikers use the trails every year during holiday breaks, on mandatory school trips, and for recreational hikes. Hiking, trails, and the ubiquitous three-striped trail blazes appear everywhere in Israeli popular culture; they are the subjects of news articles, radio programs, television shows, best-selling novels, government debates, and even national security speeches. Yet the trail system is almost completely unknown to the millions of foreign tourists who visit every year.

***

This book is a history of Israel's hiking trails that explores the origins and development of the only countrywide trail system in the Middle East. Why was hiking, in particular, such an important activity for early Zionists, before the establishment of the State of Israel? What forces and influences led to the creation of Israel's trail network? Which parts of Israel were first covered by marked trails, and who marked them? Why did the trail system grow so quickly? How does the act of painting marks on the ground, and recording trails on printed maps, relate to conflicts over territory between Israel, the Palestinians, and neighboring Arab states? Through an exploration of archival and print sources rarely explored by scholars of modern Israel, along with a series of in-person interviews with the people who built the trail network and field visits to the places where Israeli trails first took root, this book seeks to answer all of the above questions.

***

My scholarly journey into the history of Israeli trails began in 2006 when I decided to embark on a thru-hike of Shvil Israel, or the "Israel National Trail." By then, I had traveled extensively in Israel and had gained working proficiency in modern Hebrew. Once I knew about the trail, I found that no information was available in English, save for a few obscure online trail journals that offered some basic details. When I ordered a Hebrew-language guidebook for the trail and specified a shipping address in the United States, I received an email from someone at the publishing company, checking to see whether I had made a mistake. When I confirmed that I had indeed ordered the book on purpose, the bemused staffer replied, "Not many outsiders are interested in hiking in our little country."

When I began hiking the Israel National Trail, along with my brother and a friend from our hometown in Indiana, I encountered a combination of parochialism and pride. In every small-town grocery store and every bus stop, people saw our backpacks and our trail-worn appearance and assumed that we must be local hikers. Almost invariably, when they found out we were Americans, and non-Jewish to boot, they would ask us what we were doing on the Israel National Trail. When we told them that hiking across Israel was a world-class experience in terms of both scenery and history, they were amazed to think that their "little trail" might be on par with routes like the Appalachian Trail or the Camino de Santiago. But then they would usually ask the real question: "But why are *you* interested in hiking this trail?" It seemed to us that ultimately, most Israelis saw the act of exploring the country as a way of exploring themselves. They could not fathom what any non-Israeli might gain from a long journey on foot across Israel.

I learned a great deal from the full month I spent on Shvil Israel. I developed a better sense of the country's terrain and topography, along with a keen understanding of the difficulties of long-distance walking in the Middle East. I met Israelis, Palestinians, Jews, Arabs, backpackers, soldiers,

Map 0.1. Israel's hiking trail network.

yeshiva students, farmers, shepherds, and university professors. I saw the best and worst the country had to offer, from its national parks and nature reserves to its industrial sites and garbage dumps. I experienced moments that shattered the narrow world of the trail and its thru-hiking culture and which brought me back to the region's conflicts. One night, I sat around a campfire with Bedouins, eating dinner and listening to the World Cup, while in the distance, artillery shells pounded Gaza in response to the kidnapping of the IDF soldier Gilad Shalit. I learned that the trail was no place to escape politics: people often asked whether I thought the "national trail" was too right-wing or left-wing in the way it showcased the country. I didn't know enough yet to have an opinion, but my interlocutors happily offered theirs.

I returned home with questions of my own. How had Israel developed such a vibrant culture of hiking? How had it created such an enormous trail system, unique to its part of the world, and had never told visitors about it? And why—as someone who had just spent thirty days shouldering a heavy pack, sweating in the sun, ascending mountains, eating fruits from orchards, drinking water from springs, sleeping on soccer fields, being cut by stones and scratched by thorns, laughing around dinner with fellow backpackers, hitchhiking on desert highways, navigating with Hebrew maps, and becoming fluent in the ways of a foreign hiking culture—did I still feel that I was an outsider who had hardly begun to understand what Israeli trails were all about?

Two years after that first hike, I went back to Israel and trekked more than two hundred kilometers across the southern Negev from Mitzpe Ramon to Eilat, using GPS to record the most difficult section of the Israel National Trail, with the goal of creating an English-language map and data book. Later that year, I entered a doctoral program in the Department of Near Eastern and Judaic Studies at Brandeis University and shifted my focus to the academic study of modern Israel. Once there, surrounded by scholars of Jewish history and Zionist thought, I did not believe hiking trails could be a viable dissertation topic. As I got into my coursework and began thinking about collective memory, civil religion, and sacred space, I realized that all of these ideas were alive on Israeli trails. Trails, however, lay in a blind spot for most academics: for the Israelis who were personally familiar with them, they seemed too commonplace to view through a scholarly lens; for the non-Israeli scholars who might have found them interesting, trails in Israel remained essentially invisible.

When I first presented the outlines of a research project on hiking trails to a group of Israel Studies professors and graduate students, I wondered how the topic would be received. Maoz Azaryahu, a cultural geographer from the University of Haifa, was a visiting professor at Brandeis that semester and had encouraged me to pursue the project. Most others were familiar with the literature that had helped me begin laying some foundations, such as Yael Zerubavel's book *Recovered Roots*, in which hikes to sites like Masada are described as playing important roles in the formation of Israeli identity. Few in attendance, however, were familiar with the trails themselves or knew how a historian might study the origins and development of a countrywide trail system. Part of my presentation showcased a body of Hebrew-language literature that I had only begun to explore: the newsletters and magazines of nature enthusiasts who seemed fanatical about studying the country and knowing its every corner. At the forefront of these enthusiasts were the people who marked trails. For them, hiking in Israel seemed to be the ultimate expression of what it meant to be Israeli.

At the end of my talk, one of my professors raised his hand and said that the topic reminded him of a lyric from an old Israeli hiking song. Someone else remembered it, and the two of them began singing in Hebrew. As they continued, others remembered the song and joined in. The singing increased in volume, and people started tapping on the table to keep time, and before long, the question-and-answer session had been taken over by a Hebrew hiking singalong, in which academics across the political spectrum exuberantly participated. As I watched in complete surprise, not knowing what to do, another professor leaned over and shouted into my ear, "I think you're onto something."

In 2011, my family and I moved to Israel, and I began my dissertation research. Maoz Azaryahu helped me navigate Israeli archives and set up meetings with figures who had been instrumental in the project of marking and mapping the country's trails. In dusty offices and dimly lit living rooms, people like Yossi Feldman and Tzion Sheetrug (both discussed in detail later in this book) recounted stories of their exploits as young men just before and just after Israeli statehood. Through them, and through the articles and maps they had published over the decades, I began reconstructing the processes by which Israeli hikers scouted trails, marked trails, and mapped trails, so that larger numbers could go and hike trails. As I visited libraries and archives around the country, I gained a more complete picture of the culture of hiking that had preceded the creation of the trail system, and which eventually came to thrive upon it. Perhaps most importantly, I visited the places described in this book. I climbed alone up Ras Feshkha;

I descended the moonlit cliffs above Qumran; I slept under the stars in remote reaches of the Negev. Perhaps others could write honestly about the trails without doing such things, but I could not.

After defending the dissertation at Brandeis in 2013, I returned to Israel for the 2014–2015 academic year to take a postdoctoral position at the Hebrew University of Jerusalem. During that time, I also worked as a consultant for the Harvard-based Abraham Path Initiative, where I organized the research component of a World Bank trail-development grant, advised Palestinian waymarking projects in the West Bank, and helped scout the route of the Sinai Trail in Egypt. While this book builds on my dissertation work, then, it is also deeply informed by my subsequent research and real-world experiences: my engagement with Hebrew University faculty and students, my work alongside Palestinian educators and environmentalists, and my contact with the growing world of Middle East hiking and waymarking.

Meanwhile, a number of scholars have begun producing excellent material on Israeli hiking trails, particularly the Israel National Trail. Nesia Shafran's work on trails preceded mine; her excellent Hebrew-language book *The Red Rock: The Forbidden Treks to Petra* was published in 2013.[1] Noga Collins-Kreiner, who researches tourism and pilgrimage at the University of Haifa, has published articles on the reasons why people hike the Israel National Trail.[2] Tamar Hermann, a sociologist at the Open University, wrote a Hebrew-language book in 2019 entitled *Walking the Israel National Trail*, which examines the trail and its meaning in Israeli society.[3] Other scholars from an array of disciplines have delivered important papers and presentations on Israeli trails at academic conferences around the world. The dissertation I wrote at Brandeis has been cited in many of the above works; in publishing this book, I hope to offer a firmer historical foundation for further research.

A chapter-by-chapter summary of the material in this book is unnecessary; the table of contents will suffice. Instead, the rest of this introduction highlights some key ideas that are important for understanding how Israel's trail network developed over time. All trails take shape according to the contours of physical terrain, and much of the story in this book has to do with the spatial expansion of the trail network and the tools with which that expansion took place. However, as I suspected when I first hiked the Israel National Trail, Israeli trails also navigate political landscapes and sometimes flow toward or away from sites along ideological contour lines. And as I noticed during my first presentation at Brandeis, trails have existential meaning for

Israelis as well and have as much to do with the exploration of personal and national identity as they do with the exploration of beautiful places. Three threads, then—spatial, political, and existential—form the braided cord of this book's overall narrative. Here, each will be briefly examined in turn.

The Spatial Dimensions of Israeli Hiking Trails

In 2015, one of Israel's best-known hikers, a spry eighty-four-year-old named Shuka Ravek, was fined by the Nature Reserves Authority for his refusal to walk on marked trails in a protected area in the Judean Desert. After refusing to pay the fine as an act of civil disobedience, he was summoned to court. There, Ravek declared that in the 1940s, by exploring the Negev Desert in defiance of British law, the scouts of the Jewish Palmach paramilitary forces had made it possible for Israel to conquer that territory. He argued that he had not caused environmental damage and that he was being treated like a criminal for carrying on a venerated Israeli tradition. Many from Israel's hiking community agreed.[4]

The very fact that Ravek was well-known as a legendary hiker, and that his fight for the right to depart from marked trails was picked up by several media outlets, says a great deal about the place of hiking in Israeli popular culture. In his courtroom declaration, Ravek tapped into political and existential ideas that lie close to the heart of Israeli hiking, and even to the heart of what it means to be a Jewish Israeli. Later sections of this introduction will further explore those ideas. First, however, this section will examine the project that Ravek struggled against. What exactly is Israeli waymarking, and why do hikers like Ravek find it so confining?

Waymarking is the ancient and universal human practice of marking trails, and it takes many forms, from blazes of chipped tree bark in forests to stone cairns on grasslands and tundras. Modern waymarking, which originated in Europe in the late nineteenth century, is the act of systematically marking trails, usually through the placement of signs or symbols alongside a walking route. Israeli waymarking, or *simun shvilim*, which simply means "marking of trails," has been adapted to suit Israel's climate and terrain. The simun shvilim project is managed by the Israel Trails Committee (ITC), a group made up of representatives of numerous government and private organizations operating under the auspices of Israel's largest and most prominent environmental non-profit organization, the Society for the Protection of Nature in Israel (SPNI).[5] Fieldwork is conducted year-round by a small crew

Figure 0.1. Waymarking crew member with his equipment. *Photograph by author.*

of young men and women who carry their waymarking tools along the trails and renew the entire network on a three-year cycle. (See fig. 0.1.)[6]

Aside from the experimental trail marked by the Palmach on the eve of war in 1947, the first marked and mapped routes were established between 1960 and 1963 at Ein Gedi, then a remote desert outpost on the Dead Sea, facing the Jordanian-annexed West Bank. Between 1963 and 1967, a new network took shape in the Eilat Mountains at Israel's extreme southern tip, between the armistice lines with Egypt and Jordan. After Israel conquered the West Bank from Jordan in June 1967, the Ein Gedi network extended northward toward Jericho and was completed along with a new map in December of the same year. In 1973, work began on a new network in the Golan Heights, which Israel had conquered in 1967 from Syria. These networks covered most of the frontier areas where Israelis wanted to hike, and where marked trails would make them safer. After that, simun shvilim was directed at Israel's settled center, generally starting near SPNI-operated nature education schools and radiating outward. Eventually, the networks merged to form a countrywide system. Starting in the late 1980s, the border-to-border Shvil Israel, or Israel National Trail, took shape atop the existing network; it was inaugurated in 1995 by Israel's president and quickly became regarded as the crown jewel of Israeli hiking trails.

Most of Israel's hiking trails were found, not built. Simun shvilim generally involves marking and mapping existing paths and thereby dedicating them as hiking trails without making many physical improvements. Most of the trails existed as unmarked footpaths, made or maintained by Palestine's Arab population long before the modern immigration of Jews in the late nineteenth and early twentieth centuries. Some of the trails were ancient in origin, such as desert trails that were themselves archaeological relics: their switchbacks and retaining walls dated back as far as the Israelite and Roman periods.[7] As the network grew, more modern routes were brought into the network: some trails followed gravel vehicle roads, city sidewalks, and even the shoulders of paved highways. Unpaved footpaths were the priority, but through simun shvilim, almost any walkable surface could become a hiking trail.

Painted symbols, or blazes, make up the majority of Israel's trail markings. (See fig. 0.2.) At least one hundred thousand such markings are estimated to exist along the trails.[8] They measure fifteen centimeters in width by twenty centimeters in height and are composed of three vertical stripes: the outer two bars are white, and the central bar is red, black, green, or blue.

Figure 0.2. Israeli waymark, Ras Feshkha, 2012. *Photograph by author.*

Trails of the same color are never supposed to intersect. Specially colored blazes are used to mark longer super-trails that lie atop the network, including the Israel National Trail, marked in orange, blue, and white. Specially shaped blazes denote changes in direction, and blazes with no colored bar in the center—known as "transparent blazes"—indicate short side trails to nearby sites of interest. Specially shaped blazes are used to alert hikers of changes in direction and intersections with other trails.[9]

Blazes are placed according to a detailed system of rules, which were initially taken from early twentieth-century European waymarking schemes and further modified after Israeli statehood to suit the country's climate and terrain. In the ensuing decades, the rules for waymarking have hardly changed. Blazes are painted onto permanent and semi-permanent features of the landscape, including natural elements like rocks and trees, as well as built elements like walls and utility poles. They are visible in both directions of travel along a given trail. They appear more frequently in areas with short lines of sight—like forests and boulder-strewn canyons—and less frequently along trails with long lines of sight whose routes are highly visible. Some signage occurs at some well-frequented trail junctions to prevent groups from getting lost.

Marking trails on the ground represents only one-half of the simun shvilim project; the other half involves marking trails on topographical maps. In cooperation with the Survey of Israel and the SPNI, the ITC publishes a series of twenty high-resolution, waterproof 1:50,000-scale maps that are sold in bookstores and hiking equipment shops throughout the country. The maps show the entire trail network and offer an enormous amount of additional information, including contour lines for every ten meters of elevation; boundaries of nature reserves, restricted military areas, and minefields; and shadings indicating built-up areas, swamps, forests, and so on. The backs of the maps show details of certain areas of interest like cities, archaeological sites, and short day hikes, as well as drawings that enable hikers to identify birds, plants, animals, and animal tracks.

What renders the maps particularly useful for hikers, and designates them as simun shvilim maps, is the way they depict trails. The harmony between marked trails and topographical maps allows hikers in Israel to determine their exact locations in the field, even without smartphones or GPS, and to see trails depicted on maps in the same colors as their markings on the ground. (See fig. 0.3.) Whenever waymarking crews adjust the route of a trail on the ground, changes are recorded using GPS, and the new data is sent to the Survey of Israel to be included on the next edition of the corresponding

Figure 0.3. Israeli simun shvilim map. *Photograph by author.*

simun shvilim map. Even when hikers opt to use only smartphones rather than hard-copy maps, the electronic map layers depicting the trails are typically built from data gathered by the ITC waymarking teams.

The ITC and its waymarking crew work hard to maintain the unity of the physical trail system and its depiction in maps. When field waymarking personnel discover "pirate trails" whose blazes match the type used by the ITC, but which were placed without the committee's knowledge or permission, they use hammers to break the unauthorized blazes from the rocks on which they are painted.

The spread of simun shvilim across Israeli-controlled territory, and the lengths to which the ITC has gone to maintain its monopoly on trails, has led critics like Ravek to assert that Israeli waymarking is out of control. Others have argued that simun shvilim has blighted the landscape, destroyed the mystique of hiking, and placed the whole country under the shadow of an unwieldy Borgesian map.[10] In 1993, Menachem Marcus, a veteran Israeli hiker and geographer, asserted in an opinion article that the project of marking and mapping Israel's trails was megalomaniacal and that the whole country had fallen victim to "a cult of waymarking."[11]

Such criticisms did not stop the main architect of Israel's trail network, Ori Dvir, from proudly declaring in 2001 that Israel had become "the most waymarked country in the world."[12] Dvir was proud to state that proportionate to country size, Israel's trail network was more extensive than those of European countries that had been marking trails for more than a century. Modern waymarking had originated in Bohemia during the late nineteenth century and had spread quickly into Germany and across Europe in the early twentieth century.[13] Because of the European provenance of most early Zionist immigrants, Israel inherited many central European hiking traditions and waymarking methods.

In truth, Dvir was mistaken; Israel has the seventh most extensive trail network in the world, in terms of kilometers of trails per square kilometer of land area.[14] However, other factors render Israel's trail network distinctive when placed alongside others. Israel's network is uniformly marked from border to border; that is, a single system of blazes covers the whole country, almost without exception.[15] In 2009, Moti Ben-Shitrit, the coordinator of the ITC, amended Dvir's original claim by taking the simun shvilim maps into account: "It appears that Israel is the first country in the world that has completed the project of marking trails and producing maps that cover its entire territory."[16]

Perhaps the most remarkable element of Israel's trail network is not that it competes with European trail systems in size and complexity, but that it does so in the Middle East, where hiking trails are uncommon. Again, Israel's waymarking project reflects the Eastern European provenance of the Zionist immigrants who built the state's early institutions. Other Middle Eastern countries have only recently begun creating trail networks. Over the past several years, hikers in Turkey have marked a number of long-distance hiking routes. In 2009, the Lebanon Mountain Trail was officially inaugurated. In 2015, the Sinai Trail was opened as a guided route in Egypt. The same year, the Jordan Trail and the Abraham Path in the West Bank were inaugurated as waymarked trails. None of these projects, however, compares in size or duration with Israel's decades-long simun shvilim project or has met with as much local success.

Israel's trails, then, are modeled after European trails, and by all appearances, enjoy a level of local popularity similar to European trails. Yet as a space for outdoor recreation, Israel is very different from most of Europe. It lacks the iconic alpine landscapes on which much of Europe's culture of hiking is based.[17] Deserts comprise the majority of its land area. Much of the remainder is covered by cities, closed military areas, and firing zones. Safety and security are constant concerns for hikers, especially along trails near border areas and in the West Bank. One can hardly imagine a more challenging physical and political environment for hikers, or for the creation of a European-style hiking trail network. Nevertheless, on every holiday break, tens of thousands of hikers flood Israel's trails.

The eagerness of Israeli hikers to visit areas with little apparent scenic value, and to endure hardships and dangers to which few hikers in other countries are accustomed, reflects the fact that Israeli trails function as much more than mere spaces for outdoor recreation. Trails are also infrastructure elements that can channel large numbers of people into sparsely populated desert areas and contested border areas. As Ravek mentioned in his court defense, hikers have at times played key roles in conquering and controlling land. It is impossible to speak much further about the physical dimensions of the trail network without examining how, as a meeting point between people and land, the trail system has played a role in defining the boundaries of state territory and realizing Israeli control over it.

The National Dimensions of Israeli Hiking Trails

In February 2010, Israeli Prime Minister Benjamin Netanyahu took the podium to deliver the keynote address at the Tenth Annual Herzliya Conference. Six years earlier, at the same forum, Prime Minister Ariel Sharon had used his speech to announce his plan for Israel's unilateral disengagement from the Gaza Strip. Netanyahu's prime-time Israeli television audience, as well as the in-person audience of local and international government officials, private-sector consultants, reporters, and academics, therefore had high expectations for a speech on the country's most pressing national security challenges.

Instead, Netanyahu chose to speak about hiking trails. He described Israeli youth as having lost interest in the core values of Zionism and as having lost their love of homeland. Netanyahu argued that in order to ensure the long-term survival of the Jewish state, the Zionist practice of teaching youth to identify themselves with national territory needed to be resurrected. "I want to tell you that the simplest and most original way of doing so is to connect these young people to our homeland through their feet—through becoming familiar with the country, travelling the country." Netanyahu then praised the success of the border-to-border Israel National Trail and announced a plan to create two new long-distance trails that would connect hikers with Jewish and Zionist heritage sites not only across Israel but also across the West Bank and the Golan Heights—territories that Israel conquered in 1967 and has occupied ever since.[18]

"Foreigners at the conference," one reporter wrote the following day, "were bewildered by the prime minister's choice of topics." Some Israelis in the audience took issue with the speech as well, arguing that there was no reason to put trails so high on the national agenda.[19] For them, though, there was nothing strange about how Netanyahu connected the idea of "walking the land" to issues like national identity or the existence of the Jewish state. The connection was so obvious that it could hardly be articulated to an outside audience: hiking was an undertaking that lay close to what it meant to be Israeli. Historically, hiking trails had been spaces where Israelis learned who they were. If Netanyahu wanted to redefine Israeli identity, redefining Israel's hiking trails was a sensible place to start.

Later that week, when the Office of the Prime Minister released a map showing the planned routes of the new trails Netanyahu had described, the speech made sense on another level. As the leader of Israel's political right wing, Netanyahu had long worked to deepen Israeli control over the occupied West Bank. By making alterations to what Israelis across the political spectrum considered their "national trail"—a trail that did not yet touch Jerusalem or any occupied territories—Netanyahu could alter what Israelis saw as their national territory and perhaps reshape Israel's boundaries.

Netanyahu was not politicizing something that had previously been apolitical, nor was he the first Israeli leader to get involved in treks and trails. From its very beginnings in Palestine, long before the establishment of the State of Israel, walking and waymarking had been closely connected with the activities of the Zionist nation-building project. At the time, this had been nothing remarkable; Zionist hiking had been deeply influenced by the nationalist European hiking of the early twentieth century. But whereas Europeans, after the Second World War, had attempted to decouple politics from hiking, exchanging ideas of "national landscapes" for more universal ideas of "nature" and "environment," and opening their trails to foreign travelers, Israeli trails remained as political, and national, as they had ever been.

European waymarking began in the 1880s, when Czech hikers in Bohemia began placing the first modern, systematic blazes along unpaved paths and thus designated them as hiking trails. By that point, modern hiking had been taking shape in Europe for nearly a century, starting with the journeys of

Map 0.2. Historical and heritage trails proposed by Prime Minister Benjamin Netanyahu, February 2010.

Romantic writers and philosophers who popularized outdoor walking as a leisure activity, and continuing with the exploits of political thinkers who saw walking as a means of connecting people with land. In an increasingly urban and industrialized Europe, hiking and mountaineering were viewed as ways of returning not only to nature but to the landscapes that had defined peoples and cultures. Now, hiking clubs in border areas began marking trails in part to create safe routes for other hikers, but also to demarcate national territory. The first Czech trail was blazed in red and white: the traditional colors of the Bohemian crown.

Around the same time, Jewish immigrants began arriving in Palestine from Eastern Europe in what became known as the First Aliyah, or the first wave of Zionist immigration. Zionism had begun as a European political movement predicated on the idea that Palestine was the historic homeland of the Jewish people and a possible safe haven for Jews fleeing anti-Semitic persecution. When the first Zionist immigrants began arriving in Palestine in 1882, however, the country was not what many of them had envisioned. It was ruled by the Ottoman Empire, and more than 90 percent of its inhabitants were Arabs. Most of Palestine's land was either state-owned or under private Arab ownership. Arab presence was inscribed deeply upon the country's landscape: in the villages that dotted the hillsides, in the terrace agriculture that lined practically every mountain slope, in the orchards surrounding the cities and spreading across the coastal plain, and in the deeply carved wagon tracks that connected Arab towns.

Zionist leaders began working to colonize Palestine by purchasing land and settling new immigrants there. Over time, they hoped to attain a Jewish demographic majority, to own a majority of the land, and to attain some measure of Jewish sovereignty. In the meantime, they looked for meaningful ways in which Jews could otherwise make the country their own.

In his book *Zionism and Territory*, the Israeli sociologist Baruch Kimmerling argues that societies assert three types of control over land: sovereignty, ownership, and presence. A society seeking control over territory seeks all three types, and if one type is lacking, it works however possible to fill the void. As mentioned above, the Jewish community in Palestine, or the Yishuv, completely lacked sovereignty over Palestine at the turn of the twentieth century and possessed minimal land ownership. Owing to the small size of the Jewish population at that time, and its small number of agricultural settlements, the Yishuv also exhibited a limited degree of presence in Palestine. Kimmerling defines "presence" as "either (a) a basis for claims of possession without regard to ownership, or (b) demonstration of ownership upon land or the putting into effect of that ownership—especially if one's claim is contested."[20]

Zionists in late-nineteenth-century Ottoman Palestine sought both types of presence. On the land they did own, Zionists worked to demonstrate their ownership by transforming that land into the *Eretz Israel*, or "Land of Israel," that they had long imagined. They saw Palestine as unnaturally barren, particularly compared to the well-watered lands of Eastern Europe, and they believed the arid state of the country was due to the neglect of the Turks and the depredations of the Arabs. In their attempt to realize the land's potential, they hearkened to a utopian vision from Jewish scripture and liturgy that described the country as "a land flowing with milk and honey." The development of land along European lines—the establishment of planned colonies, the use of modern agricultural methods, the planting of pine trees—did not always work as well as Zionist immigrants hoped, but it became a key marker of Jewish presence in Palestine.

Walking became an important means by which Zionists established Jewish presence on land they did not own. Zionist leaders looked for ways in which Jews, and the world at large, could begin to understand the whole of the country as the ancient Jewish homeland and therefore as the legitimate domain of eventual Jewish sovereignty. They resurrected biblical Hebrew place-names and began using them in everyday speech, on printed maps, and in published guidebooks. They studied the land and described its ancient Jewish character in terms that suggested that the presence of other people groups, particularly the Arabs, was temporary and ephemeral. Almost all of these endeavors emerged from exploratory journeys, sometimes on horseback, but often on foot, along Palestine's unpaved roads and footpaths. None of them required Jews to control the land as rulers or possess it as owners. In 1903, outdoor walks became part of the first Zionist national school curriculum, and a generation of Jewish youth in Palestine began exploring the country on foot in a more systematic and visible way.

The advent of Jewish educational hiking coincided with the arrival of a new wave of Zionist immigrants who took a more aggressive attitude toward development and toward extending Jewish presence across the whole of Palestine. The Second Aliyah is generally regarded by historians to have begun around 1904, when new waves of anti-Semitic attacks spurred Jews to leave Eastern Europe, and when young activists moved to Palestine in response to a proposal that Zionist settlement activities shift to other locations. Following the death of Theodor Herzl, the radical youth who took the reins of the colonization project became the vanguard of the Zionist movement and eventually created institutions that became central elements of the Israeli state. As they began settling Palestine's frontier areas using new communal frameworks, including the kibbutz, the so-called *halutzim*, or "pioneers" of the Second Aliyah, also created organizations that aimed to guarantee the Jewish right to movement along the country's roads and footpaths.

It is worth noting here that this book uses the terms *halutzim* and "pioneers" interchangeably for the young leaders of the Second Aliyah and their ideological successors. The word *halutz* comes from the Hebrew Bible and refers to the scouts who went ahead of the Israelite invasion of Canaan in the book of Joshua. *Halutz* and "pioneer" are the terms by which the early Labor Zionists are best known in Israeli historiography. Though the terms originally glamorized the activities of the early Labor Zionists, they can be read today as highlighting the fact that the practices of Zionist settlers were similar to the practices of other groups that operated on frontier areas in other national contexts, and which also described themselves as "pioneers." The halutzim shared the vision of their First Aliyah forebears: "The ultimate aim or *pia desideria* is to take control of Palestine in due time and to return to Jews the political independence they have been deprived of for two thousand years. . . . The Jews will yet arise, weapons in hand (if need be); and, in a loud voice, they shall proclaim themselves the lords and masters of their ancient homeland."[21]

During this time, the Arab-Jewish conflict over the future of Palestine truly began to take shape. Arabs, who still constituted the vast majority of the country's population, were articulating their own political goals as the Ottoman Empire weakened and were also beginning to take Zionism seriously as a movement that sought to claim sovereignty over the land. A few Zionist thinkers pointed out that the Arabs were deeply rooted in Palestine, and that their nationalist aims were every bit as serious as those of the Jews, but most such arguments fell on deaf ears.[22] The Zionist nation-building project continued, more determined than ever, at the hands of the Second Aliyah pioneers. (See fig. 0.4.) Zionist immigration and land purchases continued, and Jewish presence became ever more visible. The same pioneer youth who insisted on "walking the Land of Israel" also insisted that on Jewish-owned land, Arab laborers give way to Jewish workers. Displaced Arab peasant farmers began moving to cities, the Jewish minority and the Arab majority developed separate economies, and violent conflicts between Jews and Arabs increased.

Because roads and paths were some of the prime locations in which members of Palestine's increasingly divided Jewish and Arab communities

Figure 0.4. Kibbutz workers on their way to work in the fields, 1939. *Photo by Zoltan Kluger, courtesy Government Press Office.*

encountered each other, walking became weaponized in the growing conflict. In 1909, Zionist pioneer youth created the Ha-Shomer, "The Guard," organization, which trained and mobilized fighters to defend Jewish settlements and to ensure free Jewish movement along Palestine's road networks. In 1912, the first Arab Scouting troop formed at the St. George Missionary School in Jerusalem. The first Jewish hiking club formed in 1916, and the Histadrut ha-Tzofim, or the "Scouting Movement" in Eretz Israel, was organized three years later, shortly after the British conquest of Palestine. In 1920, British authorities offered support to Scouting groups willing to join the international Scouting movement. Jewish Scouts, insistent on maintaining their Zionist character, chose to remain independent.[23] Arab Scouts accepted, and became increasingly political throughout the British Mandate period, working mainly in cities to organize demonstrations and protests.[24]

Throughout the 1920s, Jewish hiking became the domain of Hebrew-language schools and Zionist youth movements. As Zionist development

Map 0.3. British Mandate Palestine, 1922–1948.

extended Jewish presence across the settled body of the country in the forms of roads and settlements, Jewish hikers set out to explore Palestine's remote frontiers. Groups of young men and women began venturing into the desert east of Jerusalem, which they knew as the Judean Desert, in an effort to forge historical links between themselves and the Jews who had inhabited and ruled the country in ancient times. During the 1920s and 1930s, Jewish youth began trekking there in ever-greater numbers, sometimes risking life and limb on their journeys to and from Masada. (See fig. 0.5.) By the early 1930s, the elite hikers of the Yishuv were extending their presence to Palestine's borders and beyond, in ways that appeared less like outdoor recreation and more like conquest.

The importance of hiking in the eventual Israeli conquest of the country has rarely been examined by scholars. In 1920, the Ha-Shomer defense organization gave way to the more structured Haganah, "Defense," militia. Many historians of Zionism and modern Israel argue that the Haganah stayed more or less true to its name until the outbreak of the Arab Revolt in Palestine in 1936. Then, amid the violence that accompanied Arab protests against British rule and Zionist land purchases and immigration, the Haganah began preparing to conquer the country by force. From an institutional perspective, it is true that the unprecedented violence that gripped Palestine between 1936 and 1939 prompted the Haganah to begin organizing and training special-forces units. The Palmach, formally established in 1941, exemplified the Haganah's readiness and ability to carry out offensive military operations.

However, when Haganah leaders decided to create commando units, they found that the Yishuv's culture of Jewish hiking was already several steps ahead. Scouts who had trekked to Masada and explored the Judean Desert were already experienced at carrying equipment and weapons over long distances. The youth movement veterans who had walked to Palestine's farthest borders already knew how to navigate in the field, make incursions into Arab-controlled territory, and evade British police. Some of them had already entered the ranks of the Haganah and had learned how to use weapons. In short, the young leaders at the forefront of Jewish hiking in Palestine were practically a ready-made cadre of paramilitary fighters.

The degree to which Jewish hikers had already prepared themselves to conquer territory is perhaps best illustrated by a series of events that took place in 1934, nearly two years before the Arab Revolt began. Hikers were already beginning to face criticism from within the Jewish community on

Figure 0.5. Aerial view of Masada, 1938. *Photo by Zoltan Kluger, courtesy Government Press Office.*

the grounds that they were taking unsupervised hikes in dangerous areas, entering Arab territory as if it belonged to them, and unnecessarily inflaming tensions. Then, in the spring of 1934, two teenage hikers were killed in hiking accidents in the Judean Desert. In response, Jewish hiking leaders in Palestine pleaded for youth not to walk without adult supervision.[25] Finally, in September 1934, in defiance of youth movement leaders and their own Haganah commanders, a group of young men loaded their packs with illegal weapons and entered Transjordan under cover of darkness to begin a two-week trek around the Dead Sea. On their journey, they nearly died of exposure and thirst, struggled to navigate the rugged terrain, and on two occasions, held up Bedouins at gunpoint to rob them of their water. Upon the hikers' return, they were hailed as heroes in the Yishuv, and the story of their journey became legendary.[26]

When the Palmach was formally established in 1941, its ranks were filled with elite hikers from the scouting and youth movements, including several from the 1934 Dead Sea trek. However, some historians, portraying 1936 as the year in which everything changed in the Yishuv, have attempted to describe Jewish hiking in the early 1930s as a naïve and innocent undertaking akin to the rambles of the neo-Romantic Wandervogel in Germany. In her book *Land and Power*, the historian Anita Shapira sums up the Dead Sea trek and its participants in such terms: "In 1934 they circled the Dead Sea and discovered the splendor of the desert."[27] In truth, the armed trekkers were at the forefront of a hiking culture that had already gone on the offensive and which would soon set an example for the rest of the Jewish community in Palestine.

The ethos of Jewish hiking became the ethos of the Palmach, and the young men and women of that fighting force became regarded as the embodiment of the Zionist ideal. (See fig. 0.6.) Hiking became a key part of the Palmach's training regimen throughout the 1940s, and school and youth hikers who were too young to join the Haganah did their best to follow in the fighters' footsteps. After they hiked into Arab-controlled areas, they submitted forms to the Haganah that detailed the locations of villages, wells, bridges, and so on, and thus contributed to Zionist military intelligence.[28] Because hiking was already so popular among Jewish youth, it was impossible for the British to know whether a group of hikers belonged to a youth movement or a paramilitary group.

By 1947, when the Palmach marked the first modern hiking trail in the Middle East, the aims of Jewish hiking culture and Zionist political and

Figure 0.6. Palmach members on a brigade trek in the Judean Desert, 1940s. *Courtesy of the IDF and Defense Establishment Archives—Palmach Museum.*

military leadership were in complete agreement. Hikers wanted to be able to safely walk wherever they wanted, and the military had become accustomed to hikers playing a role in projecting Jewish presence across the country and preparing the ground for conquest. The confluence of their interests took tangible form at Ras Feshkha in the series of painted blazes that at once marked a safe route to Masada and declared to nearby Arabs that Jewish youth had claimed the path as their own.

During the 1948 War, Israel gained sovereignty over nearly all of the territory allotted to it in the UN Partition Plan and gained additional territory that had been designed to belong to an Arab state. More than seven hundred thousand Arabs, now known simply as Palestinians, had fled or had been expelled from Israeli territory during the war, and after armistice agreements were signed in the spring of 1949, Israel did not allow them to return. Through a series of laws passed in the early 1950s, ownership of the "absentee property" left by Palestinians was transferred to the Jewish state. The one hundred sixty thousand Arabs who remained within the boundaries of Israel now constituted only a small minority of the country's population, especially as waves of Jewish immigrants began arriving from postwar Europe, the Middle East, and North Africa. In short, everything changed: Israel's boundaries were different from the borders of Mandate Palestine, and within those boundaries, Israel now claimed sovereign rule and ownership over most of the land.

Throughout most of this time in Europe, hiking had remained closely tied to nationalism. Lord Robert Baden-Powell had built Scouting at the beginning of the twentieth century to teach British youth to love their country and fight for it. German hiking shifted its focus around that time from nature to nation; by 1933, the Hitler Youth had subsumed the country's other hiking and scouting organizations. In 1938, the Nazis hailed the first ascent of the Eiger North Face by a German-Austrian expedition as a triumph of the recently completed *Anschluss*. Only after 1945, amid a continent destroyed by war, did European hikers begin reimagining trails as environmental spaces.

In Palestine at that time, where the conflict between Jews and Arabs for control of the country was only intensifying, hikers did not make the same turn. After 1948, control over the former territory of the British Mandate was by no means settled; alongside Israel, Egypt controlled the Gaza Strip, and Jordan annexed the West Bank. Both countries, along with Syria and Lebanon, signed armistice agreements with Israel that left open the possibility of future conflict. In this environment, Israeli hiking retained its national and paramilitary character.

For Israeli policymakers, asserting Jewish presence across the country was a major challenge. In 1949, Israel's first prime minister, David Ben-Gurion, replaced and effectively erased Palestine's rich Arabic-language toponymy through a formal process of Hebrew-language renaming. Across the country, more than four hundred depopulated Palestinian villages were destroyed and their locations obscured by newly planted forests and newly built Jewish towns. By the early 1950s, the map of the country had completely changed. Most maps, however, still depicted certain areas along Israel's borders as blank spaces, void of Israeli presence. Palestinians moved across the porous and largely unmarked Green Line that separated Israel from the Jordanian-annexed West Bank. Bedouins moved across the southern Negev Desert as they had for centuries, crossing the Egyptian and Jordanian armistice lines in their travels between Sinai and northwest Arabia. Israel

Map 0.4. State of Israel, 1949–1967, with Ein Gedi and Eilat Mountain trail areas highlighted.

worked throughout the 1950s to realize full control over these areas but could not do so through its preferred methods of settlement and infrastructure development.

The status of the Judean and Negev Deserts as Israel's "wild south" attracted hikers who wanted to visit areas that had been largely inaccessible during the Mandate due to British-imposed travel restrictions and to familiarize themselves with the country's new boundaries. Once again, the interests of hikers aligned closely with those of the Israeli government and military. Treks to Masada and Ein Gedi in the Judean Desert, and to the Eilat Mountains in the southern Negev, heightened Israeli presence in sensitive border areas throughout the 1950s. Hikers used military infrastructure, such as jeep roads and border outposts, as staging areas for long hikes on unmarked trails and relied on the IDF to rescue them in case of emergencies. As accidents became more frequent, hikers' calls for better infrastructure resonated with the government's desire to heighten the permanent presence of Jewish-Israeli society along its borders.

In the early 1960s, marked and mapped trails answered both calls. Painted blazes again declared Israeli presence to anyone who found them, even when hikers were not physically present. On paper, the government was hardly involved; waymarking was initiated by hikers operating from an SPNI-supported environmental field school at Ein Gedi. But in the early years of Israeli statehood, few major projects took place independently of the government and military. Ein Gedi was a kibbutz that had begun as a military garrison, and it still operated in that capacity. The field school received much of its funding from the Ministry of Education. Most of the waymarking teams that painted the blazes were IDF paratroopers for whom hiking was still an integral training component and who therefore were familiar with paths and trails. Once blazed, the new trail networks enabled the Survey of Israel to print maps that no longer depicted desert territories as blank, but instead, as crisscrossed with known and safe travel routes.

The June 1967 war, in which Israel conquered the Golan Heights from Syria, the West Bank from Jordan, and the Gaza Strip and the Sinai Peninsula from Egypt, reshaped not only the physical landscape in which hikers, waymarkers, and surveyors operated but the political landscape they navigated as well. In the immediate aftermath of the war, the simun shvilim project extended across the Green Line from the southern Judean Desert to the northern Judean Desert. One of the leaders of the project at the time contacted Yigal Allon, a former IDF general who served on the Israeli

Map 0.5. State of Israel and occupied territories after 1967.

cabinet and was soon to become the deputy prime minister. Allon granted permission to mark trails across the desert east of Jerusalem, all the way to the ravine of Wadi Qelt north of Jericho. The marking and surveying were completed in about one month, and a new simun shvilim map, depicting a single trail network across a unified, borderless territory, was published in December of the same year.

At first blush, the expansion of the trail network might appear to have been a forerunner of the Israeli settlement project that would take root in the West Bank in earnest during the 1970s. Given the speed with which the trails expanded across the Green Line, one might expect the leaders of the waymarking project to have been committed to extending Jewish control over the West Bank generally and to do their part by continuing to mark trails. However, the politics of trail development were more complicated than that. After 1967, the trail system did not grow according to a coherent ideology. At times, it spread quickly and unapologetically across occupied territory. In the mid-1970s, waymarking teams blazed trails across the Golan Heights at the request of the IDF's Northern Command, after hikers had entered minefields and had been wounded or killed. However, even as the right-wing settlement movement used the tried-and-true Zionist method of increasing Jewish presence through hiking, the leaders of the simun shvilim project left most West Bank trails unmarked.

The politics of trail development after 1967 expanded to reflect all sorts of causes and divides in Israel, as border security issues became less pressing, and as trails moved away from frontiers and toward Israel's more densely settled areas. Environmental activists used trails to make people aware of encroaching urbanization. National park and nature reserve personnel established trails as the only legal means of accessing many backcountry areas. Guidebook authors used trails as catalysts for local tourism, describing interesting hikes and beautiful destinations and making lodging and dining recommendations along the way. Schools and teachers, working from models that descended from the Zionist curriculum developed during the First Aliyah, continued using trails to teach children about the "Land of Israel" and to frame the country specifically as the Jewish homeland. Whereas hikers and trails had previously been focused almost exclusively on border zones and had worked essentially in lockstep with the government and the military, the uses and significance of trails now became open to debate.

These debates only intensified in the 1980s, after Israel withdrew from the Sinai Peninsula, and hikers had to operate within a smaller and ever more congested space. Part of that space included the West Bank, where Jewish settlers began marking trails on their own and SPNI personnel began erasing them. Outside the West Bank, in areas like the Galilee, where Arab citizens of Israel increasingly identified with the Palestinian cause, trails were contentious as well. Some of the first signs for the long-distance Israel National Trail were vandalized, with the word "Israel" scratched away. Early discussions regarding the route of that trail spiraled into disputes over whether the trail should enter the West Bank. The outbreak of the First Palestinian Intifada in 1987 settled the question, and the route stayed within Israel proper. In all of these instances, trails were understood as having national implications, but the state itself was almost completely uninvolved; by this time, trails received no government funding and were sustained entirely by revenues from the simun shvilim maps sold by the SPNI.

More and more, trails reflected intra-Israeli conflicts: in the 1990s, environmentalists protested the marking of new trails in a newly opened nature reserve in the Negev, arguing that hikers would only bring damage to sensitive areas. In the 2000s, around the Sea of Galilee, activists working with the SPNI created a "Kinneret Trail" along the edge of the water, forcing private spas to open their beaches in accordance with the Israeli law that defined shorelines as public property. During the marking of that trail, confrontations between business owners and waymarking teams devolved into fistfights. Around the same time, entrepreneurs in northern Israel marked a new "Jesus Trail" with the SPNI that catered to foreign tourists and intentionally sought to bring tourism revenue to the Arab communities in the Galilee where Jesus's miracles took place in the New Testament. In response, the Israeli Ministry of Tourism created its own "Gospel Trail" that had the same beginning and end points but stayed almost completely within JNF forests and avoided Arab communities.

Given all of this, Netanyahu's 2010 speech makes more sense. While not all Israelis were consciously aware of the degree to which hiking had historically played a role in control over territory, Netanyahu took it for granted. He saw trail development as an important way to project Israeli presence across the West Bank and hiking West Bank trails as an important way to teach young Jews that all of the land between the Jordan River and the Mediterranean Sea was their historical birthright. In the end, Netanyahu's initiative did not bear fruit, for the same reason that the above-mentioned Gospel Trail failed to become a popular trail: most hikers did not seem interested in using trails that had been created solely for political reasons.

Nevertheless, similar ideas, put forth by hikers rather than bureaucrats, could conceivably take root in the future. In 2017, the Israeli hiking community was abuzz with the possibility of a new "Eastern Israel Trail" that would connect West Bank settlements overlooking the Jordan River valley and link on either end with the main Israel National Trail.[29] Moreover, Israel has not cornered the market on politically informed walking routes; in 2015, the first major Palestinian waymarking effort took place with the blazing of the three-hundred-thirty-kilometer Abraham Path, or Masar Ibrahim al-Khalil, which crossed the West Bank by way of Jenin and Hebron and was funded by a grant from the World Bank.[30] Only time will tell whether West Bank trails will be dominated by Jewish settlers or by the growing community of Palestinian hikers.

The Existential Dimensions of Israeli Trails

One might imagine Israeli hiking and Israeli trails as exclusively political phenomena, as if hikers have conspired with government land administrators, poring over maps and planning which region of historic Palestine would next fall under the domain of the Jewish state. In the early days of the State of Israel, hiker interests and state interests often overlapped. However, early Israeli hikers did not see politics as a motivation for going out onto trails; instead, they saw their politics as emerging from their underlying relationship with the Land. In the 1930s, after the British Peel Commission unveiled an early plan for creating a Jewish state alongside an Arab state in Palestine, youth movement hikers defied the mainstream Zionist support of the idea and opposed it on the grounds that it would divide the Land.[31] In the 1960s, one of the most popular songs sung on the trails was the Naomi Shemer hit "Hopa Hey," whose refrain bore the line, "Here, there is no slogan or flag."[32]

Early Zionist and Israeli hikers embraced the concept of *ahavat Eretz Israel*, or "love for the Land of Israel," as their motivation for walking the trails. It involved a particular type of "love" and a particular idea of "the Land of Israel." Both were defined by the early Zionist pioneers and were further shaped by successive generations of Israelis. "Love for the Land of Israel" remains a popular idea among Israelis today across the political spectrum, and while it can be marshaled for national ends, as illustrated in the previous section, most hikers still see their "love for the Land" as something much more personal and existential. "This land is part of me and I am part of it," writes

Meron Benvenisti, a leader of Israeli youth hiking in the 1950s who went on to become a fierce critic of the role hiking played in Israel's ever-deepening control of the West Bank. "My American friends laugh at me when I tell them that the flowers and trees in Central Park seem fake to me."[33]

The fact that such a sentiment can be expressed by a critic of nationalist hiking, and not by an exponent of it, illustrates the degree to which Israeli society takes for granted the idea that the Land of Israel is somehow more real than other parts of the world. Benvenisti demands that outsiders not simply dismiss this sense or view it as a mere epiphenomenon of Zionist political ideology, but instead take it seriously; he goes so far as to describe it as part of the Israeli national psyche.[34] For him, "love for the Land of Israel" is an existential phenomenon, born of a particular view of the Jewish people and the Jewish homeland and now bound up with Israelis' sense of individual and national identity.

Zali Gurevitch and Gideon Aran's seminal essay entitled "*Al ha-Makom*," or "On Place," uses sacred Jewish texts as a starting point for understanding the importance of the Land of Israel for Israelis.[35] If the land bears significance that causes people to regard it as the Land, it first appears in the book of Genesis, in which God brings Abraham to the land of Canaan and promises it to him and his descendants. Successive narratives in the books of Exodus and Joshua describe a process of exile and redemption, in which the children of Israel are enslaved in Egypt and eventually journey back to the Promised Land. For Gurevitch and Aran, the very concept of "place" in Judaism is fraught; in the Hebrew Bible, the term *ha-makom* can refer not only to a given physical place but also to God himself.

After the destruction of the Second Temple by the Romans in 70 CE, Jews around the world remained bound to the idea of the Land of Israel through the ongoing study and reading of religious texts. On a spiritual level, they saw themselves as intrinsically connected to the Land of Israel, where the destiny of the Jewish people would one day be fulfilled, and they deepened this connection through Hebrew-language liturgy and ritual. Meanwhile, on a physical level, they lived their lives in their immediate surroundings and carried out their everyday activities in the languages of their local communities. The very idea of "place" became bifurcated, and over time, the Land of Israel became regarded as existing more in the spiritual domain than the physical, and as belonging more to the ancient past and far-flung future than to the present.

Jewish pilgrimage to the Land of Israel in late antiquity and in medieval times, and the creation of centers there for Torah and Talmud study, only underscore the degree to which most Jews regarded the Land as metahistorical and beyond the boundaries of normal space. Pilgrimage to Palestine, study in the country's holy cities (Safed, Tiberias, Jerusalem, and Hebron), and even death and burial there, were all permitted. However, repeated rabbinic injunctions over the centuries forbade Jews from any attempt to travel there in large numbers, conquer the country, or establish a kingdom there. Such events, described by the Hebrew prophets, were associated with the messianic era, and could only be initiated by divine will. In Talmudic discussions regarding the sanctity of the Land of Israel, Jewish sages prohibit mass immigration but attach salvific meaning to the act of walking the Land. "Anyone who walks four cubits in Eretz Israel is assured of a place in the World-to-Come."[36]

Given the practical difficulties in reaching Palestine from major centers of Jewish life in Europe, the Middle East, and North Africa, the mythic Land of Israel became fascinating while the physical Land of Israel became abstract and remote. Rabbi Shmuel Yitzhaki, the famous eleventh-century teacher known by the acronym Rashi, spent most of his life in France and never traveled to Palestine, but he drew a series of Holy Land maps that were copied and recopied in Europe for centuries. None of them were intended as navigational tools, and to most modern viewers, they would hardly be recognizable as maps at all. The Rashi maps are the earliest-known examples of Jewish cartography and are pure study aids, drawn within the pages of Bible commentaries, depicting places in the Land of Israel and the surrounding countries as squares and rectangles, with no attempt at showing accurate boundaries or topography and no regard for scale.[37] They orient readers in the text, helping them understand where different Israelite tribal territories lay in relation to one another. In short, the Rashi maps highlight another sacred/secular divide in Jewish thought: they are drawn for "people of the Book," not "people of the Land."

Zionists sought to reconcile the above-described divides in Jewish space, time, and identity through a radical negation of the diaspora. They hoped to remove Jews from sacred time and restore them to history. They wanted to disconnect Jews from sacred ideas of space and root them again in physical space. They aimed to break the Hebrew language free from its religious boundaries and render it a useful, modern vernacular. In short, they sought a complete transformation of Jewish existence, and it depended on transforming Jews from "people of the Book" to "people of the Land." They saw Jewish life outside the Land of Israel, which viewed the universe through the lens of holy texts, as a condition in which life was fundamentally incomplete. It needed to be replaced with a new condition in which it would be possible for Jews not merely to exist in the world but to fully dwell in it, along the lines of what Heidegger would later describe as "being-in-the-world."

But the transformation the early Zionists sought could never be complete. If the Jewish people had any connection at all to the Land of Israel, it was by virtue of their status as "people of the Book." It proved impossible to use the Book as a means of drawing Jews to the Land and then, once there, to bury the salvific character of the Land as described in holy texts. Hence Gershom Scholem's warning in 1926 regarding the Zionist national revival, in which he described the country as a volcano: "If and when the language turns against its speakers—and this has occurred already on bitter and unforgettable occasions when the arrogance of this undertaking has become apparent—will we then have a youth which can exist in and survive the revolution of a holy language?"[38]

Israel's culture of hiking today is rooted in the lived experiences of the very people who undertook the "revolution" Scholem feared, and who initiated in their own lives the radical transformations that Gurevitch and Aran describe. In exploring these experiences, this book builds on a remarkable work by the Israeli historian Boaz Neumann entitled *Land and Desire in Early Zionism*. In it, Neumann argues that the young Zionist leaders of the Second and Third Aliyah shared a comprehensive worldview whose contours are visible in the vast body of literature they produced. He uses a phenomenological lens to examine an array of pioneer writings—stories, journal entries, songs, poems, speeches, and so on—and attempts to bring his readers into the Labor Zionist *Weltanschauung*, in which "desire" drives all interactions with the Land of Israel. He resists any impulse to explain pioneer "desire for the Land of Israel" and stubbornly insists on taking the pioneers' words at face value, especially the effusive and ecstatic descriptions of physical contact with the Land of Israel that have baffled historians.

To immerse oneself in the literature of the Zionist pioneers is to step inside a bubble—to enter the life-world of a young *halutz* in Palestine in the early twentieth century, for whom "being-in-the-Land-of-Israel" is the prime existential condition—and gaze through curvatures that cause late-Ottoman Palestine to appear as something else entirely: a land that can only be recognized as the Land of Israel. Through that bubble, one sees the Land as having an almost magnetic attraction for the pioneers: one that compels them to come into physical contact with its soil and water and to attempt to merge their bodies with it. One can then begin to understand how Israelis view themselves and their country today, and how an heir of the pioneers like Meron Benvenisti can believe, despite his rational understanding of the world, that things in Israel are more real than they are in other places.

Most historians who have seriously examined the pioneer worldview have felt compelled to rationalize it, often through complex psychoanalytic interpretations. Ultimately, scholars of Israeli history have mostly found the pioneers and their approach to land interesting only insofar as they help answer other questions regarding the nature of Zionism and its nation-building project in Palestine. But the pioneer encounter with the Land was a total experience that cannot be viewed through any single lens. Attempts to explain the pioneer mindset in the course of other studies of Zionism, or in the service of arguments about Zionism, always fall short. Even the historians most empathetic to the pioneer experience, Neumann writes, "still do not completely understand and accept the halutzim's desire for the Land of Israel; they, too, treat it reductively, as an expression of something else."[39]

Neumann, therefore, focuses on "desire," as defined by Gilles Deleuze and Felix Guattari in their book *A Thousand Plateaus*, as the driving force behind every ecstatic pioneer encounter with the Land of Israel. "For them, desire knows only to crave, to produce. It is pure energy, a fluidity that knows no origins (i.e., derives from no needs) or destinations (i.e., makes no demands) and is not essentially connected to any particular body. And this is how I understand the desire of the *halutzim* for the Land of Israel."[40] Neumann argues that below all of the political and pragmatic arguments Zionist pioneers like David Ben-Gurion made in the early twentieth century—arguments that explained and justified why the Jewish people needed to build a "national home" in Palestine—lay something deeper. They desired the Land and desired for it to desire them so that they and the Land could become one.

This desire to merge with the Land of Israel gives rise to a whole range of pioneer encounters that Neumann describes and categorizes through the book. One chapter deals with the pioneer sense of being reborn upon immigrating to the Land of Israel and engaging in physical labor. Another examines how the halutzim sought to dissolve the boundaries between themselves and the Land by burying themselves in its soil and immersing themselves in its water. Others argue that in the process of dissolving those boundaries, the pioneers' productive labor transforms the Land and actually defines its boundaries, while at the same time transforming the Jewish body into a new and muscular form that aligns with the Zionist ideal. All of these ideas, as shown throughout this book, resurface again and again within the simun shvilim project; Israeli trail developers, educated in frameworks created by the halutzim, threw themselves deep into the least-visited parts of the country and the least-defined border areas, and they left lines on the ground and on maps that clearly articulated the shape of the Land and defined it as Israeli. For now, however, Neumann's initial category is worth discussing as an example of the radical nature of the Zionist view of the Land: the desire to be reborn as a result of encountering and merging with the Land.

David Ben-Gurion's grave, situated on the edge of a scenic overlook in the Negev Desert, bears not only the dates of his birth and death but also the date of his arrival in the Land. The implication is clear: for Ben-Gurion and his contemporaries, making *aliyah*—a term that refers to immigrating to Israel but which comes from the Hebrew Bible and literally means "ascent"—marked a passage from one state of being (diaspora) to a higher state (being-in-the-Land-of-Israel). Often, transformative encounters with the Land took place on hikes. During one hike in the Negev, for example, a young man named Szymon Persky climbed up a tree and was startled when a vulture emerged from its nest. Persky's companions encouraged him at that moment to shed the name he identified with his Diaspora roots and take a Hebrew name inspired by the animal he had just encountered. He was known for the rest of his life as Shimon Peres.[41]

As accidental as Peres's encounter with the fauna of the Land might seem, it took place in the course of an intentional journey across the country, undertaken in order to better know it. To "know the Land" was to know it through acts like labor and exploration, which involved physical contact, and the pioneer generation intentionally used the biblical word for "knowing" (*yedi'ah*) that referred to sexual intimacy. The halutzim described the Land of Israel as a female lover and cast themselves in the role of her male lover. Using terminology from the Hebrew Bible, they saw themselves as the objects of the Land's desire: "I am my beloved's, and he is mine" (Song of Songs 6:3). In their everyday work and in their travels on foot, they sought physical contact with the Land and looked for opportunities to absorb its essence and even to exchange fluids with it: to immerse themselves in its waters, to bury themselves in its upturned soil, to sweat into it, to bleed into it, to walk barefoot along its unpaved paths. Having attained such knowledge, and thus having consummated their union with the Land, they described its body and theirs as one, and its fate and theirs as intertwined. Zionism's aggressive developmental ethos, then—manifest in the form of settlements, cities, highways, and other massive infrastructure projects—is intimately connected to the concurrent sense that Jewish identity and the Jewish body needed to be reconstructed.

"Desire" may seem like an abstract theoretical idea, but it surfaces in the real-life work of people involved in creating walking routes. Urban planners and trail developers use the term "desire lines" to describe the unpaved paths that form spontaneously through everyday movement. For landscapers, "desire lines" may appear to be unsightly shortcuts through bushes and across lawns, but for many planners, such paths represent ideal starting points for walking routes because they emerge from lived experience and embody the human impulse to create and to break barriers. Footpaths are organic examples of visible changes to the landscape that emerge from that impulse.

Indeed, according to Neumann, desire-driven interactions with land always involved some developmental component: the digging of a well, the paving of a road, the construction of a settlement. He therefore includes the appearance of unpaved paths, left in the wake of pioneer movement, in this framework as well. Examining this idea more closely, this book argues (contrary to Neumann) that Zionist pioneers rarely created "desire lines" as they walked the Land, but instead followed existing paths that had often been made and maintained by Arabs. However, blind to the desire of the Arabs, or anyone else for that matter, for the same land, the pioneers did not think of Palestine's unpaved paths as marks of human development but instead as pre-existing elements of the unspoiled Land. Their value lay in the fact that they enabled movement through pristine areas without sullying their virgin character. Viewed in that light, the simun shvilim project can be understood either as a developmental activity akin to other pioneer expressions of desire or as a destructive act that violates the pioneer impulse to preserve the country's natural beauty. Both ideas are explored at length in the next chapter but are worth mentioning briefly here.

Within the pioneer experience, desire for the Land of Israel is a powerful force that evokes ecstasy in pioneer youth but views the Land myopically, not merely to the exclusion of everything else but to the destruction of anything that blocks or threatens contact with the Land. The Arabs appear only as elements of the Land itself: people born in the country but not belonging to it in a sense that threatens the Zionist claim on territory. The Arab presence is regarded as ephemeral, unrooted, inauthentic; a vestige, perhaps, of how people lived upon the land in ancient times but not a presence that brings every capability to bear, including modern ones, in making the Land fruitful. As long as the Arabs stay in the place relegated to them in the pioneer worldview, they receive little notice or attention. When they challenge the right of the halutzim to the Land of Israel, or threaten their ability to possess it, the response is swift and violent.

This book takes Neumann's work seriously, along with the existential relationship between Zionists and land that it seeks to explore. However, phenomenological approaches to history, by their nature, tend to exclude critical theories that might muddy the bounded waters under observation. Once undertaken, studies like Neumann's can (and should) be incorporated into wider discussions. That is what I wish to do here. My own experiences on Israel's trails have forced me to acknowledge that for Israelis today, trails seem to be more than just trails and that this outlook seems to be a direct inheritance of the halutzim—for whom Neumann writes, "Being-in-the-Land-of-Israel was . . . *to be*." At the same time, one cannot ignore the degree to which passion for the Land, no matter its origin, can quickly circle back to nationalism and the violent effects thereof. It is difficult to use the term "love for the Land of Israel" without thinking of Michel 'Aflaq's formulation, expressed in his Ba'ath Party writings, "Nationalism is love above anything else."[42]

As mentioned earlier, figures like Shuka Ravek and Menachem Marcus have described Israeli waymarking leaders as a cult, obsessed with placing marks upon the ground. Benvenisti, who operated in that world and emerged as a critic of it, used similar terms that resonate with Gurevitch and Aran's ideas: "The obsessive search for rootedness, the need to turn the *geographia sacra* of the Diaspora into tangible reality, to make Eretz Israel a natural, not only a spiritual, homeland—to possess it through the senses by bodily contact with its soil, mountains, deserts, and streams—this is what lies at the heart of the tremendous educational enterprise properly regarded more as a cult than a subject."[43]

If, as Neumann argues, the "desire" of the pioneers was essentially encoded into the worldview of mainstream Israelis and transmitted through the institutions Benvenisti describes, then the "cult of signs" is a near-direct descendant of the halutzim. Benvenisti states that of all of the rituals carried out in the vast, pioneer-developed machinery that educates Israelis to think of their country as the Land of Israel and as the Jewish homeland, the hike is the highest.[44] It follows, then, that the people who walked alone along obscure desert paths in order to actualize their love for the Land, and then marked the paths so that others could follow, served as high priests, attempting to mediate a relationship between Israelis and a land whose physical and metaphysical significance remain in conflict.

1

The Construction of a Jewish Hiking Culture in Palestine, 1904–1935

From Walking to Hiking

Shortly after his arrival in Palestine in 1907, Yitzhak Ben-Zvi walked from Jaffa to Jerusalem. At a time when few Arabs or Jews in the Middle East considered walking a recreational activity, Ben-Zvi chose to trek, rather than travel on horseback, from Palestine's major port to its largest city. For Ben-Zvi, however, the eighteen-hour climb from the coastal plain to the central mountains was more than just a hike; it was a direct and sustained encounter with the Land of Israel. "You descend and ascend each hill," he later wrote, "feel each inch with the soles of your feet, look at each tree, tarry as you will by every spring, cave, or holy tomb. It can hardly be surprising that the impressions of the countryside of the Land of Israel, etched in my heart in those days, never fade and are imprinted in my memory as alive and fresh as when they were first experienced, when I first strode the length and breadth of the Land."[1]

At the time of Ben-Zvi's journey, Palestine had been ruled by the Ottoman Empire for nearly four centuries. Around six hundred thousand people lived in the entire country. The vast majority of the people who lived there were Arabs. Zionist settlement had been taking place for more than twenty years, but Jews only amounted to about 10 percent of Palestine's population.[2] Some were part of the religious Jewish community known as the "Old Yishuv," centered in cities like Safed, Tiberias, Jerusalem, and Hebron. Others had come as part of the first major wave of Jewish immigration, or the First Aliyah, and had built disconnected clusters of settlements in different parts of the country. Of the latter group, about half had struggled to reconcile the realities of Palestine with the "land of milk and honey" they had imagined and had left for other countries. Those who remained, and who were accustomed to European standards of transport, found travel difficult. The road from Jaffa to Jerusalem was the only all-season road in Palestine; many of the rest became impassable during the rainy season. Many Jews, conscious of their minority status, and remembering anti-Semitic attacks in their home countries, also feared violent encounters with Arabs as they traveled.

Starting around 1904, a new generation of Jewish immigrants began arriving in Palestine with a different view of the country and a stronger willingness to walk outdoors, despite any dangers they might encounter. Ben-Zvi had come to Palestine from eastern Europe, where hiking was common, during the Second Aliyah. He was part of a small group of young activists who became known in Hebrew as the *halutzim*, or "pioneers." These young men and women were small in number, comprising only a few hundred people altogether, but they laid foundations for a culture of Jewish youth hiking in Palestine and eventually rose to the leadership of their generation of Zionist immigrants. Long before Ben-Zvi became the longest-serving president of the State of Israel, he and his Labor Zionist peers built settlements on remote tracts of newly purchased land and organized efforts to patrol Palestine's road networks on foot and horseback. They also viewed hiking as a way of developing a new Jewish identity that was rooted in the soil of the Land of Israel.

After the First World War, the halutzim of the Second Aliyah and successive waves of Jewish immigration worked aggressively to build Palestine into the country they envisioned. Alongside the British, who now ruled the country under a League of Nations mandate, they began building a modern transportation network that connected their settlements to railways and ports. Travel along those routes still presented dangers for hikers, especially as the conflict intensified between Jews and Arabs over control of land. Journeying on foot across the country's wide rural spaces, where unpaved roads and paths were still the norm, was even more dangerous. Nevertheless, a robust community of Jewish hikers took shape, led by growing ranks of Labor Zionist pioneer youth who risked their lives to "know the Land of Israel." By the mid-1930s, with the country growing more densely populated, Jewish hikers began focusing their attention on the desert between Jerusalem and the Dead Sea.

This chapter charts the evolution of Jewish walking in Palestine from the furtive explorations of the First Aliyah settlers in the 1890s through the boundary-blurring hikes of the Second Aliyah pioneers in the 1900s and 1910s, the school- and youth movement-sponsored desert treks that took place in the 1920s, and the unsanctioned and rebellious desert journeys undertaken by young men and women during the early 1930s. Jewish youth across Palestine regarded hiking along unpaved paths as a means of flight from encroaching modernization; the roadless Judean Desert became an important space where hikers increasingly sought refuge from development, and the ancient fortress of Masada near the Dead Sea became the most sought-after destination for youth hikers in the Yishuv. By 1936, when the Arab Revolt erupted across Palestine and spurred the Haganah to shift from a defensive posture to an offensive posture, the Yishuv's culture of hiking had already taken on a nationalist and outward-oriented character. The hikes described in this chapter, culminating in the cross-country treks of Zionist youth movement members in the early 1930s, set the stage for the creation of Jewish paramilitary forces in the early 1940s and put in motion the forces that later gave rise to simun shvilim.

The European Roots of Modern Hiking

Hiking is generally regarded as a modern phenomenon, but the lines between it and older forms of walking can be difficult to define.[3] Some scholars trace the roots of recreational outdoor walking to the sixteenth century, when the split between Protestantism and Catholicism left many Europeans unable to make pilgrimage to Rome.[4] In the place of spiritual journeys to the center of Christianity, young nobles started the tradition of the Grand Tour, which involved sightseeing, socializing, and wandering across the Continent over a period of months or even years.[5] As Europe became safer for travelers in the early modern period, nobles moved from castles to mansions, lowered the walls of their gardens and estates, and began walking outdoors for health purposes.[6]

By the late eighteenth century, road improvements and advances in vehicular technology made travel safer and easier, to the point that Romantic authors like Jean-Jacques Rousseau and William Wordsworth were able to democratize and popularize outdoor walking.[7] That type of travel remained popular throughout the nineteenth century for people who had the time and money to move about for extended periods, and it served the interests of literary figures and political activists. Somewhere along the way, outdoor walking began to resemble what would be described today as hiking: a type of outdoor walking that was associated with its own form of dress and a specialized set of equipment, and which was understood to offer participants a certain type of encounter with nature.[8] In the United States, Henry David Thoreau journeyed outdoors to commune with nature; in German-speaking lands in Europe, Eduard Lasker walked through the Black Forest and the Alps to explore the possibilities of unifying politically divided territory.[9]

Near the end of the nineteenth century, walking became a popular activity for young men and women in Europe who wanted to become "integrated human beings," but who felt that such a goal was unattainable in modern society.[10] Student groups in Germany used hiking as a means of escaping modernity, turning to nature, rebelling against the morals of their parents' generation, and seeking a more grounded existence by returning to the soil of their homeland.[11] The activities of the Wandervogel, which became an official organization just after the turn of the twentieth century, set the tone for the larger European youth movement. The worldwide scouting movement, with its military roots, coalesced around the same time and in a similar atmosphere. Both movements encouraged young men and women to take long hikes that gave them sustained encounters with the soil, water, flora, and fauna of their home countries.

"Scouting has been described by more than one enthusiast as a revolution in education," wrote Lord Robert Baden-Powell in the introduction to his 1908 *Handbook for Boys*. "It is not that. It is merely a suggestion thrown out at a venture for a jolly outdoor recreation, which has been found to form also a practical aid to education."[12] Indeed, during the ascendant era of the nation-state, many of the activities of the youth and scouting movements were freely led and created by the youth themselves, but they were also recognized by educators as useful pedagogical tools that produced healthy, strong, and active men and women who were passionate about knowing and serving their countries. Through *Heimatkunde*, or "homeland studies," carried out in large part through walking, German youth defined the outlines of what they considered to be their country and came to see German territory as their own.[13]

Hiking in Europe at the turn of the twentieth century, then, was closely identified with nationalism and youth education. In Palestine, Zionist youth educators were not ready to mobilize Jewish youth in large numbers across rural areas, but some of them recognized the potential of hiking to serve the

Zionist nation-building project. It was an activity that could take advantage of the country's warm climate; it was a practical way of teaching the growing numbers of Jewish children born in Palestine about their home; and perhaps most importantly, given the lack of resources available to First Aliyah settlers, it was inexpensive. Given the danger and difficulty of travel along Palestine's roads, and the amount of time young men and women spent working with their families, hiking was unlikely to spring forth spontaneously as a recreational activity. Organized educational initiatives, however, were able to create some of the necessary conditions for youth hiking.

The First Hikes: Educational Walking during the Late First Aliyah Period

Most of the walking undertaken by Jews in Palestine at the end of the nineteenth century, during the period of the First Aliyah, would not be categorized today as hiking. Very little of it was recreational in nature, save perhaps for the holiday journeys people took to visit other settlements. Even then, the walk or horseback ride was but a necessary means of crossing open spaces, not an end in itself. The Jewish community had a natural interest in knowing the country's geography and connecting present-day places with sites mentioned in the Bible; starting around 1890, for example, the Jerusalem publisher Abraham Moses Luncz began writing guidebooks for traveling the country and began reprinting old religious texts on the history and geography of Eretz Israel.[14] Zionists were interested in such materials because they described the country in Jewish terms and rendered its landscapes less alien. In late nineteenth-century Palestine, however, translating this interest into a program for exploring the country was difficult. The necessary conditions that had allowed for the development of hiking in Europe about a century earlier—namely, security along road and trail networks and the existence of a leisure class interested in recreational walking—did not yet exist.

The first youth hikes in Palestine were organized by two educators: Yitzhak Epstein and Simcha Chaim Wilkomitz. Epstein, who had arrived from Russia in 1885, was a pioneer in hands-on teaching practices; one of his many accomplishments was to build on the work of fellow First Aliyah immigrant Eliezer Ben-Yehuda and teach "Hebrew in Hebrew" to his students, with the goal of resurrecting the holy tongue as a vernacular language.[15] The Russian-born Wilkomitz arrived in 1896 from Vilna and almost immediately became a leader in teaching youth about territory and homeland.[16] Both men had been influenced by then-current European pedagogical practices but taught at first in separate parts of the country. Their paths crossed in 1899 when Epstein was preparing to leave Metulla for Rosh Pina and Wilkomitz arrived to take his place.[17]

Beginning around that time, the two men worked together in northern Palestine to design a curriculum for schools in communities around Safed, and they put it into practice at a new girls' school supported by the Russian Chovevei Tziyon (Lovers of Zion) movement.[18] It built on methods that were already taking place in schools in the northern settlements, including the youth hikes Epstein and Wilkomitz had personally led. Educating students in the outdoors was appealing not only because it exposed young men and women to many of the things they needed to understand in order to live and thrive in Palestine—the history of the land, its present-day character, its plants and animals, its settled areas, its Arab inhabitants, its cultivated areas, its soil and water, and so on—but also because being outdoors in the country's warm climate was regarded as a healthy activity that cost nothing.[19] One might also note that in the above list, Palestine's Arab inhabitants are included along with the objects Jewish children studied as natural elements of the country. This tendency to view Arabs as parts of the landscape—rather than as true inhabitants of the land who had their own visions for the future of Palestine and whose presence in the country was well-established—also became a long-standing trend in Zionist education.

Epstein and Wilkomitz formally outlined their curriculum in 1903, and it quickly became the standard for Zionist schools in Palestine. It remained profoundly influential, particularly in the realm of geography education, throughout the twentieth century. In terms of hours spent per subject, geography was the fourth-most important subject in the Zionist school curriculum, after reading, writing, and mathematics.[20] The hikes that took place within the realm of geography education were modest; classes stayed together, taking advantage of safety in numbers, and were always accompanied by adults. They adhered to safe and known paths and returned to schools and Jewish settlements in a timely manner. After each hike, students took notes on what they had seen. Over time, these journeys were supposed to take students farther and farther from Jewish territory and give them knowledge of the wider country.[21]

These educational journeys can be described as the first European-style hikes in Palestine. They were not carried out in the course of everyday work but instead were intentional ventures into the countryside, with the goal of teaching students about the land that lay beyond the boundaries of their settlements. They were not strictly recreational, but since they took students out of classrooms and brought them into the outdoors, they were not regarded as regular school work either. Students brought with them the supplies and equipment they needed, gathered information while in the field, and returned to their settlements with lessons learned and stories to tell. Such hikes laid the foundation for the educational *tiyul*, which can be translated as "hike" or "field trip," and which became an important part of the curriculum in most primary and secondary schools in the Yishuv and remains a widespread pedagogical practice in Zionist schools in Israel to this day.[22]

Nevertheless, early Zionist school hikes were limited by the fact that they existed within the boundaries of educational initiatives. A true culture of hiking in the Yishuv did not develop until the arrival of a new wave of immigrants who were intent on fundamentally changing the conditions of movement and dimensions of Jewish settlement in Palestine. The men and women who led the Second Aliyah, which began in 1904, built upon the educational frameworks set up by Epstein and Wilkomitz and also journeyed across the country on their own. Under their watch, hikes evolved from furtive explorations of the areas around Jewish settlements to bold expeditions that ranged across the whole of the country. In the minds of these revolutionary-minded immigrant youth, hiking became an existential undertaking that could play a role in remaking both the Jewish people and the Jewish homeland.

How Zionist Pioneers Saw "The Land of Israel" in Existential Terms

Between 1904 and 1914, about thirty-five thousand Jews arrived in Palestine, mostly from Eastern Europe. As was the case in the First Aliyah, most of the immigrants of the Second Aliyah left their homes in the Pale of Settlement with the hope of starting a better life in Palestine. As was also the case in the First Aliyah, many were religious, and about half of them ended up leaving Palestine. Of those who stayed, a few thousand were ardent Zionists who strove, like the young leaders of the First Aliyah, to claim the Land of Israel as their homeland and, eventually, to establish a Jewish state. But the leadership of the Second Aliyah came from a different political climate: the ferment of radical ideas and action in the early twentieth-century Russian Empire. For many, anti-Semitic attacks like the Kishinev pogroms were fresh memories. A few had fled to Palestine after participating in the failed 1905 revolution.

As a group, they debated a wide range of competing political and economic ideas, but they shared a disdain for existing Zionist settlement frameworks, which attempted to maintain European-level standards of living for their Jewish inhabitants, and in doing so, depended on securing outside financial contributions from wealthy donors and outsourcing agricultural labor to Arabs. They also shared an understanding of Palestine as the Land of Israel and a determination to settle as close to the Land as possible. Despite their lack of experience, they sought to engage in agricultural labor on their own. Eventually, the young activists who rose to the leadership of the Second Aliyah became known as the halutzim, or "pioneers." The term, taken from the Hebrew Bible, refers to the vanguard scouting the country ahead of a fighting force. The halutzim were few in number but influential. One member of their ranks, the Labor Zionist leader Berl Katznelson, referred to the pioneers as "the distillate of the distillate."[23]

If the halutzim constituted a community with a shared worldview, some of the connective tissue of their outlook, such as the language that gave voice to pioneer desire, was provided by the writings of Aharon David Gordon. Gordon was much older than most of the pioneers; he moved to Palestine from present-day Ukraine in 1904, when he was forty-eight years old, and devoted himself to the same manual labor as the young revolutionaries who surrounded him in remote tracts of Jewish-purchased land in Palestine. But his revolution was not a socialist one, of the type many of the young pioneer immigrants envisioned. Gordon's ardent nationalism opposed socialism, rejecting it as too focused on materialism and individualism, and instead envisioned the individual and the collective as tied together in an organic relationship, within which land and labor were essential.

Contrary to other Zionist thinkers like Herzl and Nordau, Gordon argued that mere landlessness and statelessness were not the defining characteristics of Jews in the Diaspora. Using ideas of peoplehood, nation, and connection to land that were popular across Eastern Europe at the time, Gordon believed that the relationship between a people and the soil of its homeland lay at the root of national culture. It was not enough for Jews simply to return to the land of their origin and to build a state there, because once there, Jews might still continue what Gordon characterized as Diaspora ways of life and thinking. Gordon argued that Jews, as individuals and as a nation, needed to forge an unmediated relationship with the Land through acts of labor: "In Palestine we must do with our own hands all the things that make up the sum total of life."[24]

Gordon's writings serve as excellent vantage points for viewing land as the pioneers did. On the one hand, Gordon is a mainstream figure in Israeli history whose influence is well-known and who affected a whole generation of Zionists in Palestine across the political spectrum. On the other hand, Gordon's writings contain a mystical character that hints at an underlying cosmology. When he describes the relationship between Jews and the Land, for example, he describes sources of life that flow between people and homeland that seem to lie beyond the realm of rational understanding: "We come to our Homeland in order to be planted in our natural soil from which we have been uprooted, to strike our roots deep into its life-giving substances, and to stretch out our branches in the sustaining and creating air and sunlight of the Homeland."[25] Of his critics who suggest that Jewish life in the Diaspora is more sustainable than Jewish life in Palestine, Gordon writes, "They do not understand—they are not capable of understanding—that such life means to us as, for example, religion means to a truly pious Jew."[26]

Indeed, many scholars have had difficulty dealing with certain characteristics of the "religion of labor" that Gordon played a key role in creating among Jews in Palestine. The term *Labor Zionism* came to refer to a whole movement, but it grew from the ideas and activities of Gordon and other Second Aliyah pioneers for whom close connection to the Land of Israel, formed through labor, was essential not only for the nation-building project but for life itself. Pioneer journals, songs, letters, and poems are filled with odes to the beauty of the Land and describe, over and over, efforts to know the Land, merge with it, and become one with it. In a letter to friends in Europe, composed on a mountaintop in the Galilee, Gordon describes the country as if it is alive and as if people and land bring life to each other: "On my left is Migdal lying at the bottom of the vale like an infant reclining in its crib. Youthful forces are winding in the valley, bringing new life to the stones and making the earth fruitful. Who knows what strength they are sowing—how much of their heart, how much of their soul?"[27]

As Boaz Neumann points out in *Land and Desire in Early Zionism*, most scholars have either treated such expressions as figurative or have simply dismissed the pioneers' more effusive descriptions of their encounters with the Land. The intensity and frequency of such descriptions, however, renders them difficult to ignore. Neumann argues that they should be taken seriously because they offer genuine insights into the larger pioneer worldview—one that shares Gordon's mystical approach to the relationship between Jews and the Land of Israel and carries its anthropomorphism even further. When the halutzim write about the Land and their physical interactions with it, Neumann shows, they describe it in evocative, and often erotic, terms:

> And the deeper I dug, the sensation of the soil became more profound and spread through me, and the feeling overcame me that I [must] embrace the land, merge into it, suck from it the essence of life. The spirit of the generations blew within me from the depths of the soil and I felt, really felt, the powerful connection between me and the soil of Israel.[28]

> Here is my Land—the body of a wild ass. . . .
> Flog, flog, summer sun, the coarse body of my Land,
> We will milk dew-cream from night-breasts on its upturned earth![29]

> And as my seed proliferates in [the Land's] bosom and the sweat of my brow drenches her stiff neck, my soul is bonded to her forever.[30]

In his study of the pioneer relationship with land, Neumann attempts to encounter the halutzim on their own terms, without any preconceived notions. The intellectual roots of Neumann's phenomenological study can ultimately be traced back to the German biologist Jakob von Uexküll, whose 1926 book *Theoretical Biology* hypothesized that every being had its own *Umwelt*, or "life-world," characterized by its particular perception of the environment around it. In that work, von Uexkull famously describes the life-world of the tick—a blind and deaf insect—as existing within the narrow bounds of three external stimuli. First, it smells the specific chemical that signals the approach of a mammal; second, it senses the warmth of the passing mammal's body and leaps; third, after landing, it feels the hairiness of the mammal's skin. The confluence of these three stimuli constitutes the highest state of being for the tick, in which it is able to gorge itself on warm blood, lay its eggs, and die.[31]

Theoretical Biology opened the way for philosophers like Martin Heidegger to explore being and perception through similar phenomenological inquiries. Humans, of course, are immeasurably more complex than ticks, and Neumann limits his inquiry accordingly. Following Heidegger's concept of "being-in-the-world," Neumann defines "being-in-the-Land-of-Israel" as the prime existential condition for Zionist pioneers: "Being-in-the-Land-of-Israel was, for them, not merely being situated in a specific place. Being-in-the-Land-of-Israel was, for them, *to be*."[32] Within this state of being, Neumann identifies a basic desire for the Land of Israel as driving all pioneer interactions with the land. Through a wide-ranging exploration of pioneer literature, Neumann reconstructs how the halutzim saw and experienced the Land of Israel, and seeks to describe desire and its manifestations through that lens. To be in the Land was to desire the Land.

Neumann identifies several key characteristics of pioneer desire, some of which will be discussed in greater detail below. He describes the desire of the halutzim as "a desire for the Land's desire for them," or a reciprocal phenomenon in which the pioneers loved and pursued the Land and felt that they were loved and pursued in return.[33] Drawing on the work of Gilles Deleuze and Felix Guattari, Neumann writes that pioneer desire does not emerge from any sense of lack or deficiency; instead, it is "a primal, irreducible condition, a state of being that precedes need or purpose or any action such as farming, construction, or road building."[34] In other words, even as desire gives rise to creative activities, it does not depend on any pragmatic concern; desire simply exists as "an anarchic flow, devoid of reason or purpose."[35] As the pioneers walked the Land, themselves flowing across it, they built and transformed the Land in fulfillment of their own desire and in fulfillment of the Land's desire to be built and transformed. In the end, the halutzim carried this reciprocal relationship to its farthest end: as they transformed the Land, their own bodies and identities were transformed as well.

The pioneers did not merely want to begin a new chapter of life; they wanted to be reborn in a country that was itself being reborn. Like many Zionists, they saw Jewish life in the Diaspora as incomplete and as a state in which their existence as Jews and as humans could not be fully realized. Not all of the Second Aliyah pioneers changed their names upon arrival in Palestine, but many did. Some named themselves after heroic characters in the Bible, who they did not identify with the Diaspora but with the time period when Jews were active in history. By adopting such names, they imagined themselves as bridging the gap between ancient and modern and establishing themselves as the ancestors of the original inhabitants (or the original conquerors) of the Land. Other halutzim Hebraized their names in ways that tied their identities to the Land itself. To this day, in a marked departure from centuries of Jewish tradition, many Israelis name their children not after relatives and ancestors but after trees, plants, animals, and places found in the Land.

Connecting oneself to the Land was not always figurative, through naming, but was often literal. In Neumann's exploration of pioneer literature, examples abound of halutzim seeking physical contact with the Land's soil, sand, stone, water, flora, fauna, air, and light. Some bury themselves at night in the furrows of newly turned earth; some immerse themselves in streams and springs; some kiss and caress plants and flowers as if they are the lips and limbs of a lover. Often, encounters between pioneers and the Land are eroticized, with each playing the role corresponding to their gendered Hebrew nouns; halutzim, whether men or women, are always masculine, and *eretz*, or "land," is always feminine. Acts upon the Land, carried out in the course of labor, imply sexual acts: drilling wells, plowing fields, and so on.

Walking the Land appears frequently in pioneer literature as an important boundary-blurring activity. It offers opportunities to gaze upon the country, to view the female "body of the Land of Israel," to appreciate the beauty of its nature, and to imagine new acts of building and construction that might take place upon it. The act of exploring land, often through hiking, is described with the term yedi'at ha-aretz, a biblical "knowledge of the Land" that implies sexual intimacy. To walk the Land, to enjoy physical contact with it, and to exchange fluids with it is to experience a physical union that consummates the relationship, uniting people and homeland. Ze'ev Vilnay, one of the halutzim who became a scholar and exponent of yedi'at ha-aretz, was famous for saying, "You shall know the Land through the sweat of your feet."[36]

Even as physical interactions with the Land blur the boundaries between the pioneer body and the body of Eretz Israel, Neumann argues, new boundaries are established. In the pioneer worldview, the Land of Israel, deprived for centuries of meaningful contact with the inhabitants it desires, appears as a body-without-organs, an undifferentiated mass whose foothills, hills, and mountains are difficult to distinguish from one another and whose contours are confusing and undefined. Only through acts of exploration, like walking, mapping, and naming, do meaningful distinctions appear between one space and another. Labor further demarcates Jewish-owned land from Arab-owned land and cultivated areas from desert and wilderness. Physical boundaries like fences and barriers are constructed; settlements take shape; forests are planted; roads are surveyed and paved.

Throughout all of these activities—again, in a reciprocal process—the Jewish body is transformed as well. Deprived of contact with the Land of Israel, and languishing in the Diaspora, the pioneers saw their own bodies as *terrae incognitae* and themselves as descendants of religious and scholarly traditions that discouraged physical activity. Gordon's argument that Jews needed, as a nation, to reclaim labor was essentially a demand that Jews reestablish personal contact with soil and water. Neumann argues that the same acts of digging ditches and clearing vegetation and draining swamps that allow pioneers to absorb the essence of the Land, and to view its external and internal boundaries, create boundaries in the bodies of the pioneers as well. No longer are their bodies undifferentiated and atrophied, but instead, they become strong and muscular, flushed with color, tanned by the sun. "We came to the Land," the pioneers sang, "to build, and to be built in it!"[37]

Within this dynamic, a sort of feedback loop emerges: as the halutzim build the Land, their bodies become stronger, which causes them to build more. Carried on this upward spiral of self-actualization, the pioneers expressed love for the Land by constantly moving outward from land that had already been developed and by seeking new encounters with virgin territory. Hence the aggressive building ethos of Zionism, as expressed by Natan Alterman in his 1935 poem "Song of the Homeland": "We will dress you in a gown of concrete and cement. . . . The desert wilderness, we will cross, the swamps, we will drain."[38]

This dynamic, however, could not last forever, given the narrow limits of Jewish-owned land and, indeed, the narrow limits of Palestine itself. Another type of laborious encounter with the Land was necessary: one in which the halutzim could visit undeveloped areas and somehow engage in labor without leaving any visible marks.

The Labor Zionist View of Hiking and Paths

Hiking bore many of the hallmarks of Zionist labor. The pioneers connected with the Land through the act of walking unpaved paths—some even walked barefoot to maintain closer contact with soil, water, and vegetation. According to Neumann, hiking left its developmental imprint upon the Land in the form of lines that appeared in the wake of pioneer movement: "Pioneer desire left tracks through the land—furrows, canals, dirt paths, roads, drained swamps, trenches, excavations, wells, and more."[39] On this final point, however, Neumann is incorrect. Hiking constituted a special dimension of Zionist labor precisely because it did not enact significant transformations; for all practical purposes, after a hike was over, everything looked the same as it had before.

In a certain sense, hiking may have played roles in building and developing the land, but not in the way Neumann describes. Zionist pioneers indeed gazed upon the Land and envisioned its transformation and sometimes ventured into territory they had never visited to scout out sites for future settlement.[40] However, not all hikes across the Land constituted such scouting endeavors; many were simply oriented toward leaving settled areas and viewing parts of Eretz Israel where human development was not yet visible. The desire of the halutzim to transform the Land constituted only one dimension of their overall view of Eretz Israel and of nature itself.[41]

In opposition to the impulse to develop the Land and make it fruitful, there existed a deep veneration for pure nature—a love for the unspoiled Land that was, in the words of Charles Liebman and Eliezer Don-Yehiya, "far more evocative of paganism than of Judaism."[42] Pioneer youth drew a sharp dichotomy between parts of the Land where construction projects had taken place and the parts of the Land where they had not. To be built-up and fruitful was, in their eyes, the ultimate destiny of Eretz Israel, but the areas that were not yet developed represented the Land in its virgin state: a Land that still awaited its first encounter with the halutzim. That prime encounter was what the pioneers sought most.

That search caused youth to flee development at times—to get away from the world of building and constructing and to remember that the return to the Land was also a return to nature.[43] For the pioneers, hiking was more than a form of free recreation. It was also a sacred form of labor that blurred the boundaries between the bodies of the pioneers and the body of the Land but left no new marks of human presence because it occurred along already existing paths. Hiking along Palestine's unpaved paths enabled the halutzim to encounter a given space within the Land again and again yet maintain a sense of primacy with each visit.

Path formation is an essential part of human life; paths appear naturally in the wake of human and animal movement and constitute one of the primal means by which people transform space into place.[44] Paths precede all other forms of human development because they appear not out of intention or effort, but rather through the realization of the same kind of desire Neumann describes. Had Labor Zionist youth encountered Palestine as a true tabula rasa, upon which no paths had been inscribed, they no doubt would have relished the opportunity to create "desire lines" of their own and would thus have used hiking as a truly transformative means of articulating their desire for contact with the Land.

However, as mentioned, Palestine in the early twentieth century was not a blank slate. The Arabs who had inhabited the country over the previous centuries had formed and maintained paths that reflected their own relationship with Palestine. Because most of Palestine's desire lines formed in the wake of movement and were not planned or constructed, they underwent a continuous process of adjustment and improvement until they followed optimal routes across terrain according to the consensus of the people who used them.[45] Their utility and efficiency did not change upon the arrival of the first Zionist immigrants in the country; on the contrary, Jews and Arabs alike used Palestine's unpaved paths and roads as transportation routes in the course of their day-to-day lives. Zionist pioneers, however, blind to the existence of any desire for the Land except their own, did not recognize Palestine's paths as manifestations of the already existing relationship between the country's Arab inhabitants and the country itself. Instead, the halutzim viewed Palestine's existing network of paths—and the Arabs themselves—as part of the Land. Like abandoned ruins, paths were understood to have been originally created by humans, but over time they had become features of the landscape.[46]

As new settlements were established and Zionist development began to spread across the Land during the period of the Second Aliyah, the paved road became regarded by halutzim as a symbol of modernization and of the Zionist constructive ethos. The unpaved path, on the other hand, symbolized freedom and flight from development and the pursuit of yedi'at ha-aretz in the Land's undeveloped spaces. For example, Yosef Braslavi, a pioneer-era explorer who wrote a number of famous guides to the Land, entitled his memoirs *Along Unpaved Paths to Knowledge of the Land*.[47] Such paths haunt the background of Neumann's examination of pioneer literature; they merit little mention but together constitute the space upon which many of the pioneers' ecstatic encounters with the Land spontaneously occurred.[48]

Pioneers who wanted to leave signs of their presence upon the Land while hiking, then, did not create new paths; they placed marks alongside existing paths. They carved their names into stones and wrote their names upon ruins, thus strengthening the connection between their personal identities and that of the national territory.[49] In doing so, they engaged in perhaps the oldest form of waymarking—the sort described by Victor Turner as creating boundaries between the known territory and unknown territory, between lands that belonged to the tribe and those that existed beyond.[50] If simun shvilim had a precursor during the days of the early Zionist pioneers, this would have been it. The markings the halutzim left along footpaths, however, did not constitute systematic attempts to dedicate unpaved paths as hiking routes. Rather, they spontaneously and temporarily marked the desire lines that characterized Ottoman Palestine's transportation network as desire lines in another sense—as avenues along which the halutzim could satisfy their wanderlust and enjoy direct contact with the Land.

The 1920s: Organized Youth Hiking and Modernization under the Mandate

In the midst of journeys like Ben-Zvi's trek to Jerusalem, educational trips into the countryside, and other pioneer-era explorations of Palestine on foot, a true culture of hiking began to take shape. While Labor Zionist youth were driven by their own impulses to venture away from the safety of Jewish settlements and seek yedi'at ha-aretz, outdoor walking was increasingly encouraged by Zionist institutions during the 1910s, and increased safety along Palestine's roads and footpaths made it more feasible for larger numbers of people to go out and explore. These developments planted the seeds for an efflorescence of organized youth hiking that started during the early 1920s.

First, the Ha-Shomer defense guild, originally organized under the name Bar-Giora in 1909, aimed to provide security for Jewish settlements that were continually under attack by Arabs and worked to secure roads that connected settlements as well. Ben-Zvi, one of the organization's original members, carried a firearm at his side to discourage Arab robbers as he rode between settlements in the Jezreel Valley.[51] While Palestine's roads remained dangerous for Jewish travelers throughout the Mandate period, pioneers asserted their right to travel freely and sometimes paid with their lives. Their efforts helped create an ethos of self-defense in the Yishuv, which in turn made it possible for more Zionist youth to walk across the Land. With the defeat of the Ottomans in 1917 and the establishment of British military rule, security along Palestine's roads and footpaths improved further.

Second, Hebrew-language schools, building on the frameworks of outdoor education originally established by Wilkomitz and Epstein, continued organizing *tiyulim*, or "nature hikes," and encouraged their students to begin exploring on their own. In 1916, a teacher named Pinchas Cohen-Yardeni, who had been born in Palestine during the First Aliyah period and had studied under both Wilkomitz and Epstein as a young man in Metulla, established Palestine's first hiking club at the Reali School in Haifa.[52] The Agudat ha-Meshutatim, or "Ramblers' Association," attracted young men and women who were passionate about exploring the Land; some of them went on to write popular guidebooks for exploring the country, and later established similar clubs at other schools in Palestine. The club also laid the groundwork for the creation of the Histadrut ha-Tzofim, or the "Scouting Movement" in Eretz Israel, which began its activities in Haifa in 1919.[53]

Third, Jews in Europe were becoming increasingly accustomed to hiking as they participated in the still-developing youth movement. In the early days of the Wandervogel, large numbers of German Jewish youth joined the movement and participated in hikes alongside their non-Jewish countrymen. Beginning around 1912, however, anti-Semitism increased within the larger German movement, and Jews began forming their own athletic clubs and hiking organizations.[54] The first Zionist youth movement was organized in Germany under the name *Blau-Weiss* (Blue-White) in 1912, but the largest and most influential was founded a year later in Galicia in eastern Europe. There, Zionist youth—heavily influenced by the Wandervogel and the worldwide Scouting movement—created an organization called Ha-Shomer. Inspired by the defense organization operating in Palestine under the same name, it eventually merged with the intellectual youth group Tzeirei Tzion (Youth of Zion) to form the international Ha-Shomer Ha-Tzair youth movement. By the end of the First World War, Ha-Shomer Ha-Tzair was publishing a newsletter from Vienna, organizing outdoor excursions for its thousands of members, and preparing them for eventual immigration to Palestine. Jewish youth who immigrated during the late Second Aliyah and early Third Aliyah were therefore highly familiar with hiking and were intent on organizing European-style treks in Eretz Israel.

All of these factors combined to cause an explosion of youth hiking across Palestine during the early 1920s. On the heels of the establishment of the Scouting movement in 1919, the first Ha-Shomer ha-Tzair guides immigrated to Eretz Israel from Poland in 1920 and began the first organized youth movement hikes.[55] In 1921, the newly established Histadrut labor union began sending "wandering teachers" across areas of Jewish settlement to conduct educational hikes.[56] Some of the union's first such instructors included Shmuel Savorai, whose daughter Rachel initiated the first forbidden Israeli hike to Petra in the 1950s; Yosef Braslavi (Braslavsky), mentioned earlier as eventually becoming a well-known guidebook author; and Zev Vilnay, who had studied under Cohen-Yardeni and had participated in the Ramblers' Association in Haifa. Through the tours he personally led and the series of guidebooks he wrote, Vilnay became perhaps the greatest exponent of yedi'at ha-aretz for Jews in the Yishuv and the early State of Israel.[57]

Also at the beginning of the 1920s, the British civil administration embarked on a campaign to aggressively modernize Palestine's transportation network. In 1921, there were three all-season roads in the country, and they were paved not with asphalt but with the macadam method, in which successively smaller layers of rock and gravel were compacted atop one another to create a hard surface. The first and longest roads ran along the spine of the central mountain range, beginning at Nazareth and running south through Jenin, Nablus, Jerusalem, and Hebron before ending at Be'er Sheva; it also had a spur that ran to Tulkarm and Qalqilya. A west-to-east road ran across the Galilee from Haifa through Nazareth to Tiberias, with short spurs that the halutzim had paved along the Sea of Galilee to Rosh Pina and Tzemach. The other west-to-east road ran from Jaffa to Jerusalem and east across the Jordan toward Amman. Starting in 1922, and continuing well into the next decade, hundreds of kilometers of new roads were added to the network, mostly across the coastal plain and in the areas west of the main road through the mountains.[58]

The Zionist movement enthusiastically took part in this effort, contributing labor and funds to roads being paved between Jewish settlements. In the aftermath of the First World War, the Balfour Declaration, and the Bolshevik Revolution, a third wave of Jewish immigrants, similar in spirit to the Second Aliyah pioneers, had poured into Palestine. This affected the number and character of Zionist colonies in the country and heightened the need for establishing reliable transportation across the N-shaped area of increasingly dense Jewish settlement that was taking shape across the coastal plain, Mount Carmel and the Jezreel Valley, and the Lower Galilee.[59] It also heralded the establishment of the Gdud ha-Avoda, or the "Labor Battalion," whose main activity initially was road construction.[60] The British prioritized roads between Jewish settlements, not only because they were subsidized by the Zionists, but because in their view, the modern Jewish agricultural economy required connection to Palestine's ports and commercial centers while most Arab agriculture still consisted of subsistence farming.[61]

Against the backdrop of this wave of development, Jewish hikers found it increasingly difficult to escape the imprint of modernization as they set off to encounter the untouched Land of Israel. Schools and youth movements, having thoroughly explored the coastal plain and the Galilee, began to seek new areas where students could take long trips away from built environments. Hiking continued all across Palestine, especially to civil-religious sites like Modi'in, where the Hasmoneans had initiated the revolt against Antiochus Epiphanes in the second century BCE; Beitar, where Bar-Kochba had made a last stand against the Romans during the Second Jewish Revolt; and Tel Hai, where Josef Trumpeldor had died defending a Zionist settlement in

Map 1.1. Paved roads in Palestine, 1921 and 1938 (as shown in Reichman, "Evolution of Land Transportation in Palestine").

1920.[62] In their constant pursuit of prime encounters with the Land of Israel and their aversion to hiking through settled areas, however, Zionist youth became increasingly interested in the Judean Desert—the blank space on the map that lay within close reach of Jerusalem yet at the same time was one of Palestine's most remote and least-settled areas.

The Turn toward the Judean Desert

The Judean Desert is a rain shadow desert that lies along the eastern side of the country's central mountain range. Most of the moisture borne on the prevailing winds from the Mediterranean Sea condenses over the western side of the mountains and falls to the earth. When rain does fall on the Judean Desert, it drains quickly down the ravines that seam the plateau from west to east, producing flash floods and pouring into the Dead Sea depression from the mouths of enormous canyons. East of Jerusalem and Hebron, the desert consists of rolling hills suitable for seasonal grazing; farther east, in its relatively flat center, the land is a moonscape of rocky crags, low rises, and wide, barren valleys; and still farther east, near the Dead Sea shore, the land drops away in a wall of sheer cliffs hundreds of meters high. The shoreline itself, depending on the exact location, can be a flat plain, a maze of deep, narrow watercourses, or a vertical wall plunging straight into the water.

Historically, the desert's rugged terrain has always made it difficult for ruling powers, from the Roman Empire to the British Mandate, to access and control. The Hebrew Bible and the New Testament describe the Judean Desert, with its myriad limestone caves, as the haunt of wanderers, prophets, fugitives, and rebels, including Abraham, Elijah, David, John the Baptist, and Jesus. The religious Jewish community of Qumran isolated itself there; the Sicarii of Masada held out against Roman hegemony there; Bar-Kochba built rebel strongholds there during the Second Jewish Revolt. The earliest Christian monks sought solitude and revelation there and built numerous monasteries across the desert during the Byzantine era. After the Islamic conquest, Muslim holy men lived and died there, monks maintained their cliffside strongholds, and Bedouin tribes claimed the surrounding land. For centuries, then, the Judean Desert had functioned as a lawless area on the edge of civilization—a sort of safety valve for the pressures of Jerusalem, populated primarily by people willing to forgo the comfort of settled areas. The great historian of Christian monasticism, Derwas Chitty, writes, "It is difficult to imagine that land remaining for any long period without its ascetics."[63]

For the socialist-Zionist hikers of the youth movements, who had their own ascetic streak, the Judean Desert was irresistible. It seemed like a timeless place, almost completely untouched by human development over the centuries. No all-season roads penetrated it; southeast of the Jericho-Jerusalem-Hebron-Be'er Sheva line, Palestine's road map was completely blank.[64] The only travel routes across the desert's interior were old roads designed for armies on foot with their equipment and supply lines, the ancient footpaths whose Israelite and Roman switchbacks and retaining walls were still visible along important ascents from the Dead Sea, and the great

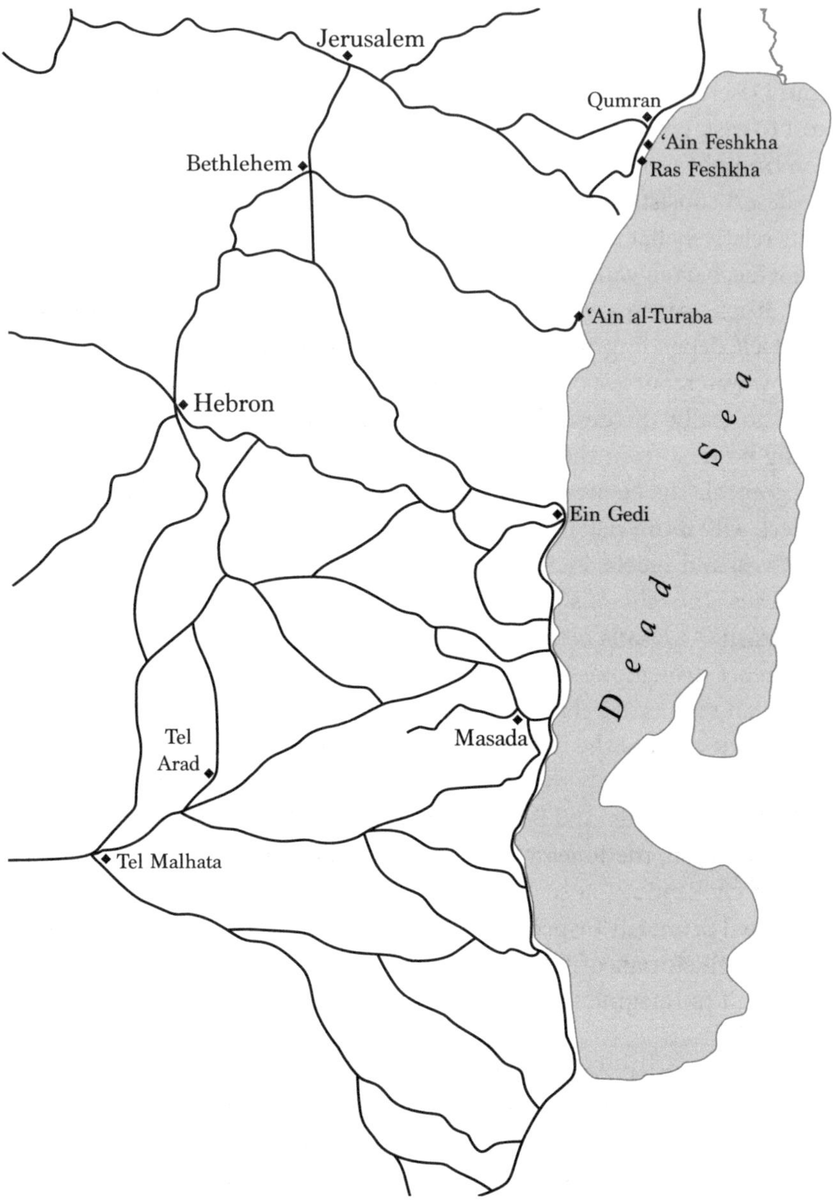

Map 1.2. Ancient roads and paths in the Judean Desert (as shown in Harel, "Israelite and Roman Roads").

watercourses that formed deep channels through the limestone bedrock as they ran down to the lowest exposed point on the face of the earth.[65] In the desert's silent and windswept spaces, Jewish youth could not only walk to important sites in Jewish history, but they could travel back in time while doing so. Here the past could be imagined in bright color, against the rich browns of the mountains and plains and the brilliant blues of sea and sky.

The ruined mountain fortress of Masada was the magnet that drew most Zionist hikers to the Judean Desert. Masada, originally constructed as a winter palace by Herod the Great in the first century BCE, was described by Josephus as the site of a prolonged siege by the Roman Tenth Legion against a band of Jewish holdouts after the destruction of the Temple in Jerusalem.[66] During the Byzantine period, the ruins atop the mountain were used as a monastery, and eventually the site and its provenance were essentially forgotten. Bedouin Arabs referred to the place as *al-Sebbeh* when Edward Robinson traveled across Palestine in 1838. Though he did not set foot on the mountain and only viewed it from across the canyon to the south, Robinson was familiar with Josephus's writings and correctly identified the site as Masada.[67] Almost three decades later, Captain Charles Warren of the Palestine Exploration Fund led an expedition to Masada from Ein Gedi, and, seeking a shortcut to the top, discovered the footpath that the rebels used to ascend the mountain, and which Josephus called the Snake Path.[68] Other Christian explorers visited Masada throughout the latter half of the nineteenth century, giving the mountain a colorful modern history well before it reentered Jewish consciousness in the twentieth century.

In 1912, the Maccabi organization brought the first tour group to Masada, but treks to the mountain on foot began in the early 1920s when Chaim Bograshov at the Gymnasia Herzliya (a prestigious Hebrew-language school in Tel Aviv) began organizing holiday hikes for large groups of students.[69] A spirit of friendly competition developed between the Hebrew-language schools and the Zionist youth movements in which hikers competed to take the farthest and boldest journeys. The Gymnasia ha-Ivrit (the Hebrew Gymnasium) and the Teachers' Seminary, both in Jerusalem, started trips of their own to the Judean Desert in the 1920s, and Vilnay began leading desert hikes on behalf of the Histadrut Central Committee.[70]

Some tours mixed hiking with other modes of travel, taking advantage of the limited transportation infrastructure that existed near the Dead Sea. In 1923, Aharon Reuveni, the brother of Yitzhak Ben-Zvi, participated in a tour that traveled by automobile from Jericho to the northern shore of the

Figure 1.1. View of Masada from the north, 1920s. *G. Eric and Edith Matson Photograph Collection, Library of Congress.*

Dead Sea, then used a boat with a hired Arab crew to skirt the Dead Sea shoreline, enabling the group to disembark at different points and take short hikes to nearby sites. In this way, the group traveled more comfortably and was able to explore a number of sites in Transjordan and Palestine.[71] For youth movement hikers, comfort was not a goal on Judean Desert trips, but the 1923 tour established the precedent of using boats to facilitate treks when necessary, particularly when timeframes allowed for one-way journeys across the desert and required faster return trips.

In 1926, Professor Otto Warburg of the newly established Hebrew University of Jerusalem organized what was by far the biggest Judean Desert trek to date: a sixty-five-person research expedition that spent seven days traveling the desert on foot. The journey, sponsored in part by the Histadrut labor union, began in Jerusalem and first traveled eastward across the desert, stopping at Herodion and the Mar Saba monastery before reaching Ein Gedi and turning north to follow the shoreline. On the return trip to Jerusalem, the group visited the springs of ʿAin al-Tureiba and ʿAin Feshkha, stopped at Jericho, and used Wadi Qelt to make the ascent westward back into the mountains.[72]

While the dangers of the Judean Desert represented attractive challenges for hikers, the lack of well-established and easy-to-follow routes there resulted in serious accidents as more and more youth ventured out. In 1927, an earthquake struck the region and caused the Roman-built ramp ascending Masada on the northwest—the primary means by which groups climbed the mountain—to drop several meters, making school trips much more dangerous. A student hiker fell to her death that same year, causing most schools and youth movements to stop visiting Masada for a brief period.[73] Not long after that, Bograshov remarked, "All treks are dangerous, but even so, walking is necessary!"[74]

Indeed, the dangers of hiking in the Judean Desert only seemed to add to the appeal of youth hikes there; throughout the remainder of the 1920s, the number of hikers and groups visiting the desert kept increasing. In the same year as the Masada tragedy, the Ha-Machanot ha-Olim ("Camps of the Immigrants") youth movement was established at the Gymnasia Herzliya.[75] It was the first such organization founded in Eretz Israel, and it was composed mostly of young men and women born in the Land. From its ranks came the Yishuv's most devoted hikers and explorers, many of whom went on to become major figures in the Palmach, the IDF, and the Israeli government. For example, Rehavam Ze'evi, who served in a number of political and military positions in Israel, began as a Ha-Machanot ha-Olim guide and became a

Palmach scout in the years leading up to the 1948–1949 war. His zeal for the Land, its exploration, and its conquest is illustrated in the names he gave his children: Palmach, Metzada (Masada), Tze'elah (a name that comes from *Tze'el*, a type of acacia tree found in the desert), Sayar (Scout), and Arava (the desert valley that runs from the Dead Sea to the Red Sea).[76] Other Ha-Machanot ha-Olim guides, including Azaria Alon and Yossi Feldman, went on to play important roles in simun shvilim and will be discussed in chapters 2 and 3, respectively.

Also in 1927, one of the participants on the 1926 Hebrew University expedition, Natan Shalem, co-founded a chapter of the Ramblers' Association with David Benvenisti at the Gymnasia ha-Ivrit in Jerusalem. Benvenisti had participated in the Ramblers' Association in Haifa as a youth under Cohen-Yardeni and had been friends with Shalem during their boyhood in Salonika. Operating from Jerusalem, Shalem and Benvenisti were able to organize student treks to Masada and across the Judean Desert with relative ease. Because the terrain of the desert was so difficult to navigate, they enlisted the help of the Arab guide who had led the Hebrew University group—a Bedouin named Hajj 'Abdallah al-'Ayan al-Ta'amri who lived in a cave near Bethlehem and had guided travelers in Palestine since before the First World War.[77] Hiking slowed down in the Yishuv after the riots of 1929 but picked up again soon afterward, and during the 1930s, Hajj 'Abdallah led many of the Ramblers' Association's most prominent treks in the Judean Desert.

The construction of the Palestine Potash Works factory on the northern end of the Dead Sea in 1930 represented a major development for hikers because it created the first safe haven for Jewish youth in the desert east of Jerusalem.[78] Prior to that time, the only water resupply points for hikers along the western shore of the Dead Sea north of Masada had been the springs of 'Ain Feshkha, 'Ain al-Tureiba, and Ein Gedi—all of which lay within territory claimed by Bedouin tribes. Such locations were safe for groups under Bedouin guidance, but they still offered no provisions other than water. Hikers who encountered Bedouin Arabs while traveling alone in the desert risked being attacked. The new island of Jewish infrastructure near the Jerusalem-Jericho highway, on the shore of the Dead Sea, became a staging ground from which hikers could mount their expeditions, and to which they could safely return.

Youth movement and school groups still typically traveled with Bedouin guides, but they were emboldened to take longer and riskier trips. In 1931, with Shalem's encouragement and blessing, a group of young men from

Ha-Machanot ha-Olim took a long trek that followed in the footsteps of the 1926 Hebrew University expedition but added Masada to the itinerary.[79] During the 1933 Passover hiking season, treks ranged all the way across the Judean Desert, into the Arava Valley, and even to Petra in Transjordan. The establishment of the Palestine Potash Company's second factory in 1934—at Sdom on the opposite end of the Dead Sea—was even more important for Jewish hikers because it lay in the most remote part of the desert, in an area that could only be reached by jeep, float plane, boat, or footpath. While the workers at Sdom were not in the business of providing services for hikers, they did not turn away youth who needed rest, provisions, or a boat ride back to the factory at Kalia on the north shore.

As youth traveled more boldly across the desert, friction began to develop between intrepid young men and women and the leaders who were responsible for their safety. The organizational frameworks for hiking established in the early 1920s had enabled greater numbers of youth to journey across the Land, but they built on the existing culture of hiking that the halutzim had created, which was inherently a boundary-blurring endeavor. Hiking, by its very nature, involved venturing out: going beyond the borders of settled Jewish territory, despite the dangers, and encountering the Land in its undeveloped form. That did not change under the youth movements and hiking organizations. The exploratory and adventurous character of hiking in the Yishuv—one that had become defined by taking great risk and facing down danger—was fundamentally at odds with the voices of youth movement and hiking club leaders who insisted that hikers travel under adult supervision.

Organized treks, then, pushed the limits of what youth could physically handle and of where guides could safely lead them. Unorganized and unofficial treks, in which youth walked without supervision or guidance, became increasingly common in the early 1930s and involved even more danger and uncertainty. During Passover 1934, two accidents took place that shook the Yishuv's culture of hiking and highlighted the degree to which Judean Desert treks had spiraled out of control. The first took place on one of the Gymnasia Herzliya's annual hikes when a student was killed by a falling rock at Masada. The ensuing outcry effectively put an end to that school's trips to the Judean Desert. The second took place during the same school break when a group of students who were all affiliated with Ha-Machanot ha-Olim, but were traveling without a guide, attempted to traverse the treacherous mountain of Ras Feshkha while walking up the Dead Sea's western shore. A fourteen-year-old girl named Sarah Rabinovitch slipped, fell from a cliff, and died. That accident effectively ended official youth movement trips to the Judean Desert.[80]

In April 1934, almost immediately after the two accidents, David Benvenisti wrote a letter to the newspaper *Davar* discussing the tragedies, the reasons why they had occurred, and the steps that should be taken to avoid more problems in the future.[81] Writing as the official voice of the Ramblers' Association, Benvenisti wrote that the Gymnasia Herzliya's hike had been carried out responsibly and that as tragic as the Masada accident had been, falling rock was one of the unpredictable dangers of the desert. The death at Ras Feshkha, on the other hand, could have been prevented. Many factors had probably contributed to the circumstances that culminated in the accident, but the key factor was a problem that was becoming endemic across the country: youth venturing out into unfamiliar places without supervision. Benvenisti argued that many young people were ignorant not only of the challenges of the desert, but also of proper behavior within Arab villages, and that an additional danger of unsupervised hiking was the further straining of relations with the country's Arab community. Misconduct by hikers could create tensions that might endanger others in the future, however well-intentioned they might be.

Benvenisti was especially sensitive to these issues, since he spoke Arabic and had developed strong relationships with Arabs in the communities where he traveled. Through the activities of the Ramblers' Association, he and Shalem had become close friends with Hajj 'Abdallah as well. Moreover, the two men had taken pains to ensure that the group's bylaws allowed Arabs to fully participate in the organization. Since the 1929 riots, though, the Association had felt increasing pressure from Jews in the Yishuv to stop depending on Bedouin guidance for hikes. Eventually, having developed their own body of knowledge about the desert, Shalem and Benvenisti began distancing themselves from Arab guides—especially those from the Ta'amira Bedouin tribe who had participated in attacks on Talpiot during the riots—and started training Jewish guides.[82] Still hoping to maintain an environment, however, in which Jews could walk safely, Benvenisti assured readers at the end of the letter that the guides of the Ramblers' Association were highly educated and well-trained, and could be trusted with the welfare of young men and women. He urged parents not to let their children participate in unsanctioned, unsupervised hikes.[83]

At that point, though, it was difficult to stop exploration-minded youth from taking trips by themselves. Even if students lacked the knowledge that could enable them to cross the desert safely, the Hebrew-language high schools and pioneering youth movements had given them all the tools they needed to at least mount an expedition. Some of the older students were members of the Haganah and knew how to procure equipment, maps, and even weapons. Many of them had already participated in organized treks through the desert and knew at least a little about how to get from one key landmark to another. The schools and the youth movements themselves gave them contacts within a large pool of willing participants. Most of all, they had internalized the pioneering values given to them by the halutzim and saw walking the Land not simply as a means of reaching points on the map like Masada, but as an end in itself.

One of the most legendary hikes that ever took place in the Yishuv was carried out in September 1934—just five months after the Passover hiking accidents—by a group of teenagers affiliated with Ha-Machanot ha-Olim. After their graduation from the Gymnasia Herzliya in Tel Aviv, they had spent a training year at Kibbutz Na'an near Rehovot. In the late summer of 1934, they met at the Ha-Machanot ha-Olim hut in Jerusalem to plan a trek whose scope was unprecedented in the history of the Zionist youth movements and competed with the journeys of the great Middle East explorers of the nineteenth century. Their goal was to walk all the way around the Dead Sea on foot in the course of a single expedition.[84]

Using a 1:250,000-scale map, they drafted their simple plan: to leave from Kalia on the northern shore, cross the Jordan River into Transjordan, and then continue clockwise all the way around the sea in an eleven-stage journey. The newly constructed Palestine Potash Company works at Sdom would be the lone rest and resupply point along the way. The chronicler of the trek, Rafi Tahon, had visited the camp at Sdom when it was opened in May of that year and was acquainted with the Jewish workers there. All of the youths were familiar with Masada, which they also planned to visit. Some of the participants had hiked in the Judean Desert under the guidance of Hajj 'Abdallah and were also familiar with the area north of Masada. None of them, however, were prepared for the challenges they would meet on such a long and sustained journey through the desert.

Against the advice of their leaders at Kibbutz Na'an and their Haganah commanders, the young men took a bus from Jerusalem to Kalia and began walking east on September 2, 1934. They crossed the river into Transjordan under heavy loads of food, water, and other equipment, including nine illegal guns. Their journey down the unfamiliar eastern shore of the Dead Sea was difficult; in the vicinity of the Arnon gorge (also known as Wadi Mujib), the hikers could not find a way across the broken terrain and ran out of water in their futile attempts to proceed south. After a long process of surmounting those obstacles by way of the sea, the group continued on its way but had to cross through the village of Mizra'a, where there was a British police post. There, the hikers escaped arrest by claiming to be students whose boat had broken down during a school trip on the Dead Sea.

Having spent a full week in the desert, the group finally made it to Sdom, where the workers were astonished to see a group of Jewish youth approaching from the east. After a day of rest, and after filling their water bottles and restocking their packs with food, the hikers continued north along more familiar routes and ascended Masada as planned. Shortly thereafter, though, the group ran out of water and survived only by accosting a group of Bedouin Arabs at gunpoint in Wadi al-Si'al, later known as Nahal Tze'elim. According to Tahon, the group regretted having to take such an action, and each member limited himself to drinking two and a half cups of water. However, shortly thereafter, the hikers needed water again and nearly repeated the action upon encountering more Bedouins. This time, though, one of the Arabs was armed with a rifle, and the group backed off.

Eventually, the hikers found water and, continuing north along the Dead Sea shore, came to Ras Feshkha, the mountain where Rabinovitch had fallen five months earlier. Using knowledge they had learned from Hajj 'Abdallah, Tahon and two of the other hikers guided the rest of the group up a narrow path ascending the south side of the promontory and back down a little-used route that descended the north side.[85] From there, the group crossed the remaining distance across the plain to Kalia, where the journey had begun twelve days earlier. The hikers, of course, returned to the settled body of Jewish territory with amazing stories to tell, and their return journey established a route that would serve the Palmach and other youth hikers throughout the 1940s. In the course of their travels, though, they had accomplished exactly what David Benvenisti had feared. First, they had gravely endangered their lives, as evidenced by the detail at the end of Tahon's narrative stating that each participant in the hike lost more than ten kilograms of weight.[86] Moreover, in their failure to adequately plan for the journey, they had taken precious water by force, and had thereby soured relations with the Bedouins in the southern Judean Desert.[87]

Though the Dead Sea trek was one of the last successful major hikes to take place in the Judean Desert before the outbreak of the Arab Revolt in

1936, it inspired at least one other unsuccessful and unauthorized hike.[88] In June of 1935, five youth hikers left Bethlehem with a vague plan of circling the Dead Sea. The group made it to Ein Gedi and planned to continue south to Sdom and move around the sea in a counterclockwise direction. However, the hikers quickly ran out of water and decided to travel north toward Kalia instead. They avoided catastrophe only when they were rescued by a boat that was plying the Dead Sea's western shore.[89] Newspaper reports subsequently stated that the hikers were affiliated with a Gdud ha-Avodah (Labor Battalion) group in Ramat Rachel and had left without permission and without a guide.[90]

Other unsanctioned Jewish youth hikes continued unabated across Palestine. Less than two weeks after the character of the failed Dead Sea hike was outlined in the press, an unnamed author wrote an article in the *Davar* newspaper entitled "Less Arrogance and More Caution!" In it, the writer described an out-of-control situation in which youth could be found everywhere along Palestine's less-traveled byways, walking at all hours of the day and night without any apparent concern for the dangers that might befall them or for the way Arabs in rural areas might be offended by their relatively immodest clothing. The article called on the Histadrut to try to impose order on all of this "freedom" and urged responsible adults to forbid children under the age of fifteen from taking night hikes. It also argued the need for explaining the dangers of the Palestinian countryside to new immigrants from Europe, who were accustomed to more comfortable hiking environments and put their lives at risk when they walked across the country without adequate knowledge.[91]

Conclusion

By the mid-1930s, Zionist hiking had left a remarkable imprint on Palestine, not in terms of visible trails or dedicated hiking routes, but rather in terms of the physical presence of Jewish youth across the country's open spaces. It had also left its imprint on Jewish identity in the Yishuv; to engage in hiking outside the boundaries of Zionist settlement was to risk the dangers that existed in the Palestinian countryside and engage in a form of pioneering, even if one lived in Tel Aviv. To engage with the Land as the halutzim did—to know it through exploration and physical contact—was to possess the Land and to be possessed by it. Jewish youth who did not belong to the generation of pioneer immigrants, but instead had been born in the Land, were steeped in the Labor Zionist culture of Mandate Palestine and sought this sense of possession no less than the halutzim had, and perhaps more so.

The question over who would possess the country in terms of sovereignty over land became immediate during the course of the Arab Revolt and the corresponding studies regarding the partition of Palestine between Jews and Arabs. Jewish youth who were passionate about knowing and exploring the Land had not refrained from hiking through the country, even after accidents had caused Zionist organizations to clamp down on unauthorized treks. The violent confrontations that took place across Palestine between 1936 and 1939 did not seriously curtail youth hiking, either; on the contrary, it brought about the establishment of paramilitary groups like the Palmach, who drew their members from the ranks of the kibbutz and youth movements and whose training and reconnaissance journeys across the Land inspired more hikers to follow in their footsteps.

However, the fears articulated by David Benvenisti in 1934 regarding the tendency of youth hikers to venture into the desert without knowledge remained on the back burner; while movement of youth across Palestine contributed in new ways to the Zionist nation-building project, it also exposed youth to great risks and eventually gave rise to more accidents and deaths. Safety concerns—along with the rise of the native-born "Sabra" generation, the contest over control of Palestine, and the establishment of the Palmach—helped shape the character of hiking in the Yishuv in the years leading up to the 1948–1949 war. The confluence of those forces in the Judean Desert, and their role in the creation of Palestine's first marked hiking trail, will be discussed at length in the next chapter.

2

The Palmach and the First Marked Hiking Trail in the Middle East, 1935–1948

Spying Out the Land

When twenty-two-year-old Szymon Persky set out in 1945 on a long-distance trek across the Negev Desert, he could never have guessed that the journey would play a key role not only in defining his personal identity but also in shaping the future boundaries of the State of Israel. As mentioned in the introduction to this book, the young man found himself face-to-face during the hike with an enormous bird, known in Hebrew as a *peres*. Later, viewing that event as his rebirth in the Land of Israel, he changed his last name; as Shimon Peres, he became one of Israel's best-known leaders and statesmen. But the hike was more than a personal journey: it was an intelligence mission in a section of British Mandate Palestine where Jews were forbidden to enter. David Ben-Gurion, then the chair of the Jewish Agency Executive, had sent young Persky and his companions undercover as hikers to gather information on the country's southern reaches.

Just north of Umm Rashrash, the former Turkish border station on the shores of the Red Sea, Persky and his group were arrested by a British-led camel patrol. After being transported to Beersheba, Persky escaped from police custody, traveled north, gave his information to Ben-Gurion in Tel Aviv, and then went back to Beersheba to rejoin his companions in jail. "The escapade made newspaper headlines at the time as a daredevil sort of prank," Peres later wrote, "But it was to prove its value during the War of Independence, when Ben-Gurion asked me for the maps we had drawn up—and asked [chief of the Haganah General Staff Yitzhak] Sadeh and me to plan a route for the army units sent southward to take Umm Rashrash."[1] Today, the site of Umm Rashrash is better known as the Red Sea resort city of Eilat.

If this had been an isolated occurrence, it might be possible to look at Peres's hike merely as an interesting footnote in Israeli history, in which one hike served as cover for an intelligence-gathering mission that happened to shape the boundaries of the Jewish state. By 1945, however, long hikes had been a key component of Zionist education in Palestine for more than four decades. By the time Peres's generation came of age and the Jewish community in Palestine began to prepare itself for war, the Yishuv's military leaders and special forces were drawn, almost to a person, from the ranks of the hiking clubs and Scouting organizations that had passionately explored the country in the hopes of knowing it intimately and thereby knowing themselves. Spying out the Land under the cover of hiking had become a well-established Zionist practice.

Peres was not present when the first European-style hiking trail in the Middle East was marked at Ras Feshkha on November 22, 1947. But as mentioned in the opening paragraphs of this book, the waymarking effort, like Peres's hike two years earlier, was approved at the highest level of the Yishuv's leadership and involved a territorial claim. While the volunteers who carried their equipment from Kibbutz Beit ha-Arava to the cliffs on the Dead Sea's northwest shore really were members of Jewish hiking clubs and youth movements, they were also trained paramilitary fighters. The marks the Palmach scouts painted on the rocks at Ras Feshkha declared that no matter what happened in the upcoming UN vote on the partition of Palestine, Jewish hikers would continue risking their lives to trek to Masada, the ancient mountain fortress that had become a national shrine.

This chapter tells the story not only of that first trail but the hand-in-hand development of Jewish hiking and Jewish paramilitary organizations in Palestine. Until the outbreak of the Arab Revolt in Palestine in 1936, the Haganah saw itself as a defensive organization and worked to limit the incursions of Jewish hikers into heavily settled Arab areas. After 1936, when the Haganah began adopting an explicitly offensive stance against the Arabs, it was able to draw from a culture of hiking that had never been content to stay within the boundaries of Jewish settlement in Palestine and which had understood itself as having the right to walk anywhere in the country and sometimes beyond. With the creation of Haganah special forces units in the late 1930s, culminating in the establishment of the Palmach in 1941, elite hikers became the culture heroes of the Jewish community in Palestine. The processes they pioneered as they marked the first hiking trail in the Middle East served as templates for the development of trails in Israel over the ensuing decades and in occupied territories after 1967.

The Rise of a Native-Born Generation of Jewish Youth in Palestine

By the mid-1930s, three decades had passed since the arrival of the first Zionist pioneers in Palestine. A whole new generation of Jews, born in the land they knew as Eretz Israel, were now coming of age as young men and women who were ready to take their place as leaders in the Yishuv. The Arab Revolt, which began in 1936 and continued through 1939, was a watershed event that changed the whole dynamic between Jews and Arabs in British Mandate Palestine and marked the shift in dominance from the "generation of the fathers" to the "generation of the sons," or from the "pioneer generation" to the "Sabra generation." The Palestine-born children of the mostly immigrant Labor Zionist halutzim articulated their relationship with the Land of Israel in ways their parents had not. Boaz Neumann describes the ascent of the underground Palmach paramilitary organization as marking the end of the dominance of the halutzim in the Yishuv: "In the mid-1930s, the pioneer ethos began to undergo a fundamental change. The halutz came to be perceived also as a warrior defending his nation and land. As such, he had not only to defend but also to attack, kill, and be prepared to be killed. His knowledge of the land and his ability to navigate it now served not only the goal of developing it but also of fighting for it. This 'new halutz' became the man of the elite fighting force of prestatehood Palestine known as the Palmach."[2]

Oz Almog similarly describes the "Sabra generation" as symbolized by the Palmach and consisting of the group of men and women whose formative years coincided with the formative years of the new Israeli society as they reached adulthood between 1930 and 1960:

> The Sabra generation includes the Jews born in Palestine toward the end of World War I through the 1920s and 1930s, who were educated in social frameworks belonging, formally or informally, to the Labor movement of the Yishuv, as well as immigrants who arrived in Palestine as youngsters (alone

> or with their families) and were assimilated into the same milieu. These social institutions included the kibbutzim, the moshavim, and their schools; the Hebrew gymnasiums (academic high schools) in the large cities; the agricultural youth villages (agricultural vocational boarding schools); the pioneering youth movements; the premilitary youth corps . . . the Palmach and its brigades in the War of Independence . . . and the first elite units of the Israeli Defense Forces (IDF) . . . who continued the Palmach tradition.[3]

Not everyone who came of age between 1930 and 1960 exhibited all of the well-known characteristics that defined that generation's leadership. According to Almog, the number of actual "Sabras" who fit into the above categories numbered between five thousand and eight thousand during the 1930s and as high as twenty thousand at the time of the establishment of the State of Israel. Just as the Labor Zionist halutzim always constituted a tiny minority within the Jewish population in Palestine, the "Sabras" who served as the vanguard of their generation never constituted more than 10 percent of the Yishuv. Moreover, "perfect Sabras," who were the vanguard of the vanguard or the "generational nucleus" as described by Almog, never numbered more than a few hundred.[4] Anita Shapira describes their relationship with the Land of Israel as visceral and passionate, similar to that of the halutzim:

> When the poet A. Hillel described the generation of the Palmach, he depicted them all as adoring one beloved, a love that evoked no jealousy among them: "That beloved was the homeland, the country, the soil—in its simplest meaning." The feeling of concreteness was conveyed in the following description: "They are waging the war for their love; out of true love—of the kind that is sucked with the thumb, absorbed with the songs of pioneers, stuck with briar thorns in the bare leg!" It was not by chance that they chose to make so many treks and excursions throughout the length and breadth of Palestine. They developed a new area of studies whose very name hinted at the erotic connection between them and Palestine: Yediat ha-Aretz (Knowledge of the Land).[5]

The men and women who defined the Yishuv's culture of hiking and yedi'at ha-aretz, and who later played important roles in creating the first networks of hiking trails in the State of Israel, emerged from that elite few—the cadre of Palmach and youth movement scouts who were the most dedicated to walking across the Land, knowing it, and conquering it. They were the heirs and beneficiaries of the halutzim and, in many cases, had been taught about Eretz Israel by the leaders of that earlier generation. Clear chains of transmission can be traced back from the elite Palmach hiking guides to the yedi'at ha-aretz experts of the Second Aliyah and even the educators of the First Aliyah. Lines of descent from the pioneer hikers to the Sabra hikers, as well as the exploits of the Palmach guides themselves, will be discussed at length later in this chapter.

The mid-1930s mark the beginning of an important period in the history of simun shvilim—Israeli waymarking—not only because the Palmach and youth movement guides who rose to prominence during that time played an important role in finding and marking trails but also because the father of simun shvilim immigrated to Palestine during that time and almost immediately had an effect on the training of the Yishuv's paramilitary youth. Hillel Birger was not a member of the Sabra generation, nor had he taken part in the halutziut of the pioneer generation; on the contrary, he was a bespectacled engineer from Poland who spoke at least five languages and had an intellectual bent. He was a natural mentor, though, for kibbutz youth who wanted to know how to move safely across the country, and who wanted to gain an edge in combat through skillful navigation. Even as Birger helped the scouts and guides of the Palmach reach the apex of their abilities, he made the first moves toward creating a trail network that would allow Jews to move across the country without the aid of such guides. Whereas hiking had been one of the only activities of the halutzim that did not transform the land in terms of development, the trail Birger marked with a detachment of Palmach fighters at Ain Feshkha near the Dead Sea in November 1947 laid the foundations for the system of colored blazes that would eventually spread across all Israeli-controlled territory.

Hillel Birger: The Father of Simun Shvilim

Hillel Birger was born in Lodz, Poland, in 1902. As a teenager, he was a member of the Ha-Shomer ha-Tzair youth movement, and during the 1920s, he began leading hikes for the organization. His early treks led him out of the plains of Poland and into the Tatra Mountains beyond the Czech border. On those hikes, he came into contact with European waymarking systems and learned how to use topographical maps to navigate on his own. Birger eventually went on to study engineering in Graz and became interested in topographic mapping. He continued to hike and think about the difficulties of navigating across unfamiliar terrain. In association with his coursework, he read professional literature describing how to scientifically chart positions and make land surveys but found little that was immediately useful for his own needs.[6]

For lack of scholarly materials to guide him, Birger learned much through firsthand experience. Later in the 1920s, he and a group of friends from the university took a long trek through the mountains of Austria. Birger describes the group's attempts to navigate the country with a set of maps that had been published before the First World War and which clearly depicted a railroad track that could lead them through a forest toward a mountain they were interested in climbing. Birger plotted a route that took them to the end of the track and then across a negotiable set of contour lines up the mountain. Everything went according to plan until everyone reached the end of the railroad and realized that they were nowhere near where they wanted to be. In the years since the publication of the map, the line had been extended fifty kilometers; by abandoning themselves to an inaccurate map, and not taking into account the features of the land around them, they had ended up in an entirely different part of the country.[7]

After receiving his degree, Birger returned to Poland and served in the army engineering corps, moved to France and worked there for five years as an engineer, and then immigrated to Palestine in 1935. Upon his arrival, Birger immediately found employment as a work leader under the British Mandate government. Late in 1936, during the Arab Revolt, he lost his job and began searching for other opportunities. Birger heard that Plugot Hapoel, the Histadrut-sponsored youth sports organization, was looking for instructors. Physical conditioning fell outside his expertise, but he suggested that he teach topography and navigation. Birger thought he could translate the scientific understanding he had gleaned from academic texts into practical knowledge that would help youth movement members. He was hired, and in early 1937, he set out for northern Palestine to begin teaching youth in rural Jewish settlements.[8]

Birger's first students lived on the neighboring kibbutzim of Geva, Tel Yosef, and Ein Harod and were affiliated with Aliyat ha-Noar, or "Youth Aliyah," an organization that settled refugee German youth in Palestine and helped them culturally assimilate.[9] Most of the students, by virtue of their exposure to the European youth movement, were already experienced hikers. They knew nothing, though, of the unique challenges that Palestine presented to Jews who wanted to walk across it. Birger later described the Yishuv at that time as a series of disconnected islands separated by large spaces of Arab-owned land, many of which were difficult and dangerous to cross. Newly immigrated youth therefore needed to learn, first, what Birger called *topografia*, or "topography"—the skill of reading the land's physical features and their representation on paper maps—and second, what Birger called *azimut*, or "azimuth"—the ability to measure directional bearings with the aid of a compass and to use those measurements to chart safe routes across the country with the aid of a map.[10]

However, Birger was himself a relative outsider in the Yishuv, and as he got started, he faced numerous challenges. First, the kibbutzim were ambivalent about whether Birger's courses were necessary and could not agree with the Histadrut on how Birger should be paid. Second, Birger found that maps and compasses were scarce in the Yishuv—according to him, even the Haganah had few of either in 1937—and in the end, everything had to be purchased by Youth Aliyah.[11] Third, Birger lacked the deep knowledge of the country that he knew would be necessary for his students, so he had to study.

One of the books he read was the newly published guide to Eretz Israel written by Pinchas Cohen-Yardeni and David Benvenisti, two of the greatest figures in the Yishuv's culture of yedi'at ha-aretz and the founders of some of the oldest hiking clubs in the country. While reading, Birger checked the information in the book against his own maps and concluded that parts of the book were dangerously inaccurate. In the interest of warning people against making potentially fatal navigational errors, Birger wrote a detailed criticism of the book. This put him at odds not only with Cohen and Benvenisti but also with Zev Vilnay, whose own red-bound *Guide to Eretz Israel* was already famous in the Yishuv. According to Birger, Vilnay later accused him of "murdering" Cohen and Benvenisti's book.[12]

Such obstacles notwithstanding, Birger made quick progress both as a learner and as a teacher. He scoured all the professional literature he could find in all the languages he knew—Russian, Polish, German, French, and Hebrew—and turned his personal understanding of topography and navigation into practical disciplines he could teach to others. By late 1937, his courses had grown in breadth, depth, and popularity. As they became available for more and more kibbutzim in the north, they began attracting the attention of important leaders in the Yishuv. On November 4, Yitzhak Sadeh, then the leader of the newly created *Fosh* commando arm of the Haganah, attended one of Birger's lectures at Kibbutz Ayelet ha-Shachar and approached him immediately afterward.[13] Sadeh asked for Birger's help in enabling troops to position and maneuver accurately across a wide area during nighttime operations.[14]

Birger's advice—as well as the Youth Aliyah compasses Sadeh requisitioned, since the *Fosh* had none of its own—proved successful and convinced

Sadeh that knowledge of topography and navigation would give Haganah troops a distinct advantage in the field. Systematic study of both disciplines was heavily emphasized thereafter throughout the Haganah, and Birger became the militia's primary instructor. In 1938, he communicated with the British Survey of Palestine, whose maps of the country were by far the best available at the time, in the hope that it would publish maps not only in English but also in Hebrew and Arabic.[15] This effort failed, but Birger visited the Survey, learned about its methods and activities, and used this knowledge to create a *Fosh* technical department, which conducted its own surveys and produced its own maps.[16]

In December 1938 and January 1939, Birger taught the first course for *Fosh* topography guides at Giv'at ha-Rambam near Tel Aviv with the aid of a slide projector and his five languages' worth of material.[17] Around the same time, he wrote his best-known work on topography and navigation, simply entitled *Topografia*. In 1940, he cowrote a reconnaissance manual entitled *Siyurim u-Masa'ot*, roughly translatable as *Explorations and Treks*, which established a means by which scouts could move undercover through the countryside as hikers, record what they saw, and thus contribute to Jewish military intelligence.[18]

Birger later described the study of topography in the Yishuv as evolving along with the Haganah throughout the Arab Revolt and in its aftermath. In his view, the Haganah had begun as a static force, and as it oriented itself more and more toward dynamic field operations, it established the *Fosh*, the more-permanent *Hish*, and finally the Palmach.[19] At each step, route finding and navigation became increasingly important.[20] Also at each step, Birger stayed involved in refining the ability of the Haganah's special forces to move safely and effectively in the field. With the formal establishment of the Palmach in 1941 and under the leadership of Yitzhak Sadeh, Birger began instructing guides in that organization as well.[21]

Finding Paths in the Desert: The Hiker-Fighters of the Palmach

Many of the young men and women who joined the Palmach had already trekked across the country in the course of their upbringings on kibbutzim, their education in Hebrew-language schools, or their participation in youth movements. Not all of them, however, were able to safely and skillfully navigate across the countryside outside the body of settled Jewish territory in

Map 2.1. Paved roads in Palestine, 1947 (as shown in Reichman, "Evolution of Land Transportation in Palestine").

Palestine. The few who could were the ones who had been trained as youth movement hiking guides. Even these, however, were limited in their abilities because they had not been able to travel freely across the whole country. The excursions of the Hebrew-language high schools to the Judean Desert had essentially ended after students died in hiking accidents in 1934 and after British-imposed travel restrictions in the wake of the Arab Revolt had curtailed the Jewish exploration of the Negev.[22] Palestine's desert areas, then, remained *terrae incognitae* even for the most knowledgeable youth movement and Palmach guides.

Those same factors, however, rendered Palestine's deserts attractive destinations for Zionist hikers in the early 1940s. Hiking in the Yishuv was characterized, just as it had been in the days of the halutzim, by venturing out from known territory into unknown territory and by seeking prime contact with the unspoiled Eretz Israel. After the Arab Revolt, and with the possibility of the eventual partition of Palestine between Jews and Arabs, the stakes for exploring and knowing the country were much higher. The Palmach saw the land as theirs by right, but as land that needed to be conquered nonetheless. "In all places, the scout's job is to discover the enemy's country and help conquer it," said Benny Maharshek, the Palmach's political officer. "With us, his job is to discover the homeland and help conquer it."[23]

Azaria Alon was one of the Palmach's first reconnaissance scouts and, in almost every way, fits into Almog's model of the idealized Sabra. Born in the Ukraine in 1918, Alon immigrated to Palestine with his parents at the age of seven and was educated at the Reali School in Haifa. He studied under Pinchas Cohen-Yardeni, who, as mentioned in the previous chapter, had been a student of Simcha Wilkomitz and Yitzhak Epstein at Metulla during the First Aliyah period and who, despite being attacked by Birger, was recognized as one of the country's experts in yedi'at ha-aretz. Alon also participated in the Agudat ha-Meshutatim hiking club and joined the Ha-Machanot Ha-Olim youth movement. In 1938, while still leading cross-country hikes for the youth movement, Alon became one of the founding members of Beit ha-Shita, the first kibbutz established by Ha-Machanot ha-Olim. In 1942, he was inducted into Plugah Alef (Company A) of the Palmach and started laying the groundwork for the organization's first large-scale treks, or *masa'ot*, in the Judean Desert.

Masa'ot were popularized by the Palmach but were similar to other types of hikes that had been established earlier by youth movement hikers; indeed, the divisions between *tiyulim* (hikes), *siyurim* (reconnaissance expeditions), and masa'ot (challenging training journeys) were not always clear. For example, Zev Vilnay had begun leading tiyulim on behalf of the Histadrut Central Committee in the 1920s that went far beyond the boundaries of Jewish settlement to the very edges of Palestine. If these had occurred later, such hikes, as well as the long 1926 and 1934 expeditions to the desert, would likely have been described as masa'ot. Even in 1940, Birger's reconnaissance manual entitled *Siyurim u'Masa'ot* describes both sorts of treks in passing as tiyulim.[24] In any case, the Palmach took the long and challenging cross-country treks that had become increasingly common during the 1930s and turned them into structured paramilitary training exercises. Through the pioneering youth movements affiliated with the Palmach, masa'ot eventually became the standard type of excursion for serious hikers in Eretz Israel.

Almog describes the Palmach *masa'* as being different from the educational tiyul in seven ways. First, it involved a long stay in the field—usually at least three days and nights. Second, it required physical exertion and psychological stamina; it was designed to test the mettle of young recruits. Third, it involved navigation with a topographical map. Fourth, the destination was more important than the process of getting there; much of the walking actually took place at night. Fifth, the *masa'* involved elements of conquest; it typically required participants to reach key landmarks like springs or mountain peaks. Sixth, it usually isolated groups of hikers by sending them to remote desert areas. Seventh, it was conducted within the framework of military discipline; participants walked in columns, rationed food and water, and sometimes carried illegal weapons. All of these characteristics rendered masa'ot dangerous, and this was part of their appeal.[25]

Palmach masa'ot took place all across Eretz Israel, starting in 1942, but increasingly gravitated toward the Judean Desert, with Masada serving as a key destination. (See fig. 2.1.) Alon and the other Palmach guides charged with leading groups safely across such areas, however, first had to learn to traverse the country themselves. For Alon, learning how to cross the desert was a process that had begun for him a few years before his enlistment in the Palmach, when he walked with a Ha-Machanot Ha-Olim group that started in Jerusalem and followed the circular route that passed through Sdom, Masada, and Beit ha-Arava. The first stop south of Jerusalem en route to Sdom on that trip was Yata, an Arab town in the mountains near Hebron. There, the group met a Jahalin Bedouin named Hasin, who was already legendary among Zionist hikers as a man who knew every trail in the Judean Desert; it was the first of several trips Alon took in which Hasin served as a guide.[26]

Figure 2.1. Palmach masa' near the Dead Sea, 1940s. *Courtesy of Palmach Museum, Tel Aviv.*

In a later account, Alon describes the deep sense of insecurity he felt as he descended toward the Dead Sea for the first time. He had a rudimentary map, but its features were meaningless to him, and he could not imagine ever actually using it to cross the desert. Hasin, for his part, had no map and did not need one. At one point the group encountered a lone Jewish hiker who had walked alone from Masada and reported to Hasin that there was no water at the mountain fortress. Alon was awed by this figure and could only dream of what it would be like to know the territory so well and to move through such dry and dangerous areas with such calm and confidence. Hasin told the group they would find water elsewhere and led them down the canyon later known as Nahal Tze'elim, the great wadi that drains into the Dead Sea north of Masada. Sure enough, high on the side of the deep canyon was a bank of rushes, and inside it, a spring. Alon spent his first night in the Judean Desert next to that spring, which he would later know as Ein Anava, and resolved to learn the desert's trails for himself.[27]

On subsequent hikes with Hasin, Alon filled the blank spaces of his mental map with known places that corresponded with the points on his printed topographical map. He learned the important routes across the desert and became familiar with the Bedouin *rujum*, or "stone piles," that had long guided travelers along safe paths when the terrain was too difficult to read. After his enlistment in 1942, Alon was tasked with leading a Palmach group through the Judean Desert without the assistance of a guide. Until that point, Bedouin guidance had been the norm; indeed, no Palmach group had yet undertaken a *masa'* without Bedouin assistance. Often, it was Hasin himself who walked at the vanguard of Palmach groups.[28]

In Alon's account, the trip was mostly uneventful until the Palmach scouts reached Ein Gedi. There, the unescorted hikers were ambushed by Bedouins but managed to stave off the attack. The group continued the rest of the way to Masada. When Alon and his comrades reached the approaches to the mountain, Hasin was there waiting. The Bedouin guide and the Palmach guide now greeted each other as old friends, but according to Alon, Hasin was not happy to see Jews hiking across the desert without his guidance. From that point, self-guided Palmach masa'ot became the norm, and clashes between Bedouin Arabs and Jewish hikers became more frequent. A year later, while Alon was leading Plugah Alef through Nahal Tze'elim—the very place where he had spent his first night in the Judean Desert under Hasin's guidance—the company was attacked by Jahalin Bedouin, whose tribal territory the Palmach was now crossing without permission.[29]

For the Palmach scouts who led the way on masa'ot and were regarded as knowing the desert better than anyone else, the only way to stay safe was to stay on well-trodden paths. Like Alon, many of them had learned directly from Bedouin guides and along the way had developed an unimpeachable faith in the ability of established desert paths to carry travelers to their desired destinations. Rehavam Ze'evi, who was recruited into Plugah Dalet (Company D) in 1944, wrote, "An experienced reconnaissance soldier knew that the trail was the product of the experience of many who had walked here before. Therefore, he shouldn't be tempted to make a shortcut."[30] Alon later wrote an advisory description of Judean Desert paths that further illustrates this view:

> Remember this well: The trail is wiser than the one who walks it. If you ascended upon it, do not abandon it, because it's always right. Here it takes you to the edge of the sea, right at the moment when you're looking to the mountains, and you want to depart from it and "shorten" it; you've arrived at the cliff edge and want to descend, but the trail goes indirectly, up and down, and brings you someplace. Beware of shortcuts! Rely on the generations of robbers and shepherds who were in as much of a hurry as you are, and in this way blazed the trail through their footsteps. Don't you understand? Anyway, try to. Go your own way, and you'll arrive either at the top of a waterfall without

> any path, apart from ashamedly retracing your footsteps; or at a high and deep canyon opening that drops you to a void of gravel and limestone; or just to a maze of wadis and hills in which you will wander aimlessly and in vain. A "shortcut" like this is the shortest, and the longest![31]

However, not everyone knew the Judean Desert as well as scouts like Alon and Ze'evi did. As youth movements followed in the footsteps of the Palmach and began organizing their own masa'ot to sites like Ein Gedi and Masada, safety became a serious issue. All of the dangers that contributed to the romance of the Judean Desert and rendered hikes there such valuable training exercises for the Palmach meant that even the slightest procedural missteps by armed and inexperienced youth could prove fatal. The first major accident took place in 1942 and had to do with the mishandling of weapons: on a Ha-Shomer Ha-Tzair trek, a grenade exploded in someone's backpack and killed eight people.[32] More often, accidents took place along the lines described earlier by Alon: youth either got confused and followed false trails or tried to take shortcuts away from established routes; in any case, such mistakes caused them to get lost in the desert and run out of water. Trails were lifelines, and those who did not know them, or who strayed away from them, walked in the Judean Desert at their own peril.

The number of Jewish hikers in the Judean Desert continued to increase after 1942. Masada rose to prominence once again as a national-historical symbol and a civil-religious pilgrimage destination in response to the presence of Rommel's *Afrika Korps* in Egypt and the possibility that German forces could reach Palestine.[33] In 1943, the Palmach began sending whole companies, comprising hundreds of members, on mass treks across the Judean Desert. By 1944, Masada was the "central station" for Palmach masa'ot and retained that status through 1947.[34] All the while, accidents kept taking place, but few people seem to have given much consideration to addressing the problem; the risks of hiking in the desert were well-known, and the Palmach allowed its scouts to offer their expertise as guides for youth movement treks. The desert itself, however, remained essentially as it had for centuries, with its web of paths that, save for the graffiti of Jewish hikers and the *rujum* of the Bedouins, had remained mostly unimproved and unmarked since the days of the Roman occupation of Palestine.

The Turning Point: Hiking Accidents in the Judean Desert

Hillel Birger believed as early as 1943 that many accidents could be avoided if hikers were better able to stay on trails. His days as a Ha-Shomer ha-Tzair guide in eastern Europe had taught him the value of trail networks marked on the ground and depicted on corresponding topographical maps. Birger began thinking of ways similar networks could be created in Palestine, and he began contacting parties he thought would be interested in funding such an endeavor. He approached insurance companies, thinking they would want to save money by preventing accidents. One official, noting Rommel's recent drive into North Africa, asked Birger, "And what will happen if the Germans come back, and they see the markings?" "I saw that this wasn't serious," Birger later said, "and I left."[35]

At that time, few were yet willing to listen to Birger's waymarking scheme, in which signs and maps would conduct hikers safely along desert trails. During Birger's time in Palestine, though, the ground had shifted under his feet. He had begun as an outsider in the Yishuv's culture of yedi'at ha-aretz, whose input on hiking guides had gone unheeded except to arouse the wrath of Vilnay. Now he was a "voice in the wilderness" of a different sort: a man whose understanding of maps and navigation had rendered him valuable to the Yishuv's fighting youth. Birger's status as a teacher of the Yishuv's human repositories of yedi'at ha-aretz now placed him near the vanguard of the Zionist movement and at the center of the culture of Jewish youth hiking in Palestine.[36] Birger's connections simply needed to be convinced that waymarking was important.

The turning point came in 1947 when a series of hiking accidents aroused the attention of the Zionist leadership. Numerous accounts of ambushes and accidents appear in newspapers from that period. In January 1947, for example, a group of thirty Jewish hikers was attacked by Arabs in an attempted robbery near the village of Tubas, about ten miles north of Nablus; the hikers disarmed the robbers but were subsequently detained by the British.[37] In February, fifteen Jewish hikers were arrested by Syrian police, who claimed the hikers had crossed the border illegally; the hikers were jailed in Kuneitra and released only after paying a fine of one thousand Palestinian pounds.[38] In April, a group of hikers was returning home in two trucks after a trip in the Negev when they were stopped near Gaza by Arabs in police uniforms; when the hikers realized the "police" were actually robbers, they attacked the highwaymen and "routed" them.[39] In May of that same year, two Jewish hikers were attacked near the Kfar Uriah settlement after being mistaken by local Arabs for settlers involved in a grazing dispute; one of the hikers was injured, and the other was killed.[40]

Hiking anywhere in Palestine, therefore, remained a dangerous enterprise. It is unclear exactly which hiking accidents finally spurred the Yishuv's leaders to action, but Birger states that after a series of high-profile incidents in 1947, the Haganah General Staff listened to his proposal for waymarking and took it seriously. Yitzhak Sadeh, who had approached Birger a decade earlier for help in teaching his special forces how to move in the field, now advocated the idea as head of the General Staff. Yigael Yadin and Ya'akov Dori supported the effort as well. Birger received a modest allocation of one hundred Palestinian pounds to begin marking an experimental trail in the Judean Desert.[41] Shortly thereafter, in a meeting at Birger's house in Tel Aviv, Yitzhak Rabin, then a young officer in the Palmach, agreed to send a detachment of troops to support the effort.[42]

From Birger's point of view, waymarking needed to begin in the Judean Desert, where the Palmach trained, where most hikers gravitated, and where most accidents occurred. The question, though, was which trail should be marked. Most Palmach masa'ot and youth movement treks to Masada took place along a few important routes through the desert. The main trail followed almost the exact route (but in reverse) that Rafi Tahon's expedition had originally established in 1934 as it completed its circumlocution of the Dead Sea.[43] Groups of hikers generally came down the main highway from Jerusalem to Jericho and disembarked from their vehicles at Kibbutz Beit ha-Arava, which, beginning in 1939, housed Jewish workers from the Palestine Potash Company's factory near the northern end of the Dead Sea. From there, hikers walked a route that more or less paralleled the sea's western shore and stopped at Ein Gedi and Masada before completing their journey at the workers' camp of Sdom—Beit ha-Arava's counterpart at the southern end of the Dead Sea. They could then return to Beit ha-Arava by boat and thence to Jerusalem by bus.[44] Variations on this route generally involved beginning at Yata, as Alon had on his first hike with Hasin and Ha-Machanot Ha-Olim; or beginning at Bethlehem and taking Nahal Arugot all the way to Ein Gedi; or continuing past Sdom and thence pushing west into the Negev, perhaps as far as Kibbutz Revivim via the Large Crater and the Small Crater.[45]

Birger's long-term goal was to mark the entire route of the "shore trail" from Beit ha-Arava to Sdom. Given his interest in safety, he did not think it was necessary to immediately mark the trail from beginning to end, but rather to start with the sections that were the most difficult to traverse and then expand from there. The whole trail south of Ein Gedi, which was located at roughly the halfway point between the sea's northern and southern ends, was straightforward; travelers could simply follow an ancient road that

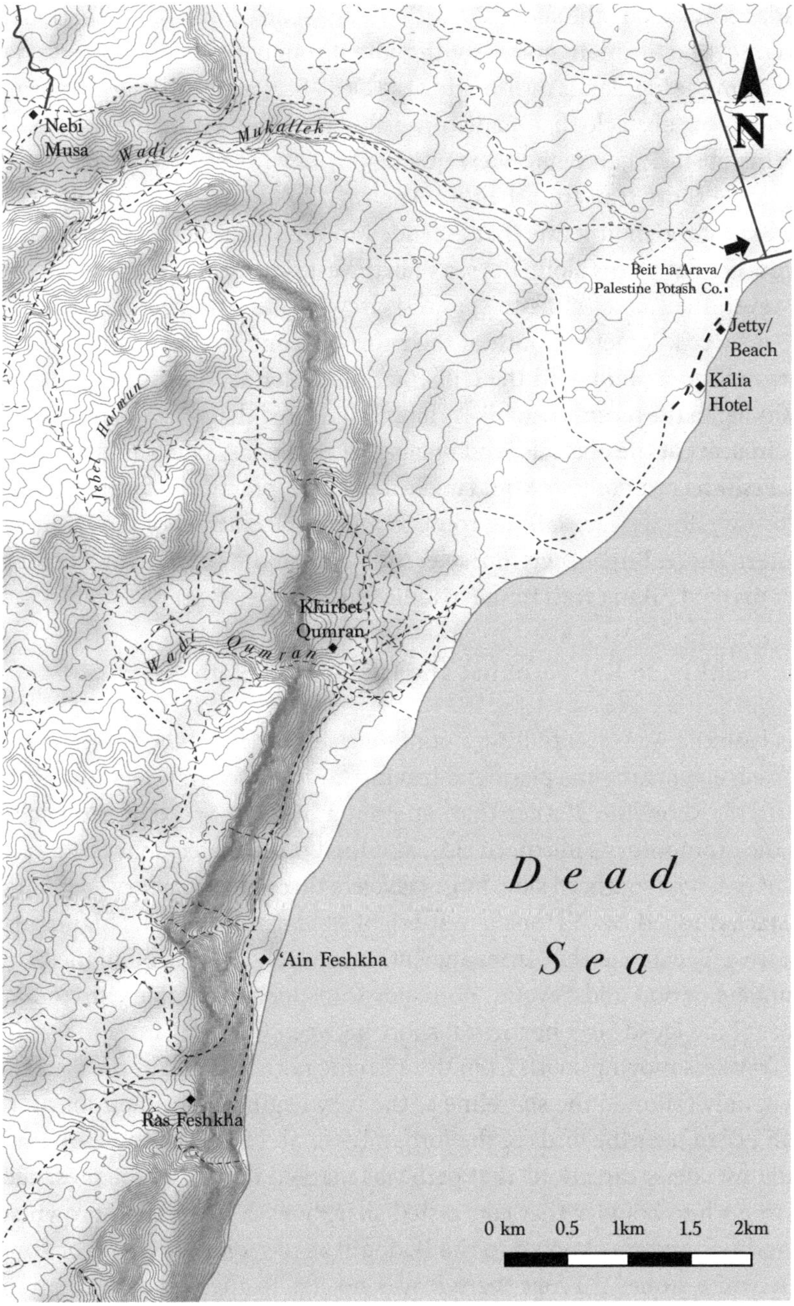

Map 2.2. Northwestern shore of the Dead Sea, early 1940s; note the triangular plain that narrows to 'Ain Feshkha and Ras Feshkha.

made its way along the shore.[46] North of Ein Gedi, though, the situation was reversed, and the main north-south route through the Judean Desert stayed mostly in the highlands overlooking the Dead Sea, mainly because of a single topographic obstacle that made travel along the shore difficult.

This obstacle came into view quickly for any hiker who departed south along the shore trail from Beit ha-Arava. At first, one could simply stay to the east of the mountains that ascended toward Jerusalem and walk south across the flat plains along the sea's northwest side. As one continued south, however, the line of cliffs to the west drew nearer and nearer. Eventually, about three kilometers south of the ruins of Qumran, the triangular plain narrowed to a point, and the cliffs met the water at a headland called Ras Feshkha. In the recent past, hikers had endangered their lives trying to climb or circumvent the obstacle, and one had even died. A safe trail up and over the Feshkha promontory would make it possible, practically for the first time in history, for a clear walking route to follow the entirety of the Dead Sea's western shore. Birger therefore selected Ras Feshkha as a worthy site for the first marked hiking trail in the Middle East.

Ain Feshkha to Ras Feshkha: The History of a Path

Ras Feshkha was essentially a mountain that pushed all the way to the water's edge, blocking the plain and leaving no room for travelers to continue along the shoreline. Rather than attempt a difficult and dangerous climb up the promontory's northern side, and then immediately make a steep descent down its southern side, most travelers throughout history avoided the obstacle altogether and took a well-established detour into the highlands to the west. Because of this, from ancient times all the way through the British Mandate period and beyond, no major transportation route existed along most of the Dead Sea's northwest shore between Qumran and Ein Gedi.

Travelers moving south from the extreme northern end of the Dead Sea, then, only followed the shoreline at the very beginning of their journey. A path began near the fords of the Jordan River and followed the shoreline in a southwesterly direction. That path was marked in part by the presence of a large white boulder that contrasted sharply with its reddish-brown surroundings and was known to the Bedouin as *al-Hajar al-Asbah*, or simply "the white stone."[47] From there it was not far to the ruins of Qumran—then known as *Khirbet al-Yehud*—which stood on an elevated plateau at the mouth of a deep wadi. Qumran was where the main trail departed the shore and climbed an ancient path to the Hyrcania Valley—a flat area that ran north and south across much of the Judean Desert. The valley was bounded on the west by higher mountains and guarded by the ruin of an eponymous ancient fortress.[48] By walking south along the old road that crossed the desert longitudinally through that valley, travelers could move a considerable distance past Ras Feshkha before using a different wadi to descend again to the shoreline.[49]

Travelers generally only proceeded past Qumran along the shore if they wanted to visit a group of freshwater springs that lay along the northern flanks of Ras Feshkha. In ancient times, the springs at Ain Feshkha had served the Qumran community and allowed date palms to grow there; in modern times, they served Bedouin shepherds who raised flocks on the wide strip of vegetation that grew along the coast. Beginning in 1900, a researcher from the Palestine Exploration Fund—the British organization that had invested in the study and mapping of the Holy Land since the 1860s—began visiting the Ain Feshkha area for entirely different reasons and literally left a mark on Ras Feshkha that exists to this day. The writings of E. W. G. Masterman shed considerable light on the challenges that Ras Feshkha presented to travelers—and the possibilities of surmounting them—in the early twentieth century.

Masterman was the resident physician and director of the Anglican Hospital in Jerusalem at the turn of the century and was involved in the activities of the Fund.[50] In 1900, as a response to inquiries about rising and falling Dead Sea water levels, the legendary Charles Wilson, who had carried out some of the Fund's most notable mapping and surveying activities in its early days, expressed his hope that "a mark be cut on the rocks near 'Ain Feshka" to help keep track of the changing water levels over time.[51] Wilson had been referring, of course, to the sheer walls at the foot of Ras Feshkha, where changes in the water level would be easily visible and measurable. Beginning later that year, Masterman began journeying to the Dead Sea on horseback twice annually to mark the water level and check it against previous marks. He carved a horizontal line into the rock as a standard reference point exactly fourteen feet above the lake level at the time, and below it, chiseled the initials "P.E.F."[52] In 1902, he wrote an article for the Fund's quarterly journal describing the rock and the arduous journey to it.

> The rock on which the P.E.F. mark was cut is a huge mass of conglomerate, fallen from the mountain above, which breaks the long line of reeds skirting the shore between 'Ain Feshkhah [*sic*] and Râs el-Feshkhah. It is nearly a mile

Figure 2.2. Ras Feshkha, early 1900s. *G. Eric and Edith Matson Photograph Collection, Library of Congress.*

> south of the 'Ain, and is approached by a faint track parallel to the shore, the last half of the way being a scramble from rock to rock. I always have to leave my horse at the 'Ain. . . . It is possible that nearer to the Râs a surface of rock really perpendicular might be found, but this advantage would, in my opinion, be slight compensation for the extra length of scramble in the sweltering heat.[53]

Traveling any farther along the shoreline in an attempt to clear Ras Feshkha would have been futile at that time; almost two kilometers lay between the observation rock and the point to the south where flat ground prevailed again for good. In effect, as one looked south from the ruins of Qumran, the area around Ain Feshkha was a cul-de-sac, hemmed in by the salty sea on one side and the cliffs on the other, with no reasonable way out for travelers except to turn and head back north. (See fig. 2.2.) However, in a separate account, Masterman describes the path crossing the plains along the shoreline, the view of Feshkha from Qumran, and the existence of a path that exited the Feshkha enclosure by ascending the mountain to the south.

> To the west, the mountains, from the steep crater-like head of Wady Kumran, all the way to Ras el-Feshkhah, are composed of exceedingly rugged and broken limestone and conglomerate, more than 1,500 feet (Tristram) in height, and almost precipitous. There is only one exit from this district to the south, and that an exceedingly rough ascent, about 40 minutes steady climbing, which commences near 'Ain el-Nahr ('Ain Feshkhah). This is the pass described and depicted in Tristram's "Land of Israel," and marked in some maps as if it were a made road. It may have been so once, but now in many places it is almost impassable for led horses. I have returned to Jerusalem this way three times, but on the last occasion almost lost a horse over a declivity.[54]

The young Jewish men and women who negotiated Ras Feshkha about three decades after Masterman wrote the above account were more likely to use a narrow and direct path, despite its dangers, than a circuitous and time-consuming detour that ran all the way up into the Judean Desert highlands. Encounters with the Bedouin had always been risky for outsiders traversing the area, and in the relatively flat expanses of the Hyrcania Valley, such encounters would have been considerably more likely. Robinson describes the highland route as "the great Arab track through the desert along the Dead Sea" and declares that throughout history it was a well-used Bedouin road that allowed tribes from the eastern side of the Rift to penetrate deeply into the territory of their enemies.[55]

For Jewish hikers, then, safety lay in connecting the dots of Jewish territory as efficiently as possible, not in venturing farther into remote Arab-controlled areas. The scarcity of water in the desert as a whole—and especially on the journey north from Ein Gedi to Ain Feshkha—gave hikers additional motivation to shorten distances and timeframes wherever possible. Both of the famous treks that encountered Ras Feshkha in 1934 opted to attack it head-on rather than take long detours through the highlands. The path Masterman describes as ascending the mountain from the springs on the northern side was a necessary element in successfully making any such attempt.

The hikers on the Passover 1934 trek associated with Ha-Machanot ha-Olim actually arrived at the mountain from the west and therefore did not have to climb Ras Feshkha. Having descended into the desert from Jerusalem by way of the Mar Saba monastery, they were able to cut straight eastward across the Hyrcania Valley to arrive at the top of the headland, where it overlooked the Dead Sea. The group's plan was to descend to the Feshkha springs using the very path mentioned above by Masterman and then move quickly across the flat plain to Kalia. On the face of it, the idea was sound and perhaps worth the risk inherent in climbing down the steep trail; again, the alternative would have been to take a longer route through more densely inhabited Bedouin territory, and that presented its own dangers.

After the hikers rested atop Ras Feshkha, they began making their way slowly down the mountain's northern side. During the descent, the hikers spread out and became scattered along the length of the path. When Sarah Rabinovitch lost her footing, she fell between eight and ten meters down the side of the mountain and was wounded both from the fall itself and from the rocks that came tumbling down after her. In the aftermath of the accident, the other dangerous characteristic of Ras Feshkha became clear: from it, Kalia was visible in the distance, but it was still far enough away that help could not arrive in a timely manner. The wounded fourteen-year-old lay on the rocks for six hours before finally succumbing to her injuries; half an hour later, at eleven o'clock at night, a boat finally arrived to bring her body to Kalia.[56]

David Benvenisti wrote afterward that Ras Feshkha did not present life-threatening dangers to hikers, but that fatigue and lack of knowledge of the desert could lead to fatal mistakes.[57] However, since Kalia to the north was the closest place to the mountain where Jewish hikers could truly rest, anyone coming from the south or west would only reach Ras Feshkha after a long and difficult journey. Fatigue, therefore, was almost always part of the equation. Lack of knowledge could lead to hikers losing the trail, but in the case of the Passover 1934 trek, two of the group's young leaders had navigated the cliffs on multiple occasions in the past and were familiar with the path. The fact was that the route down the mountain was treacherous, and once a group became scattered along the length of the path, it was impossible for guides to point the way down every difficult section.

The Passover 1934 tragedy at Ras Feshkha took place in the course of a hike that only had to deal with one-half of the problem the mountain typically presented to travelers making long-distance journeys across the Judean Desert. Nineteenth-century travelers and twentieth-century youth hikers alike often encountered the promontory while trying to make uninterrupted journeys along the shore. Indeed, continuing along the shore rather than making the long inland detour was so tempting—and so dangerous—that Bedouin guides typically tried to dissuade travelers from seriously considering it. In 1863, Henry Baker Tristram, an English clergyman and naturalist traveling through Palestine in the footsteps of other explorers, refused the advice of his guides and decided to set himself apart from his predecessors as he approached the mountain from the north.

> Lynch had only passed in his boats from Ain Feshkhah to Ain Terabeh; Robinson, De Saulcy [*sic*], and all our predecessors by land had mounted the ridge, and descended inland to the south. We inquired of the Sheikh whether we could not pass by the Ras (headland), and thence up the gorge to Marsaba [*sic*]. He replied that it was quite impossible, and that no one had ever been by that route. I told him that the English for 'impossible' was 'we will try,' and set off, with my barometer, prismatic compass, and gun, to see what it was, determined to round the headland and map five miles of coast for my day's work.[58]

Tristram's attempt to "round the headland" in such a manner was extremely difficult, requiring him to wade through the water at certain points and to scramble up cliff faces at others, but it was eventually successful and he made it to Wadi al-Nar (Nahal Kidron) on the southern side. On returning, however, he decided to find a way up and over Ras Feshkha and, in doing so, ran out of water. Tristram does not describe exactly which paths he used to return to his camp near the springs at Ain Feshkha, but he writes that the following day, his party sent its baggage and mules "by the circuitous but more easy road to the north," referring to the detour through the highlands, while the rest of the men in the group ascended with their horses to the top of Ras Feshkha.[59] Masterman's assumption that his path and Tristram's were one and the same, given the lack of other paths ascending the mountain, is reasonable.

The second 1934 trek associated with Ha-Machanot ha-Olim was the journey of Rafi Tahon and his companions around the Dead Sea, which took place in September and was one of the last great Judean Desert hikes of the 1930s. Like the first group, it approached Ras Feshkha from the south, but unlike the first group, its members had the advantage of having learned a reliable route from the Bedouin for ascending and descending the mountain. Tahon writes, "Reuven [Har-Tzvi], Ezra [Kadourie] and I had already passed this way with Hajj 'Abdallah in the winter of 1931. Hajj 'Abdallah had explained to us that one could not pass Mount Feshkha along the sea. We climbed the trail that ascended to the 'Naqab Arubai' [an Arabic name for part of the headland, and labeled as such on British maps] and from the top of the Feshkha cliffs, we descended to the springs."[60]

On the southern side of Ras Feshkha, then, a path apparently existed that not only gave Tahon and his companions access to the top of the mountain from the seashore but had probably also given Tristram similar access when he climbed the mountain while returning to his camp. No such path appears on British maps, but as mentioned, Survey of Palestine maps tended to be unreliable as far as walking routes were concerned, especially in desert areas where data was gathered primarily through aerial photography. Since the trail on the north side was narrow, steep, and unimproved, and because it crossed such rugged terrain, it makes sense that the better-beaten track ascended to the highlands via the Qumran ravine and bypassed Ras Feshkha through the Hyrcania Valley. The lesser-known path beginning at Ain Feshkha and ascending the headland had probably always existed, though, and some desert researchers have more recently categorized it as one of the Dead Sea's ancient, if lesser-known, ascents.[61] The trail on the south side, too, had probably existed for a long time, enabling lightly burdened travelers without livestock to pass over the mountain and travel along the Dead Sea shore.

The idea of circumventing Ras Feshkha along the water's edge never completely went away, though. In May 1943, Plugah Gimel [the equivalent of "Company C"] of the Palmach undertook a seven-day company-wide trek that began in the mountains of Samaria and ran south along the Jordan River Valley and followed the Dead Sea shore trail all the way to Masada and Sdom. Reconnaissance scouts moved ahead of the group as part of their own training, and upon reaching the north side of Ras Feshkha, they used the footpath that ascended the headland from the springs. (See fig. 2.3.) One of the company's scouts was Uri Yafeh, who had joined Tahon's 1934 journey at Sdom and walked with the group up the Dead Sea's western shore. Yafeh was likely one of several Palmach scouts who had learned about the paths at Ras Feshkha from the Bedouin and used that knowledge to find a safe route for the company that followed behind.[62]

However, that larger group—composed of more than four hundred young men and women, all traveling on foot and carrying their own provisions—was informed by some of the residents of nearby Beit ha-Arava that it was possible to sneak around the protruding headland by way of a narrow goat path that stayed just above the level of the water. Traveling in such a manner had not worked well for Tristram eighty years earlier, nor had it even appeared possible for Masterman in 1902. However, Tristram made his exploration around the headland on his own, without a guide, and does not seem to have first scrambled upward to gain a vantage point from which he might have seen such a narrow path. Masterman actually mentions in passing that a path around Ras Feshkha had once existed but that it had become submerged by the Dead Sea's unusually high water level at the turn of the

Figure 2.3. Palmach scouts atop Ras Feshkha, 1943. *Courtesy of the IDF and Defense Establishment Archives—Palmach Museum.*

century.[63] By the end of the 1930s, though, the water level had dropped by several meters, exposing a considerable amount of shoreline all the way around the lake.[64] By 1942, ledges and narrow paths may have been visible that had still been submerged in 1934.

In any case, the Palmach company's officers decided to take the shorter, riskier, and potentially faster shoreline route around Ras Feshkha. It took between three and four hours for the whole group to arrive at the mouth of Wadi Kidron on the beach at the other side of the promontory, but everyone made it safely.[65] Company Gimel took great pride in having been the first Palmach unit to blaze a new route around the Feshkha headland and continued its journey south to Masada and Sdom before returning to Kalia by boat.

Opening such a path, though, raised the chances that unsupervised groups of youth movement hikers would try to follow in the footsteps of the Palmach and further endanger their lives in doing so. The ascent from Ain Feshkha to Ras Feshkha may not have been a "made road," in the words of Masterman, but it was a well-enough established trail that had led men—if not their horses—safely over the headland in the past. Compared to the alternatives—climbing into the more heavily inhabited Bedouin territory in the highlands overlooking the Dead Sea, or skirting the cliff faces that hung over the water—the path up Ras Feshkha represented the best way for young hikers to travel from Beit ha-Arava to Masada. That was the path Birger planned to mark and, in doing so, to establish as the main travel route for the Palmach and the youth movements.

Marking the Trail: Birger and the Palmach at Ras Feshkha, November 22, 1947

On the morning of November 22, 1947, Hillel Birger and a group of Palmach scouts and volunteers from Beit ha-Arava set out across the plains on the northwest shore of the Dead Sea to begin marking the first hiking trail in Palestine. The group made its way past Qumran, along the old shore trail that led to Ain Feshkha and its springs, all surrounded by cane and rushes, and assembled near the foot of the mountain. Azaria Alon, the scout from Plugah Alef, walked with Birger as one of the trailblazers and was familiar with the place and with its history. In a later account, Alon describes what it felt like to mark the first hiking trail in the Judean Desert, far outside the body of the Jewish settlement in Palestine, under the gathering storm of war:

> On November 22, 1947, the Judean Desert waymarking initiative began, and let's remember that time: Only a week before the United Nations' announcement of the establishment of the state, we still didn't have a state or an army, and our actual foothold in the Land was infinitely smaller than it is today, and in all of the Judean Desert—from Beit ha-Arava to Sdom—we didn't have one single bit of ground that was ours. But we had a doubtless sense of possession over the whole Land, and of the whole Land's possession over us. The Judean Desert was a magnet for the youth movement trips, although it wasn't a pleasant site. There was a long list of those who had fallen in the tiyul era, who had slipped from cliffs, died of thirst, had fallen victim to murderers' bullets, and even to our own weapons by accident. There were still hikers who depended on the mercies of Bedouin, or on dubious trails, and different groups became aware of the need to mark the trails of the desert.[66]

Birger intended to eventually mark the entire route from Beit ha-Arava to Masada with painted blazes, modeled after the sort he had seen in central Europe. His scheme seems to have come from the Czech system, which he had encountered in the Tatra Mountains where trails were marked with rectangular signs composed of three horizontal stripes. The top and bottom stripes were white, and the middle stripe was a different color, thereby enhancing visibility through contrast and enabling multiple trails to be marked in different colors simply by changing the middle stripe. The main route to Masada that ran longitudinally across the desert would be marked in red and white, with side trails marked in other alternating colors should the need arise. At the time and for at least awhile thereafter, he referred to the overall endeavor not as simun shvilim but as *simun netivim*, whose meaning is more along the lines of "path marking" than "trail marking."[67]

Since nothing like this had yet been attempted in Palestine, Birger's plan also involved documenting the exact route of the trail and the location of each painted blaze. Charting the exact route of trails onto maps was a difficult procedure that could not be undertaken easily in the field, and in any case, the best 1:20,000-scale maps of the area that the British had produced at the time were based on unreliable aerial photographs and outdated topographic surveys.[68] Instead, Birger meticulously recorded the placement of the trail's first blaze by triangulating it against known landmarks and then used ground measurements and compass bearings to record the locations of subsequent blazes in relation to each other.[69] This was a relatively common practice at that time, and if undertaken carefully, it could yield accurate results; in 1838, Robinson and Smith employed similar methods using a compass and a measuring tape to collect data that produced the best-quality map of Palestine theretofore produced.[70]

Part of Birger's recording system involved assigning ordinal numbers to the trail markings and painting them onto the rocks alongside each blaze. Since this marked section of trail represented only a small part of the larger path, Birger designated the first blaze number twenty so that he could come back later and place the first nineteen blazes along the flat section between Beit ha-Arava and Ain Feshkha.[71] Each numbered blaze was recorded in a journal, along with its location, a physical description of the area around it, bearings of nearby visible landmarks, and so on. This would ensure that the data on the location of each blaze would be well-organized enough to ensure that the trail's route could be mapped later on. It seems, however, that Birger was more concerned with making sure hikers would have as much data as possible so that even if the markings were to disappear, anyone trained in the use of a compass could still find the trail. This was a marked departure from European waymarking, in which walking routes were never recorded with such detail and redundancy but were simply marked so that hikers could move from blaze to blaze. It seems that Birger sought to tailor waymarking in Palestine to suit the conditions of the country—the most problematic of which was the conflict over control of land between Jews and Arabs.

The masa'ot of the Palmach extended Jewish presence across the whole of Palestine, but this marked trail was something new: its markings did not simply signify the presence of a trail but of the Jewish right to place signs upon the ground as they saw fit and to permanently sanctify a corridor of movement for Jewish use. A marked trail showed not only that Jews had passed through the area before, but that they would pass through it again. Even when Jewish hikers were physically absent, the trail markings announced to anyone who might see them that the area between Ain Feshkha and Ras Feshkha was a place where Jews claimed the right to walk. The impending United Nations vote on the partition of Palestine stood to place this territory under the sovereignty of an Arab state, but this had little bearing for Palmach hikers, who intended to continue using Beit ha-Arava as a bridgehead for treks across the northern Judean Desert. To mark this trail at this time, then, was to mark territory, and Birger knew that his act would be interpreted as such by Arabs.

Conscious of the degree to which the placement of colored markings along the seashore would attract the attention of the Bedouin—and the degree to which such markings would constitute a threat to the system of rock cairns and boundary-stones the Bedouin already used to signify their own control over the area—Birger and the trail crew took precautions to make sure the markings would not be erased. The paint and paintbrushes the Palmach scouts carried were already unusual additions to the equipment they typically carried into the desert, but the ladder they carried up the side of the mountain must have seemed even more unorthodox. Where possible, the crew climbed the ladder and painted blazes high on vertical rock faces so that they would be easy for hikers to notice but difficult for the Bedouin to remove.[72]

With each blaze being painted with such care, recorded with such precision, and described with such detail, the extension of the trail up the mountainside took place slowly. By the end of the day, the group had completed its goal and had placed dozens of blazes along the entirety of the ascent, but the marked trail itself was only about two kilometers long. Birger had only spent one-quarter of the budget he had received from the Haganah, though, and since the most difficult section of the trail had been completed, marking the remainder of the route to Masada would likely take place much more quickly.

The 1948 War and Its Immediate Aftermath

Birger was never able to return and mark the rest of the trail. On the night of November 29, 1947, one week after the experimental waymarking project had begun, the United Nations General Assembly approved the plan to partition Palestine. The decision set the stage for the termination of the British Mandate, the withdrawal of British troops from the country, and the establishment of an independent Jewish state. Civil war began almost immediately thereafter as Palestinian Arabs started attacking the Yishuv's roads and communications networks. The Jewish community dedicated all of its resources to the war effort, including the Palmach troops who had been marking the trail and the seventy-five pounds that Birger had not yet spent.

Over the course of the war, Kibbutz Beit ha-Arava and the Palestine Potash Company works at Kalia were overrun and destroyed by Arab forces. The Judean Desert north of Ein Gedi became part of the Jordanian-occupied West Bank. The red-and-white markings painted on the rocks above Ain Feshkha were abandoned to the elements, without a single Jewish hiker having followed them. Masada and the surrounding southern portion of the Judean Desert remained in Israeli control, but most of the old routes leading

Map 2.3. United Nations Partition Plan, 1947.

to the mountain were cut by the Green Line. After the 1948–1949 war, Israeli hikers faced the task of rediscovering their country—making their way along its new boundaries, exploring its newly opened desert areas, and finding new trails to replace the old ones that could no longer be traveled.

Compared to the network of marked trails that took root and grew around Ein Gedi, and that eventually spread across the rest of Israel, Birger's short and untraveled first trail might seem to be little more than a footnote in the history of simun shvilim. It was an important beginning, though, and served as the foundation upon which all subsequent trails were based. The knowledge Birger gleaned from marking the experimental trail from Ain Feshkha to Ras Feshkha made him Israel's lone expert on simun shvilim after the war, and the only man with a plan for transforming the country's lonely desert paths into safe highways for intrepid hikers. It took time, though, for the impulse to mark trails to rise to the surface again in the aftermath of the war. For about a decade, as Israeli hikers set about exploring the country within its new boundaries, Birger again became a voice in the wilderness, calling for a system of marks and maps to guide youth across the Land of Israel in a way that guidebooks and human guides could not.

3

The First Israeli Hiking Trails, 1949–1963

The Challenge of Hiking within Boundaries

The "pioneer generation" of early Labor Zionists was responsible not only for building a Jewish culture of hiking in Palestine but also for founding the central institutions of the eventual State of Israel. Both projects were infused with the Labor Zionist imperative to go beyond existing boundaries, to seek new spaces for unmediated encounters with the Land of Israel, and to actualize Jewish existence through those encounters. The culture of hiking created opportunities for Jews to embody the Zionist values of strength and initiative by leaving the "safe" areas of Jewish settlement, to explore the whole country, and to come into intimate contact with it—and in doing so, to preserve what they saw as the Land's virgin, unspoiled state. Other Labor Zionist institutions, from the labor union to the kibbutz, aimed to transform the Land wherever possible through the act of building, constantly seeking new spaces to consummate the pioneer-Land relationship, and leaving indelible marks of development. Both the imperative to build and the imperative to walk were parts of the ongoing process of Zionist colonization; the former was limited to Jewish-owned territory, and the latter ranged freely across the whole of Palestine, creating possibilities for eventual conquest as Jewish hikers came to "know the Land," including Arab-owned land, as their birthright.

With the creation of the State of Israel, the Labor Zionist imperative to build took on new dimensions as the flight and expulsion of more than seven hundred thousand Palestinian Arabs, the Israeli expropriation of their land and property, and the destruction of more than four hundred of their villages created a tabula rasa in the eyes of the state upon which new spatial and economic visions could be projected. Across the relatively well-watered northern areas of the country, all the way down to the coastal plain, the state resettled masses of new Jewish immigrants in formerly Arab areas, created new towns and settlements for further immigrant placement and population redistribution, and connected those settlements to the main body of the country with new road networks.

In Israel's remote desert spaces, the new Jewish state was unable to put Zionism's cement-and-mortar ethos to work on a large scale. However, the state was able to encourage the other side of the Zionist relationship with the Land, which involved the efforts of pioneering youth to explore and to intimately know the country's undeveloped areas. Meanwhile, elite scouts and guides, whose identities prior to statehood had been based on their knowledge of Eretz Israel, were unsettled by the incorporation of large and unknown tracts of land into Jewish territory. Spurred by an existential urge to know the Land and define the contours of its body, the young leaders of Israel's culture of hiking walked across unmapped deserts and along unmarked frontiers. At the same time, frustrated that the realization of the Zionist dream had created finite limits to the knowable Eretz Israel in the form of hardened boundaries, some youth sought to continue their exploration horizontally by walking across the border to sites like Petra in Jordan. Others directed their energies vertically, digging downward and seeking deep historical, geological, and archaeological knowledge of the Land.

Simun shvilim reappeared in the late 1950s and early 1960s at Ein Gedi, where all of these forces came together at the farthest extremity of Israeli territory. There, after having extensively explored Israel's deserts, Yossi Feldman established a hostel and field school on the Jordanian frontier where youth could stay and deeply develop yedi'at ha-aretz. Meanwhile, the demand for desert hiking—particularly to the national-historical site of Masada—had far outpaced the development of infrastructure and the training of guides. Hiking accidents—due to navigational and route-finding difficulties, the rugged and arid character of the Judean Desert, and the proximity of enemy armistice lines—grew in frequency and severity, causing regional governing authorities and the military to expend large amounts of time and effort in search and rescue operations. In response to renewed calls for simun shvilim, Feldman used his knowledge of the Land, as well as his familiarity with the people who lived and worked in the Judean Desert and the Negev, to assemble a team of experts and create a sustainable framework for marking and mapping desert footpaths.

This chapter begins by examining Israeli hiking in the 1950s against the backdrop of the state's efforts to establish a greater Israeli presence in its peripheral desert areas. Yossi Feldman's experiences in Israel's deserts—his explorations as a youth, his military service in a Nahal settlement unit, his participation in archaeological field research projects, and his leadership in rebuilding ancient Nabatean ruins—serve as an illuminating lens for understanding the character of the Negev after statehood, the way trails stood to serve as a lightweight and low-cost means of developing the desert and keeping hikers safe, and the reasons Feldman was able to succeed where others had failed in creating Israel's first marked and mapped trail network. Finally, by discussing how the trail network existed from the beginning within the tension created by the Zionist desire to know the unspoiled Land on the one hand and to transform and develop it on the other, this chapter lays a foundation for understanding how the mark and the map became such dominant mediators in the relationship between Israelis and the Land of Israel and how trails came to play a prominent role in ongoing processes of deepening state control of contested territory.

The First Israeli Hikers and Their Identity Crisis

Yossi Feldman, the figure most responsible for laying sustainable foundations for large-scale waymarking and trail mapping in the nascent Jewish state, was only seventeen years old when Israel and its Arab neighbors signed armistice agreements in the spring of 1949. Feldman fit the category of the archetypal Sabra that Oz Almog describes as part of the small "generational nucleus" of pioneering youth who charted the course for the Zionist movement between the 1930s and the 1960s.[1] Born in Tel Aviv in 1932, Feldman was steeped from early childhood in the Hebrew-language Zionist educational system. His kindergarten teacher was Chaya Brenner, the wife of the writer Yosef Chayim Brenner. He later studied outside the city at Mikve Israel Agricultural School, the institution founded in 1870 to teach Jews in Palestine how to farm. As a teenager he joined the Ha-Machanot ha-Olim youth movement—which was the first such movement native to Palestine and the most fervently dedicated to exploring and knowing the Land—and trekked across the country on every school break with elite scouts like

Map 3.1. State of Israel and surrounding countries, 1949–1967.

Azaria Alon and Motta Gur.[2] Feldman was too young to fight in the War of 1948, but when the armistice lines were drawn, he and his friends were some of the first to walk to the country's farthest edges.

The great triangle of the Negev now comprised more than 60 percent of Israel's land area, but it was almost completely unmapped and unknown to Israelis. Even the British, who had enjoyed sovereignty over the desert territory for three decades, had never produced accurate maps of the area; the Survey of Palestine's series of 1:100,000-scale maps extended only as far south as Be'er Sheva.[3] Beyond that frontier, British-made maps of the Negev were based on topographic data obtained before the First World War and updated only through unreliable aerial surveys. During the late Mandate period, British-imposed travel restrictions made it difficult for the Jews of Palestine to explore the Negev at all. After the war, Israel, with its limited resources, could not yet heavily settle and develop the desert, but it could work on multiple fronts to research the Negev and begin establishing presence there.[4]

In July 1949, Prime Minister David Ben-Gurion established the Negev Names Committee, a group of geographers tasked with assigning a new Hebrew toponymy to the country's south and eventually to the whole country.[5] Within the IDF, agricultural settlement units like Nahal were created so that young men and women could continue the Zionist pioneering tradition during their mandatory military service.[6] Civilian efforts took place as well under the IDF's security umbrella; university scholars, yedi'at ha-aretz enthusiasts, and youth movement hikers all explored the desert throughout the 1950s.

During Passover 1949, Feldman and some of his friends from the Ha-Machanot ha-Olim youth movement decided to trek across the desert on the heels of the Negev Brigade, which had raced to establish a bridgehead on the Red Sea only a month earlier, during the last Israeli campaign of the war. The hikers began at Revivim, which was the southernmost Jewish outpost in Israel until one reached Umm Rashrash or the newly conquered Eilat.[7] The shortest distance on the map between the two points was about one hundred fifty kilometers. The planned route for the hike, which was much longer because of the desert's mountainous terrain, ran through the great crater of Makhtesh Ramon, into the broken highlands of the western Negev around Be'erot Oded, to Har Sagi overlooking the Sinai border, and then south across wide, shadeless plains crisscrossed with dry watercourses before reaching the Eilat Mountains and, eventually, the Red Sea.

The journey was overwhelming for everyone involved. As the group descended into the crater, a *hamsin* (a type of hot desert storm) blew into the area. The group's guide, a scout from Revivim, became disoriented and could not find the right way to exit the southern side of the crater. This caused the hikers to be in the wrong place for their planned rendezvous with the jeep that was supposed to come and replenish their water supply. Eventually the despairing and exhausted group became spread across a three-kilometer area before Feldman and a friend assembled everyone atop a hill that became known thereafter as *Giv'at ha-Metim*, or "Hill of the Dead." From there, Feldman was lucky enough to spot the jeep, and the group eventually made it all the way to Eilat.[8]

Feldman found his first encounter with the Negev unsettling, not because of the hardships he and the group endured there—after all, he had already faced all sorts of dangers and difficulties when hiking elsewhere in Mandate Palestine—but because the country he and his companions had taken pride in knowing suddenly seemed different. In one sense, this was exhilarating. The boundaries of Jewish territory had expanded not only beyond the narrow confines of pre-state Jewish settlement but even beyond the wider areas allotted to the Jews under the Partition Plan, thus opening new frontiers for exploration. At the same time, though, that expansion had brought huge and unknown spaces into Israel's domain, rendering the once-knowledgeable scouts novices once again in yedi'at ha-aretz. The scout from Revivim could not make his way out of the Ramon crater. The group had no name for the hill it climbed. No one knew where to find water. Similar dynamics had turned the Judean Desert east of Jerusalem into a fascinating and frightening place for pre-war Jewish hikers, but the Negev was many times larger and much less familiar.

If it was true that a person was, as Tchernichovsky wrote, "but the image of his homeland's landscape," then the incorporation of huge and unknown spaces into the body of Jewish territory represented nothing less than an identity crisis for the scouts and guides who, before the war, had identified themselves most closely with a particular conception of the Land of Israel.[9] In order to regain an understanding of their own existence, they had to go and explore the country. "With the founding of the state," Feldman later wrote, "the conditions for hiking and knowing the Land changed. There was a tremendous urge to move and to scout the open spaces of the Land to find new horizons. We, the generation that passed from the pre-state era to the era of statehood, found ourselves lost and perplexed."[10]

Though hiking through the Negev was difficult, the guides and scouts who had served as leaders in the youth movements and the Palmach were able to explore the country fairly quickly—especially in the absence of the obstacles to Jewish movement that existed prior to the establishment of the state. For example, by 1952 Arik Megger and a small group of Israeli hikers from the Hebrew University of Jerusalem had not only crisscrossed the country's interior but had also traced all of the country's borders with their footsteps.[11] They soon realized that while the fulfillment of the Zionist dream had indeed opened large portions of Eretz Israel for exploration, it had also resulted in the creation of finite boundaries. Their horizontal journeys across the Land in search of yedi'at ha-aretz could only take them so far. For youth like Meir Har-Zion and Rachel Savorai, who felt that there was little left to know in Israel, the answer was to keep going—to push across the armistice lines and enter truly unknown territory once again. In 1953, they became the first Israelis to hike to Petra in southern Jordan.[12] They returned safely, and Har-Zion became famous (and to some, infamous) for his continued cross-border exploits as an IDF commando.[13] Other hikers, however, were not so lucky; Megger and several others were killed in various attempts to reach Petra throughout the 1950s.[14]

Feldman, too, explored the country in his own attempt to define and connect Israel's unknown spaces to its known and settled places. Like other elite hikers, he had the sense that horizontal explorations could eventually become unsatisfying. After his long Negev trek, though, a good deal of the country still lay open for him to see, so in the spring of 1950, he embarked on a hike through the Judean Desert that helped him to articulate the type of knowledge of the Land he would seek in the long term. Rather than sneak across borders to explore lands that were not his own, Feldman decided to find places in Israel that aroused his curiosity and attain a yedi'at ha-aretz that was vertical, not horizontal. On his first long trek through the Judean Desert, the oasis of Ein Gedi became anchored in his mind as a point where he wanted to seek this kind of knowledge; he describes his first experience there as the beginning of a "love affair" that lasted for years and years.[15]

A New Frontier in the Judean Desert: Ein Gedi on the Green Line

Ein Gedi possessed a certain mystique for Israeli hikers in the 1950s. It was a green oasis, full of Jewish history and situated at the very edge of the Land.[16] In the days of the Palmach, the site had been but a way station for hikers

Figure 3.1. Nahal soldiers at Ein Gedi, 1953. *Courtesy Government Press Office.*

traveling the Jerusalem—Beit ha-Arava—Masada—Sdom route, but after 1948, that route had been cut off by the Israel-Jordan armistice line. To reach Ein Gedi from Jerusalem, then, or anywhere else in the settled body of the country, travelers had to follow the swell of the Green Line west and south around the Hebron foothills all the way to Be'er Sheva. There, the paved road continued west toward Nitzana on the Sinai border, and an unpaved jeep track continued east toward Sdom. The old boat route to Sdom from the Palestine Potash Company's northern works at Kalia had been similarly cut off during the war, so the southern works, which had once been the only site of significant Jewish presence in that part of the desert, now lay inactive and rusting on the salt-crusted shore. One traveler described the rest of the journey as follows: "From Sdom, at the southern tip of the Dead Sea, a track runs northward, following the western shore. . . . Further along the coast, the track crosses dry river beds winding their way down the steep sides of the bare, rocky mountains of the Wilderness of Judah to reach the sea. It passes the hot springs of Zohar and the Brook of Bokek, where fresh water streams over the stones of a river bed. . . . Nine and a half miles to the north is the foot of legendary Massada [*sic*]; beyond it, Ein Geddi [*sic*]."[17]

Farther north near the Dead Sea, the Green Line swung northeast again to form a narrow triangle of Israeli territory hemmed in by the

Jordanian-occupied West Bank on one side, and the Dead Sea on the other. Ein Gedi lay at the apex of that triangle, only a few kilometers away from the border where the great wadis of Nahal Arugot and Nahal David flowed down from Jordanian territory and met near the sea. During the 1948 War, the Jordanians had placed an Arab Legion garrison there; near the end of the war, when the Israelis made an amphibious assault from Sdom on Ein Gedi, they wiped out the garrison and replaced it with an outpost of their own.[18]

One year later, the military camp at Ein Gedi was almost as isolated as the ruined Roman fortresses farther down the Rift had been in ancient times, back when the lines of the Limes Arabicus guarded the Empire against the incursions of nomads from the south. Feldman describes Ein Gedi at that time as "a place of punishment for the IDF, faraway and inaccessible, where they would throw anyone they didn't want around." The soldiers stationed there were lonely, and their nerves were frayed from constantly being on the lookout for Bedouin incursions and attacks. The camp consisted of some old buses and ramshackle buildings, all surrounded by a wire fence that had empty cans strung all over it, and "at night, when animals wandered around the camp, or when a *soroka* wind blew, the cans would rattle around, and all of the soldiers would open fire, shooting into the darkness in all directions."[19]

Feldman and his youth movement companions soon experienced this firsthand. They began their spring 1950 hike at Rosh Zohar, where the Romans had set up one of their frontier forts centuries earlier and walked to Ein Gedi by way of Nahal Ye'elim and the Dead Sea shoreline.[20] The hikers, one of the rare civilian groups to visit the new Israeli outpost, approached unannounced. The soldiers inside saw the hikers from a distance, but identified them as hostile Bedouin. They immediately began throwing grenades and firing their weapons. Feldman, walking at the head of the group, was hit in the chin by a piece of shrapnel as everyone took cover.[21]

When the soldiers realized their mistake, they rushed to the group's aid. Feldman was the only one injured, but he needed medical help. No road yet connected Ein Gedi to any other settlement in Israel. The nearest military clinic was at Ein Hatzeva, another remote outpost in the Arava Valley about seventy kilometers away on the map. The soldiers therefore took Feldman by boat to Sdom, where the decaying Palestine Potash Works was still guarded by a small detachment of workers. From there, the soldiers took Feldman the rest of the way by jeep, left him at Ein Hatzeva, and returned to Ein Gedi the way they came.

After the doctors at Ein Hatzeva stitched him up, Feldman was on his own. He left alone on foot to return toward Ein Gedi. Upon his arrival back at Sdom, Moshe Langosky, who had been Moshe Novomeysky's right-hand man at the potash factory and was now supervising the guards at the site, detained Feldman and refused to allow the teenager to continue alone through the desert to Ein Gedi. Feldman then waited until nightfall, sneaked away from the workers' camp, and began walking north again, armed only with a staff and some rocks in case he needed to defend himself.

Feldman is not clear in his account of the trip exactly how much time elapsed between the initial friendly fire attack at Ein Gedi and the moment of his escape from Langosky's men at Sdom, but it is likely that by that point, Feldman had been on the move for several days. Even without counting the first stage of the journey between Rosh Zohar and Ein Gedi, he had spent a fair amount of time on foot. The walk from Ein Hatzeva to Sdom alone was nearly forty kilometers, and in the late spring, Feldman would have walked it under a hot sun and a heavy load of equipment and water. He seems to have covered it in a single day and then to have embarked again from Sdom late the following night.

Unable to take a straight line by boat toward Ein Gedi, and therefore forced to navigate the terrain on the ground, Feldman could expect a walk of about another fifty kilometers north along the Dead Sea shoreline from Sdom, lasting the better part of two days. This would realistically have required him either to ration water or to try to find some along the way, perhaps at the freshwater springs of Ein Bokek. In any case, the trek Feldman faced was difficult, and it makes sense that Langosky, out of a sense of responsibility for the young man's life, had tried to keep him at Sdom. It would have been reasonable for Feldman to try to get back to Ein Gedi by the shortest route possible, so as to rejoin his group—especially considering the fact that he was still nursing a shrapnel wound to the face—but he did not. "I decided to take a detour to Masada," Feldman later wrote.

He approached from the east, from the broken plains ascending toward the mountain from the seashore. When he got to the foot of Masada, he could see silhouettes of hikers along the heights, and he recognized them as his companions who were now returning from Ein Gedi. Shvil ha-Nachash, or the "Snake Path," had not yet been brought to the public's attention, so Feldman took Shvil ha-Ratz, or the "Runner's Path"—another ancient trail—around the mountain until he arrived at the Roman ramp on the northwest. As the group atop the ruined fortress watched the lone, fast-moving figure far below, everyone began arguing over who it was. Feldman recounts, "Some of them said, 'That could only be Yossi.' Others said, 'That's not Yossi—that's an Arab.'"[22] Upon his arrival at the top of the ramp, the dispute was settled, and the group gave Feldman the name "Yossi ha-Aravi," or "Yossi the Arab."[23]

Feldman's journey was a turning point for the young man because it helped him to feel less "lost and perplexed" as it renewed his sense of identity as someone connected with the Land. Like the Palmach masa'ot, Feldman's pilgrimage in the desert, which took place on the cusp of his graduation of high school and his entry into the military, was a rite of passage. He had been taken out of familiar territory, had received marks upon his body, and had been exposed alone to the challenges of the desert by day and by night. Finally, he found himself at the mountain of Masada—which in the eyes of the pioneering youth movements was essentially a holy site—and upon ascending the mountain, received a new name. "Yossi ha-Aravi" left the Judean Desert with a renewed sense of self-confidence and also with a sense of place in the desert. No longer was the territory near the Dead Sea a blank and unarticulated space on the map of Eretz Israel; large parts of it were now filled in with familiar landmarks and known lines of movement, and he felt more at home there.

Perhaps more importantly, Feldman's desert travail caused him to fix his eyes on Ein Gedi as a place where, once he had attained a strong knowledge of the Land's horizontal spaces, he could direct his energies vertically, down through layers of earth and time, and attain a deep sense of yedi'at ha-aretz that penetrated the Land's every dimension. Feldman's desire to know Ein Gedi, which was first stirred during his initial brief and violent encounter with the site, only grew stronger over the years and eventually gave rise to his decision to plant himself at the oasis, establish the Ein Gedi Field School, and create the first marked and mapped hiking trail network in Israel. The love affair could not be immediately consummated, however. "Nine years passed for me in the desert before I moved to Ein Gedi," he later wrote.[24]

Israeli Hiking and Government Development in the Negev: 1950–1959

Upon his enlistment in the IDF in 1950, Feldman was inducted into the Nahal youth settlement corps of the IDF and stationed at Revivim to help build and develop the kibbutz. During this time, he made important contacts within the civilian administrative bodies responsible for development of the Negev, and also within the IDF Southern Command, which Moshe Dayan described as "the broad-shouldered body to whom [Israelis in the Negev] could turn for everything, from educational and medical services to plowing and paving access roads."[25]

After Feldman finished his army service in 1953, he became a member of Kibbutz Revivim and maintained his contacts with the Negev Development Authority and with the military as he devoted himself more fully to exploring the desert. At Revivim, he did extra work to compress his weekly labor quota into a three- or four-day period so that he could spend long weekends hiking.[26] Then, in an effort to make the most of his free time, he would subject himself to long-distance treks that led him to the Nabatean ruins at Shivta, to the deep wadis of the Western Negev, and to the outpost of Nitzana on the Egyptian border. Feldman became well-acquainted with the soldiers at Nitzana, and eventually they started sending a vehicle to pick him up at Revivim so that he could join them on hikes. Afterward, Feldman usually had to return to Revivim alone on foot, which was more than forty kilometers away on the map and considerably longer on the ground.[27] Then he would begin another grueling burst of work so that he could take another tiyul as soon as possible.

In 1956, while returning from Nitzana to Revivim by way of the ancient Nabatean city of Shivta, Feldman discovered that IDF soldiers had used stones from old ruins while constructing an army camp. Incensed, Feldman called Yigael Yadin, who had recently retired from his work as IDF Chief of Staff and was beginning his career as a full-time archaeologist. Yadin put an end to the theft and used the incident as an opportunity to bring the ruins at Shivta to the attention of the Public Committee for Landscape Improvement, which had been established a year earlier under the auspices of the Prime Minister's office for the purpose of developing Israel's tourism industry. The Committee decided to renovate the site and offered Feldman the job of coordinating the reconstruction of Shivta's ruins. Feldman accepted, and the Prime Minister's office sent him fifty newly arrived immigrants from the development towns of Dimona and Yeruham to help with the work.

In the course of exploring, excavating, and rebuilding the city walls, Feldman and the immigrant workers discovered other walls and water channels that had been used in antiquity for irrigation and farming.[28] It was not the first of Feldman's archaeological discoveries. By the mid-1950s, Feldman had developed extensive connections not only with the Israeli government and military, but also with the network of local and foreign scholars who were studying the desert. While living at Revivim, Feldman served as a field guide for virtually every Israeli and foreign researcher who studied the Negev. Though Feldman had no formal training in history or archaeology, his personal explorations of the desert, combined with the work he carried out at Shivta, caused expert academics to regard him as an established scholar in his own right. Feldman was one of the lead figures in the American archaeologist Nelson Glueck's foundational survey of the Negev. In the introduction to *Rivers in the Desert*, Glueck credits Feldman—along with a few other Israelis, including the prominent archaeologist Yochanan Aharoni—with discovering and correctly dating a number of theretofore unknown ancient sites in the Negev.[29]

For Feldman, who was one of the only Israelis exploring the farthest and most remote sites in the Negev on a frequent basis, one discovery tended to lead to another. While conducting an aerial survey in association with Glueck's project, Feldman noticed geoglyphs, or man-made shapes build from stones, atop a mountain called Har Karkom. Upon further exploration, Feldman found that the mountain was littered with flint points and rock drawings. He mentioned the place to Emanuel Anati, one of the archaeologists working with Glueck.[30] Anati went on to find tens of thousands of cultic artifacts at the site and made the research of Har Karkom his life's work.[31] Similarly, on one of Feldman's journeys near Nitzana, he discovered ruins that were later found to constitute the largest prehistoric site in the Negev.[32] While these represented major breakthroughs for formal academics, they were footnotes in Feldman's personal quest to intimately know as much of the country's open spaces as possible. He studied sites as long as they piqued his interest and then turned them over to others so that he could go and explore elsewhere. "When Glueck came to expose the antiquities of the Negev," read a newspaper profile, "Feldman participated in the expedition, and then went back to his own way."[33]

When Feldman found the remnants of the Nabatean farm at Shivta, then, he contacted desert researchers with whom he had become acquainted in the course of his unofficial scholarly pursuits. One of them was Prof. Michael Evenari, who, along with his colleagues from the Hebrew University of Jerusalem, decided to rebuild the ruins and create an experimental Nabatean farm that would utilize ancient runoff irrigation methods. Feldman, already engaged in rebuilding the ruins of the ancient city, was the ideal candidate to manage the farm since he had received intensive agricultural training as a youth at Mikve Israel and since he was already familiar with the site and with the whole area surrounding it.

Few others would have been willing or able to stay at Shivta in the 1950s. Evenari describes the western Negev as a dangerous place, even on short trips: "In those days, field trips were made in convoy style, with about one-fifth of the party acting as security guards in case of an attack by marauders. This was the era of hard-desert living, when we camped under the open starry sky. Many of us grew beards during the trips and on our return to Beersheba we would look like gun-packing frontiersmen from the Wild West."[34] Feldman was less concerned about "marauders" and began working full-time for Evenari in 1958, first as the guardian and caretaker of the farm site, and then as the manager of its reconstruction and day-to-day operations. With the winter rains that came in 1958, the planted terraces filled with water, and the Shivta farm achieved its first successes; olives, pomegranates, grapes and almonds were some of the first fruits of Evenari and Feldman's labor.[35]

By 1959, Feldman was receiving widespread recognition for his work. The *Davar* newspaper, then one of the most widely read publications in Israel, published a long article in April describing him as "the Mayor of Shivta." In September, the state held a formal ceremony celebrating the completion of the reconstruction of the Nabatean city. Government ministers and military leaders attended, as well as Ogden Reid, the new American ambassador to Israel. Yigael Yadin delivered the opening remarks, and Feldman gave the main address: a detailed explanation of the restoration work on the city and the operation of the farm.[36]

Ten years after the end of the 1948–1949 war and his first tiyul across the Negev, Feldman had developed enough firsthand expertise on the desert and its antiquities that he was delivering lectures to statesmen and scholars. It is worth noting, however, that all of this took place during a time when the boundaries were blurred between archaeology as a science and archaeology as a national project. Yadin had appointed Feldman to rebuild Shivta even though the latter had no archaeological training and was himself involved in archaeological work aimed at legitimizing the Jewish state.[37] Ben-Gurion's Department of Landscape Improvement, which supervised Feldman's work, was notorious for enacting "improvements" that served government goals, but which were enormously destructive. While Feldman had real knowledge, much of it was in line with the narrative of Jewish presence in the Land that the state sought to advance. He also embodied the image of the tough, resourceful Israeli that had just been popularized in Leon Uris's 1958 novel *Exodus*. At the time of Reid's visit, the book was the biggest runaway bestseller since Margaret Mitchell's *Gone With the Wind*.

In terms of yedi'at ha-aretz, there was little more Feldman could accomplish by walking across the Negev again or by digging deeper at Shivta. A profile of Feldman written a few years later described his time in the Negev as follows: "He scouted the Land from border to border, all the way to the sun, until he had absorbed all there was to absorb from moving horizontally across the territory of the state. One of two things will happen to anyone who arrives at that stage: he will reach satisfaction and will abandon everything, or he will search for a new dimension. Yossi turned away from length and width, and turned toward depth; he discovered that in this dimension, there were no boundaries."[38]

Feldman was fully committed at this point to developing a yedi'at ha-aretz of depth, not of width, but Shivta was running dry and, in any case, was not the wellspring he had sought. Throughout his time at Revivim, he had dreamed of Ein Gedi and had returned there at every opportunity.

Renewed Attempts at Judean Desert Waymarking in the 1950s

During the years since Feldman's 1950 tiyul, development had slowly penetrated the Judean Desert. In 1952, a state-owned company was created to restart mineral production from the Dead Sea, and work began to restore and reconstruct the processing plant at Sdom. In 1953, a group of Nahal youth constructed two permanent huts at Ein Gedi and announced that the military camp would become a kibbutz.[39] That same year, the former Palmach scout Shmaryahu Guttman led the excavation of the Snake Path, which attracted youth movement hikers who wanted to climb Masada along the same route the ancient Jewish Zealots had used.[40] By 1954, the industrial work at Sdom had populated the southwestern corner of the Dead Sea with enough workers that a youth hostel was established there. Yehuda Almog, the Third Aliyah pioneer who now headed the Tamar Regional Council—the government administrative unit responsible for the southern Judean Desert—announced in August of that year that the hostel would be expanded as part of the larger project to develop the Dead Sea shore.[41] In 1955, a road was finally paved from Sdom to Be'er Sheva, which restored the transportation link between Sdom and the settled body of the country that had been severed since the 1948–1949 war.

The flow of everyday Israelis into the Judean Desert south of the Green Line along the new road was still little more than a trickle, but it represented enough of an increase that hiker safety became an issue. In June 1949, Hillel

Birger had written an article in the military journal *Ma'arachot* arguing the need for simun shvilim in the Judean Desert and describing the lessons he had learned from the experimental initiative in 1947.[42] It had fallen on deaf ears. With the exception of mass tiyulim like the 1950 "March of the Thousand," during which the Gadna pre-military youth organization organized a large-scale trek to Masada, relatively few Israelis visited the Judean Desert during the first half of the decade.[43] Hiker safety therefore was not a priority; rather than spend time and money on infrastructure that could prevent hiking accidents, local and national governing authorities were content to let the military shoulder the burden of search-and-rescue operations.

In 1956, as larger numbers of hikers entered the desert via the Be'er Sheva to Sdom road, Birger returned to the Judean Desert to mark trails. In June of that year, at the initiative of a youth movement leader, Birger and a group of volunteers marked the two trails that ascended Masada: the Snake Path, marked in red, and a trail winding around the mountain that led to the Roman ramp, marked in green. A wooden sign was erected at the point where the two trails divided, and it showed the colored symbol for each. The marking system was the same as Birger had used at Ras Feshkha in 1947; each blaze consisted of two horizontal white stripes with a colored stripe in between.[44] Little seems to have come of this effort, perhaps because the two trails ascending Masada were some of the least problematic to be found anywhere in the Judean Desert.

However, the brief reappearance of simun shvilim seems to have gotten Birger thinking again about the need for marked trails in the Judean Desert. In July of 1957, Yehuda Almog wrote a letter to the editor of the *Davar* newspaper outlining a series of development projects that the Tamar Regional Council hoped to complete around the Dead Sea with the help of volunteers.[45] On August 18, Birger responded to Almog's letter with a letter of his own, entitled "On the Margins of the Popular Initiative in the Dead Sea Area," and addressed Almog directly as the party responsible for the welfare of travelers in the Judean Desert. Birger wrote that waymarking should be viewed as an important part of developing the desert and mentioned the efforts he had made at Masada the previous year. Birger argued that the security of hikers in the desert should be the first priority of anyone arguing for the desert's development.[46]

Birger continued working with youth movement leaders to develop a system for marking desert trails. In December 1957, he drafted a plan for a standardized system of waymarking to the leadership of the tiyulim department of Ha-Shomer ha-Tzair—the same youth movement to which Birger had belonged in Europe before immigrating to Eretz Israel. The document is essentially a list of twenty-three principles that outline every aspect of the waymarking process, from a network's conception to its completion, and is remarkable because many of its ideas are still in use today.[47]

Rules zero through three emphasize clarity and ease of use from the point of view of the hiker; for example, markings along a given trail should only appear in one color; markings of a given color should lead hikers from one landmark to another, and so on. Rules four through eight deal with the proper appearance of blazes—including their shapes (rectangular, with one colored horizontal stripe flanked by two white stripes), measurements (fifteen centimeters high by twenty centimeters wide), colors (red, blue, green, yellow, and black), and orientation (stripes should be horizontal)—and ways of depicting parallel trails following the same route, forks in trails, and so on. Rules nine through thirteen outline the placement and appearance of markings in the field, including the frequency with which blazes should appear, the placement of ordinal numbers alongside each blaze on a given trail, and the strategic placement of map grid coordinates at key landmarks so that hikers could be sure of their exact positions. Rules fourteen through twenty-two cover the mechanics and procedures associated with the actual painting and maintenance of markings in the field and emphasize durability; for example, paints were to be chosen for their resistance to fading and abrasion, blazes were only to be painted on firmly fixed landscape features, and rocks were to be cleaned with wire brushes before any markings were placed on them.

Some of the rules are interesting because today, they may seem counterintuitive to Israeli hikers. Rule number eight, for example, states that blazes should always be horizontal, not vertical, and should never be shaped like an arrow. In the language of semiotics, signs in the latter category would be indexical; that is, their shapes would communicate the proper direction of a hiker's movement.[48] Similarly, vertical blazes might imply that the colored stripe in the center of the painted mark represented the trail and that the trail was continuing forward in a straight line. Birger's signs, however, were iconic, not indexical; that is, the presence of the marking simply signified the presence of a trail and said nothing about its direction, with the exception of the fork-shaped blazes depicted in a diagram—apparently drawn by Birger's own hand—beneath rule number six, which deals with dividing trails.

Birger's system also does not presuppose the existence of a map depicting the routes of trails. In fact, it says nothing about how a marked route might be recorded for future placement on a topographic map or how trails on a map could be depicted on paper using the same colors with which they appeared in the field. Instead, the document mandates that trails begin and end at distinct landmarks (rule two) and suggests that map grid coordinates be painted alongside blazes in certain places, with the Hebrew letters *nun* and *tzadi*, standing for *nekudat tziyun* and designating a navigational waypoint, painted alongside (rule thirteen). The assumption seems to have been that hikers would be using topographic maps but that the trails would not appear on those maps. Therefore, the system contains multiple layers of safeguards. A path blocked with numerous obstacles, such as one following a boulder-strewn ravine, should either not be marked or the character of the trail should be noted on a sign placed at the trailhead, and hiking there should not be encouraged unless an experienced guide was present (rule zero). Even on a clear path, ordinal numbers should be stenciled alongside blazes so that it can be possible for waymarking crews to note every feature of the landscape in the immediate vicinity for future reference. This last rule is one Birger followed during the 1947 initiative.

While Birger's system is influenced by the trail networks he saw in Europe while hiking as a youth, some of the rules are particularly suited to the Israeli context and reflect Birger's engagement with the terrain of Eretz Israel. Rule eighteen mandates that no markings be placed on archaeological features or international border warning signs. Rule nineteen suggests that on trails that pass near to international borders, warning signs should be erected. The final rule—rule twenty-two—reflects the lack of organization that existed in Israel at that time for people interested in marking trails. "On every signing," Birger writes, "arrange an explicit protocol and report it to: . . . ." The dotted line, presumably, is supposed to be filled in later with the name of a person or an organization who would keep track of where and when trails were marked. In 1957, though, no such person or organization existed in Israel.

While Yehuda Almog did not make a public response to Birger's call for waymarking in the Judean Desert, he did work to create the bare outlines of an infrastructure that could benefit hikers. In January 1958, on behalf of the Tamar Regional Council, Almog announced plans to construct a youth hostel at Masada with one hundred fifty beds and large group camping areas outside.[49] Hikers from Israel's center and north could now take buses to Sdom via Be'er Sheva along the recently paved road and could stay at the youth hostel near the Dead Sea Works. After a full day of walking, they could make it from there to Masada, where the new hostel offered lodging and water and served as a rudimentary resupply point. From there, Ein Gedi was the next logical destination, and it too could be reached after a full day of walking. Despite the allure of the desert oasis, though, it was still disconnected from Israel's road network and public transportation system and offered no official services for hikers. Most groups, then, explored the desert between Sdom and Masada. Typically, the largest numbers of visitors came during long school breaks—Sukkot in the fall, Hanukkah in the winter, and Passover in the spring—when high school and youth movement groups organized tiyulim to Masada.

In late March 1958, during the Passover holiday, a forty-five-person group from the Maccabi ha-Tzair youth movement got lost in the desert on its way to Ein Gedi from Ein Bokek south of Masada. The group's guide had taken the wrong path and then succumbed to heat exhaustion. Leaderless and running out of water, the group sent two runners for help in what they hoped was the right direction. While the group suffered in the shadeless desert, the runners made it to Ein Bokek with one of them muttering the words "Accident . . . police . . . airplane" before passing out. Yehuda Almog led the rescue attempt from Ein Bokek while the call went out to Be'er Sheva for more help. By the time two police jeeps arrived from Be'er Sheva, volunteers and soldiers were conducting a nighttime search, and the group still had not been found. In the end, a group of elite scouts assembled by Almog made contact with the hikers near Ma'ale Ye'elim—the Ye'elim ascent—and managed to bring them water, escort them to safety, and narrowly avert disaster.[50]

None of the hikers died, but the event was covered by the Israeli press, and the search effort was a fiasco. The hikers were rescued at 3:00 AM, but the lack of communication between Almog's rescue party and the police from Be'er Sheva resulted in the jeeps scouring the desert for the remainder of the night, with their exhausted drivers returning to Ein Bokek in the morning to find that the group had already been found. One week after the accident, Hillel Birger wrote a scathing letter to the editor of *Davar*, pointing out the dangers inherent in placing the welfare of a large group on the shoulders of a single guide and placing the blame for the accident squarely on the shoulders of Yehuda Almog.

> No one had bothered to paint signs to mark trails, as is done in the mountainous regions of every civilized country in the world. And if this has been done outside the Land, then how much more should it be done in the Judean Desert?

> Waymarking is cheap. A kilogram of paint is enough to mark kilometers of trails. There is no reason why youth will not be willing to do this as volunteers. It is not nearly as hard as paving the road to Rosh Zohar. It is Yehuda Almog's job to take care of the Judean Desert region. He knows that if he does not mark trails, it will put more hikers in danger. It was a miracle that these hikers were saved.[51]

Again, Almog offered no immediate public response to Birger's letter, but he and the Tamar Regional Council appear to have become aware of the need to create additional safety measures for hikers in the Judean Desert. Of all the arguments Birger put forth, the most convincing seems to have been "Trail marking is cheap." The status quo was costly and unsustainable: as more and more groups came to the desert with greater and greater numbers of hikers, it became less and less feasible for individual guides to ensure safety. When those guides did fail—either due to the physical demands placed on them or due to the lack of available navigational aids, such as visible landmarks and accurate maps—the burden fell to the police and army. Neither of those organizations wanted to waste time, money, and manpower on finding lost hikers, but under the prevailing situation, they had to be prepared to do so ahead of every hiking season.[52]

In February 1959, Almog finally responded to the voices calling for increased hiker safety in the Judean Desert by writing a letter of his own to newspapers including *Davar* and *Herut*. In the letter, entitled "To the Hikers on the Trails of the Negev," Almog did not make any apologies but mentioned hiking accidents and the high cost of search and rescue efforts, and he wrote that it was unrealistic to expect government and youth organizations to "scamper around after every tiyul to 'search for a path.'" Instead, Almog announced that the Tamar Regional Council, with the help of the staff of the Masada Youth Hostel, would start marking trails throughout the region that could be used for tiyulim, particularly around Sdom and Masada.[53]

The first large-scale waymarking initiative in the Judean Desert took place from April 15 to April 17, 1959. Almog and the Tamar Regional Council worked with the military and the police to gather all of the necessary resources, which in the end included floodlights, flares, radios, hired Bedouins and their camels, and a Piper Cub airplane.[54] Hillel Birger and the Masada youth hostel staff organized the actual waymarking process, evidently training the volunteers—who came from the Gadna youth corps, the Scouting movement, the army, and the police—to work according to the rules set forth in the 1957 document Birger had created for Ha-Shomer ha-Tzair.[55] An article in the *Ma'ariv* newspaper described Birger's scheme to an interested

Israeli public: "Each trail will be marked in its own color, and with special numbers. The paints, which will be marked on the faces of the rocks and on rock piles alongside the trails, are special paints that can withstand heat and moisture."[56]

During the three-day initiative, four groups of volunteers marked trails from Rosh Zohar to Sdom, Ein Bokek, Masada, and Ein Gedi. The *Ma'ariv* article states that Almog justified the effort in view of safety and financial considerations: "The army and the police lent their assistance to the campaign, which itself was initiated by Mr. Yehuda Almog, head of the Tamar Regional Council, after he explained that the trails of the Judean Desert, crowded during this season with hundreds of hikers, constitute a danger because of their complex topography and their lack of water; and they are supporting it in view of the high costs of gathering manpower from the army and police, which are called up every time there is a search for lost hikers."[57]

A continuation of the waymarking effort took place in early June of 1959 and focused on the mountainous desert area between Masada and Ein Gedi. This initiative, too, was led by the staff of the Masada youth hostel, but was more modest in scale.[58] Little was written about this project, either in the Israeli press or retrospectively by the people involved in the eventual creation of the country's trail network.

It is possible that the Masada youth hostel staff was motivated to mark trails north of the mountain because of the April 1959 announcement by Egged that a new bus line would run once a week to Ein Gedi.[59] The Egged transportation cooperative was not just Israel's largest bus service; it also trained guides and organized tours all over the country. Running a bus line to Ein Gedi was actually not profitable in the short term, but the cooperative worked closely with the government and sought to extend travel and tourism all the way to the farthest edges of Israeli territory. The bus route's first trial run to Ein Gedi via Sdom for hikers in early April 1959 featured an overnight stop at Sdom, where participants met Yehuda Almog and listened to a lecture by Ori Dvir, the founder of Egged's division of yedi'at ha-aretz.[60] The successful trip heralded Ein Gedi's connection to the public transportation system, which, combined with the increasing flow of youth groups to the Judean Desert during school breaks, made it likely that more hikers would soon begin trekking north of Masada, closer to the Green Line.

In any case, the early Masada-area trail network seems to have represented an important beginning for future initiatives, but it suffered from several problems that prevented it from taking hold and truly changing the character of hiking in the Judean Desert. First, the network was not well-publicized; aside from the initial newspaper articles covering the waymarking projects and the word-of-mouth guidance hikers received from the staff at the Masada hostel, few even knew about the trails' existence. Second, even if hikers encountered the trails in the field and used them, they had no way of knowing where the markings eventually led and therefore could not rely on them as navigational aids. In fact, the trail markings could have constituted a danger to hikers who found them, followed them, and then abandoned themselves to a marking system that could lead them to destinations other than the ones they intended to reach. Guides and scouts who still operated under the watchword "the trail is wiser than the one who walks it" would likely pay more attention to a visible footpath than to any markings placed alongside. The publication of maps showing the trails' routes could have alleviated both of these problems, but no such maps were ever conceived, much less published. Finally, no system of checking and maintaining the trails' markings was ever put in place; even though the project had the support of the Tamar Regional Council, there was no authority, volunteer or otherwise, that took responsibility for the upkeep of the trails.

Birger's system provided an effective template for how to mark trails in the field, but the missing element was organization. The Tamar Regional Council had come to understand the need for waymarking and could pull together the necessary resources for doing so, but officials like Yehuda Almog were not field men nor did they have the time to supervise projects like simun shvilim. The personnel at the Masada youth hostel could handle themselves in the field, knew the routes of the backcountry trails, and had an interest in simun shvilim, but had not devoted the time and thought to waymarking that Birger had. Birger himself, with his organizational skills and mind for detail, might have been a good long-term coordinator of waymarking activities, but he had a full-time job and a family, and he lived in Tel Aviv. Feldman, however, was well-acquainted with every notable civilian and military leader in the Negev and had already proven himself as a field man and an effective project manager. After Feldman established himself at Ein Gedi in late 1959, he was able to pull the necessary forces together in a way no one else had.

Yossi Feldman and the Ein Gedi Field School

Yossi Feldman already knew Yehuda Almog. Feldman had visited Ein Gedi frequently during his time at Revivim—so frequently, in fact, that when the kibbutz opened its membership to civilians, Feldman went to Sdom in the hope of catching a ride with the trucks going up to establish the new settlement area. The leader of the convoy recognized Feldman and refused to take him. "Three times I've seen you at Ein Gedi," the man said. "You've been there enough." Feldman, determined to witness the formal dedication of the new settlement site, set off on foot. Upon finding a group of Bedouin on one of the backcountry trails after nightfall, Feldman ambushed them in the dark and took one of the men and two camels at gunpoint. Feldman and his hostage then rode hard across the desert under a full moon in pursuit of the convoy. When they got close to the kibbutz, Feldman gave the camel back to the Bedouin and went down to the settlement alone on foot. Just as he arrived, so did the convoy, with Yehuda Almog riding in the lead jeep. Almog recognized Feldman and shouted to the convoy leader, "You don't know who you're dealing with. Otherwise it would have been clear to you that if you didn't bring him, he'd get here by himself."[61]

Feldman's adventurism in the desert is reminiscent of the behavior of the group of Haganah-affiliated youth who trekked around the Dead Sea in 1934 and stole water from Bedouins. It also bears resemblances to Meir Har-Zion's cross-border hikes to Petra and infamous cross-border revenge attack on Bedouins. Like Har-Zion, Feldman was a standard-bearer of the tradition of the pre-statehood paramilitary underground; insofar as his own relationship with the Land was concerned, he bowed to no authority.[62] He seems to have cared little about the effect of his behavior on people whose relationship with the Land he viewed as less valid than his own.

The expanded settlement site of Kibbutz Ein Gedi was at the bottom of Nahal Arugot. The two huts and other small buildings originally constructed in 1953 on the site of the old military camp were now being abandoned at the bottom of Nahal David. Feldman told Almog that he wanted to create an outdoor youth education center at Ein Gedi, and Almog gave Feldman permission to renovate and repurpose the old huts. "Nobody knew what a field school was, not even me," Feldman later wrote.[63] With an initial outlay of ten thousand Israeli lirot from the Ministry of Education, Feldman began by turning the two huts into a youth hostel and using the hostel as a base for guiding and exploration.[64] The hostel, which consisted of little more than open rooms with mattresses on the floors, was named "Beit Sarah," after Sarah Rabinovitch, the girl who had fallen at Ras Feshkha in 1934.[65] With a hostel at Ein Gedi, the constellation of lodging and resupply points for hikers across the southern Judean Desert was complete; Sdom, Masada, and Ein Gedi were each separated by about one full day's walk.

Trails remained a vital link between Masada and Ein Gedi, though; the weekly bus service from Sdom to Ein Gedi was enough to bring hikers for weekend visits, but those who wanted to cross the desert on their own schedule still had to do so on foot. With the hostel in place, the first educational activities Feldman conducted at Ein Gedi were guided tiyulim in the nearby canyons and desert highlands for anyone who came to visit. The guiding services were not just an amenity offered by the hostel; they were necessary because Ein Gedi's proximity to the Green Line meant that hiking was still a dangerous undertaking. In February 1960, one of the residents of the kibbutz, Giora Barzilai, was climbing Mount Yishai—the promontory of rock in Israeli territory between Nahal David and the Green Line—and was shot by Jordanians in a cross-border attack.[66] The incident underscored the dangers that were still present, especially for visitors who might approach or cross the Green Line simply by following natural lines of travel.

However, this did not mean the area near the border should be avoided completely. Kibbutz Ein Gedi established its presence as much as it could on Israeli territory, farming the lands north of the kibbutz almost all the way up to the Green Line. This was common practice in Israeli border settlements. When Moshe Dayan was the head of the IDF Southern Command in the early 1950s, he promoted filling in empty territory along boundaries as a way of stopping Arab infiltrators. Israeli border settlements established presence where Jewish claims on the Land might otherwise be contested and were regarded by Ben-Gurion and the Zionist leadership as the first lines of defense against cross-border attacks.[67]

By 1960, border incursions near Ein Gedi had become a major issue, in part as a result of the treasure hunt originally spurred by the discovery of the Dead Sea Scrolls in 1946. After the 1948–1949 war, the Ta'amira Bedouin tribe started scouring all the most remote and inaccessible caves along the wadis in the Jordanian West Bank, beginning at Qumran near 'Ain Feshkha, where the first scrolls were found, and working their way south.[68] During the 1950s it became apparent that scroll fragments and other artifacts on the antiquities market were being found on the Israeli side by Bedouins who were crossing the Green Line via the old trails and footpaths they knew so well. In some cases, Bedouins who brought scroll fragments for sale on the Jordanian market claimed to have found them on the Israeli side of the border so that they would not be found guilty of breaking Jordanian antiquities laws. Sometimes those claims were true and sometimes they were not.[69] In any case, Israeli archaeologists who were particularly interested in scroll fragments connected to Shimon Bar-Kochba, the leader of the Second Jewish Revolt, realized that they needed to go on the offensive and excavate Judean Desert caves themselves, lest the sites be picked clean by treasure hunters.[70]

Feldman already knew the archaeologists in charge of the 1960–1961 expedition that focused on Nahal Mishmar and Nahal Hever; he had worked with Yochanan Aharoni in the course of Glueck's Negev survey and knew Yigael Yadin from Shivta. Kibbutz Ein Gedi became a base for the field research project, which eventually yielded important discoveries in the Cave of Treasure in Nahal Mishmar and the Cave of Horror and the Cave of Letters in Nahal Arugot. Feldman oversaw some of the practical work involved in reaching the remote sites, including using cables and winches to lower soldiers to cave entrances on sheer cliffsides.[71] Feldman and students from the Field School were even more directly involved with Benjamin Mazar's excavation of Tel Goren near Kibbutz Ein Gedi in 1961 and 1962.[72] The archaeological surveys and digs were undertaken, as all major projects in the Judean and Negev Deserts were, with significant help from the IDF. Feldman's participation in the work further cemented his connections with Israel's academic community and the military and gave him the chance to witness how Ein Gedi could serve as a base for carrying out complex and labor-intensive projects.

Meanwhile, Feldman built his reputation as a skilled field educator, and Ein Gedi became known as a "center out there" for the study of yedi'at ha-aretz. The border kibbutz quickly became attractive for teachers and institutions intent on educating Israeli youth about the Jewish homeland. Azaria Alon and Amotz Zahavi, the founders of the Society for the Protection of Nature in Israel (SPNI), were also acquaintances of Feldman's. As mentioned, Alon had been one of Feldman's guides in Ha-Machanot ha-Olim; and not long after Feldman's arrival in 1959, Zahavi brought a group of students to Ein Gedi to help clear the old settlement's garbage dump at the mouth of Nahal David. In those days, the SPNI was at the leading edge of Israel's nascent environmental movement but was looking for ways to engage larger numbers of people. Zahavi suggested to Feldman in 1960 that it would be natural for the outdoor education center to partner with the SPNI, and Feldman agreed.[73]

With renewed funding from the Ministry of Education, the youth hostel and guiding center became the Ein Gedi Field School—the first of a series of government-financed and SPNI-operated outdoor education centers that eventually spread across the country. The long-term partnership in the field school was momentous for everyone involved. The Ministry of Education had placed a high value on yedi'at ha-aretz as part of the public school curriculum since the founding of the state and now had an institutional framework in the field to which it could direct outdoor education initiatives. The increased funding made it possible for Feldman to expand the field school's facilities and activities and to further develop the sort of deep yedi'at ha-aretz he had first imagined at Ein Gedi more than a decade earlier. For the SPNI, working with the Ministry of Education was a two-edged sword; on the one hand, it guaranteed the nature protection organization large amounts of funding and access to a wide segment of the Israeli public, but on the other, it threatened the group's status as an NGO and sometimes made it difficult for the SPNI to criticize the government's activities. This partnership, with all of its problems, continues to this day.[74]

During the early 1960s, then, Ein Gedi became an important base from which soldiers, hikers, and scholars fanned out on their separate pursuits across the southern Judean Desert. None of the initial activities of the Field School constituted a permanent presence, though; when hikes, patrols, and research expeditions were over, the desert returned to its normal state, and the Green Line remained a porous and mostly unmarked frontier. Anyone who ventured into the desert around Ein Gedi either had to have substantial knowledge of the area or had to be accompanied by someone who did. The problem was the same that had existed in the Judean Desert before the 1948–1949 war: the culture of hiking depended on the ability of knowledgeable guides, and no infrastructure existed that could help less-experienced hikers in the event of an emergency. Feldman first sought to solve the issue by stepping up the Field School's guiding services but eventually realized, as Yehuda Almog had written in 1959, that guides could not realistically accompany every group through the desert and ensure their safety. In light of all this, Feldman wrote later, "the dream of *simun shvilim* came together at Ein Gedi."[75]

Marking and Mapping Israel's First Trail Network

In late 1960, Feldman made a first attempt at creating a trail network in the Judean Desert. During the winter, Feldman gathered a group of volunteers and made an initial effort to place "signs and temporary markings" along the trails between Ein Gedi and Masada.[76] Wooden stakes and metal signs were among the navigational aids placed by the volunteer crews, but these were quickly removed by Bedouins and did little overall to keep hikers from getting lost.[77] Feldman replaced the missing signs with Bedouin-style stone piles so that the planned routes would at least remain visible until a more sustainable system of marking and mapping could be put in place.[78]

Feldman redoubled his efforts in early 1961, and this time he set about creating a massive front of funding, resources, and volunteers to ensure that simun shvilim would be a success. He had heard about Hillel Birger but had never met him, so he visited Birger at his apartment in Tel Aviv and asked his advice on how to create a useful and sustainable trail network. He recruited Birger to join a larger team consisting of desert scouts and guides, professors and other experts, and "anyone who had a hand and a foot in the Judean Desert and the Dead Sea, in order to build as a team a method of signing that was efficient and simple, and in order to determine the important arteries that would be marked."[79] Feldman called the group the "technical committee" for simun shvilim, and it was the foundation for what would become the Public Committee for Waymarking in Israel and eventually the Israel Trails Committee.[80]

Drawing on all of his contacts in the Judean Desert, Feldman obtained financial and material support from the Prime Minister's office, the Ministry of Development, the Ministry of Education, the Arad Regional Endowment, IDF Southern Command, Egged, SPNI, the Dead Sea Works, the Committee for Landscape Improvement, and others.[81] Feldman also pulled together knowledgeable and motivated volunteers; rather than draw primarily from the youth movements, he recruited workers from the Ein Gedi Field School, the SPNI, and the Sayeret Tzanchanim paratrooper unit of the IDF. That elite unit, commanded by Feldman's friend Dov Tamari, set up a temporary base at the Field School and not only marked trails but also carried weapons and communications gear and provided security for the overall effort.[82]

The first stage of the work took place in the spring of 1961. A network of twenty-one trails was planned within the area encompassed by the Arad region on the west, the Green Line on the north, the Dead Sea on the east, and the Sdom-Be'er Sheva highway on the south. Most of the marked trails already existed, either as footpaths or vehicle tracks. Because of the orientation of the desert's natural lines of travel in relation to the Green Line, though, Feldman had to make sure that in the area around Ein Gedi, foot traffic moved along more of a north-south axis than an east-west axis. Some new routes, therefore, had to be created in addition to the old paths. Marking was carried out according to Birger's system, with blazes painted in red, black, green, and blue.[83]

Feldman played a large role in making sure the plans he made with consultants like Birger were executed in the field, but he delegated a good deal of the work to the paratroopers as well. "The most serious help came to us from the army," Feldman said in June 1961, when the initial work on the trail system was completed.[84] The paratroopers offered manpower, security, and a sense of professionalism to the project, and the IDF Southern Command as a whole offered equipment that made the work much faster and easier. The area that fell within the scope of the project constituted approximately eight hundred square kilometers of terrain that was largely inaccessible by motorized vehicles and difficult to cross even on foot. Army trucks and jeeps, however, were able to move waymarking crews a fair distance away from paved roads and pick them up at pre-planned points at the end of the day so that they could sleep back at the hostel. Radios enabled far-flung crews to stay in contact with other workers and with the headquarters at Ein Gedi. Aerial photography allowed Feldman to look at possible marked routes in relation to all of the surrounding terrain and to have a better picture of the territory than maps could then offer.[85]

For the volunteer scouts in the field, though, the work was still difficult and dangerous. The use of army vehicles and equipment made the desert more accessible, but the whole raison d'etre for simun shvilim was that there was no transportation network of any sort in that part of the Judean Desert, except for the trails themselves. When spring rains fell in the western mountains, torrents of mud and rock roared through the canyons and washed out bridges and roads, sometimes leaving crews stranded in the field. In the best cases, they simply had to walk back to Ein Gedi or spend the night outside; in the worst cases, they were nearly killed by flash floods. On one occasion, a powerful flood in Nahal Tze'elim forced one of the crews to scramble up the sides of the wadi and take shelter in a cave. After the danger passed, they regrouped and returned to their work.[86]

The trails that appeared on the ground were not quite the same as those that were envisioned by Birger in his 1957 rules for simun shvilim. For the most part, they adhered to the prescribed system. Blazes appeared in the right colors, sizes, and dimensions. Frequency of blazes depended on how visible the footpath itself was and what kinds of obstacles or false trails might cause hikers to lose their way. Other rules, however—including the system of numbering each blaze, writing detailed descriptions of the environment around each blaze, and the labeling of key terrain features with map grid coordinates—were not carried out. Birger's system made sense for short trails like the one between Ain Feshkha and Ras Feshkha and the ones that ascended Masada. Some of the trails in the Ein Gedi network, though, reached thirty-five kilometers in length and were marked with hundreds of blazes. Numbered blazes and grid coordinates would have served as useful stopgaps until the trail system was mapped, but might have doubled the amount of time spent on marking the network on the ground.[87]

Instead of offering hikers a journal with written descriptions of trails and their markings, Feldman and his volunteer crews erected three signs at key points in the desert where people were most likely to access the network: Sdom, Ein Gedi, and Arad. The signs explained the appearance and function of the markings and showed the destinations of the different trails. Feldman's primary focus, it seems, was putting the marked network on the ground and then working afterward to make sure it would not fade into obscurity as the 1959 Masada trails had. Most of the work was finished by the time summer began descending upon the desert. "Organizers of the initiative say they have succeeded in 'networking' the trails and the central axes of movement in the area," read a June 1961 news article.[88] Work continued on a smaller scale, though, throughout the remainder of the year, and by December 1961, the marked network was essentially complete.[89] The trail network could not have come at a better time; during the 1961 Hanukkah break, six thousand hikers—mostly from youth movements—climbed Masada. While there were no serious hiking accidents, perhaps partly as a result of the newly marked trails, both Yehuda Almog and Shmaryahu Guttman pointed out the need for more safety measures for hikers at Masada and in the surrounding desert.[90]

Mapping the trail network was the final goal and the next necessary step. The three explanatory signs were not enough to render the Judean Desert easily accessible or safely navigable by the trail network. More than three hundred kilometers of marked trails now extended across the eight-hundred-square-kilometer space.[91] If anyone happened upon the network without having seen one of the signs, the meaning of the blazes might be a mystery. Even if someone had seen the signs, they would have no way of knowing where a given trail led unless they had copied or memorized the information. Birger the engineer and Feldman the field expert both knew that maps were the key to making the Judean Desert trails truly effective, but neither of them knew how to go about creating a map that could accurately depict both the area and its trails.

As mentioned earlier, the British 1:100,000-scale map series covered Palestine only as far south as Be'er Sheva. Much of the work of the Survey of

Israel during its early days involved extending those maps south to cover the Negev. The Judean Desert, however, did appear in the Survey of Palestine 1:100,000-scale map series, which were the basis for subsequent Israeli maps. By the early 1960s, these maps had only been minimally updated by the Survey of Israel and remained the most accurate maps of the Dead Sea region.[92] The 1944 edition of Sheet 10, "Jerusalem," includes the area northwest of the Dead Sea and is the most accurate of the series. Its data was based on information from 1:20,000-scale maps revised in 1941 and 1942, and the Jerusalem area itself was based on 1:10,000-scale maps revised during the same years.[93] The part of Sheet 13, "Dead Sea," that shows the northern and central Judean Desert is based wholly on air photos taken in 1935 and 1936.[94] Similarly, Sheet 16, "Jebel Usdum," which shows the southern Dead Sea region around Mount Sdom, is based on aerial photography from 1936 and 1937.[95]

These maps, and the ones that succeeded them, were notorious among hikers for their inaccurate depiction of footpaths. The actual trails known by the Bedouin, the Palmach, and the post-statehood Israeli guides were hard enough to find and follow on the ground, but when viewed on photographs taken from above, they were indistinguishable from other lines that appeared upon the land, like false trails and dry washes. The topographic data on the maps was accurate enough for navigation, and indeed, the Survey of Palestine 1:100,000-scale maps were the main operational maps used by the Palmach, but trails were often inaccurately depicted. The Palmach scout Rehavam Ze'evi wrote that for the purposes of exploring the Land he generally preferred to use the nineteenth-century PEF maps because in certain areas they offered details that did not appear on the Survey of Palestine maps.[96]

Feldman set up a meeting at the headquarters of the Survey of Israel in Tel Aviv with Joseph Elster, the organization's director, in the hopes of convincing him that trails in the Judean Desert needed to be depicted on maps in order for the new network at Ein Gedi to be effective. "I was very concerned about the meeting," Feldman writes. "I came, barefoot and disheveled from the desert, to the Holy of Holies of order, punctuality, and organized clerical work, and I had to give a lecture about desert trails."[97] To Feldman's surprise, Elster not only listened and understood but also promised that the Survey would create a 1:100,000-scale map of the southern Judean Desert and its trails and would task someone from the Be'er Sheva office to do the field work. At Be'er Sheva, Feldman met Tzion Sheetrug, who happened to be filling in at the office in place of his supervisor and who therefore became responsible for charting the trails onto topographical maps.[98]

However, Sheetrug was not a cartographer. Born in Tunisia in 1928, he had served in the French underground during World War II as a youth and in the Haganah in Europe. In 1948, he fought with a Machal foreign volunteer unit and saw action near Be'er Sheva. He stayed in Israel after the war, studied land surveying, and then took part in the state's efforts to map its newly conquered territory. He was sent to Eilat in 1950 to help set up a triangulation grid for the extension of the 1:100,000-scale maps across the country's south. Then he participated in various border-marking projects, including efforts to place markers along the Jordanian border near Be'er Ora in 1951 and along the Negev-Sinai border near Nitzana in 1952 and 1953. Throughout the remainder of the 1950s, he had assisted in the establishment of development towns like Dimona and Kiryat Shmona, the planning of the route of the National Water Carrier, and the creation of cadastral land registries around Jerusalem and Nazareth. In the wake of the 1956 Sinai-Suez Crisis, Sheetrug even worked in the Sinai Peninsula and on the island of Tiran to establish triangulation networks before Israel returned the conquered lands to Egypt.[99] Like Feldman, then, Sheetrug was a field man; though he had participated in almost every stage of the map-making process, he had never been in charge of actually making a map.

Sheetrug needed to find a way to make exact records of the trails' routes in the field and then transfer that information to existing topographical maps. He decided to solve the problem through a combination of field triangulation and aerial photography. Sheetrug began the triangulation process in 1962 by going out with Feldman along the marked trails and finding landmarks that could be easily identified on aerial photographs, such as boulders and isolated trees. From such a landmark, Sheetrug could use his surveying equipment to find the exact bearing, or angle on the compass, from that point to another known point on the map, such as a distant mountain peak. Once he had at least two such bearings, he could draw lines on the map from the known points along the angles he had recorded and the intersection of those lines—the apex of the triangle—would show the exact point of the landmark Sheetrug had found along the trail. As he followed Feldman, then, he could not draw the exact route of the trail onto the map, but he could make a series of dots showing the positions of different features visible from the air. Back at the office in Be'er Sheva, Sheetrug could examine aerial photographs, compare them with the dotted maps he had made, and see not only the landmarks, but also the footpath that connected them.

Without the dots, Sheetrug would have been exactly where the British mapmakers had been and would have struggled to differentiate between dry watercourses and actual trails. Armed with the knowledge he had gleaned through field triangulation, though, he could be confident that the lines connecting the dots were the actual trails. Sheetrug drew the trails' routes onto films of the aerial photographs and then projected them onto topographical maps. By making sure the scale of the projected marked images were exactly the same as the scale of the map, he could trace the lines he had drawn on the photographs directly onto the maps; those maps could then be copied and printed through the Survey of Israel's normal processes.[100]

By the end of 1962, Feldman and Sheetrug had gathered all of the necessary data and were waiting for the Survey of Israel to publish the map. Meanwhile, the Israeli government and the Tamar Regional Council had worked to connect Ein Gedi to the rest of the country by paving the road along the Dead Sea shore from Sdom. Before the existence of that road, Masada was the practical limit of civilian vehicle travel, and the record number of people visiting Ein Gedi in a single day was one thousand. That record was shattered almost immediately after the completion of the new road in October 1962. Twenty-three thousand visitors came to Ein Gedi during the Sukkot break.[101] During the Hanukkah break in December, an estimated thirty-five thousand hikers visited the site.[102]

In short, the new road changed everything. Kibbutz Ein Gedi was no longer an isolated border settlement; it was now an important destination for Israeli tourists. The Ein Gedi Field School was no longer a center of yedi'at ha-aretz only for the relative few who knew how to find their way to Israel's farthest corners; it was now poised to become a center of yedi'at ha-aretz for the whole country and a platform from which Feldman, the SPNI, and the Ministry of Education could teach large numbers of people. The trail network, too, could now become more fully realized. The new road not only brought civilian traffic to the foot of the trails that branched out from Ein Gedi but also ensured that the number of Israelis demanding safe conduct through the desert would far exceed the ability of expert guides to provide it. The marked trail network in the southern Judean Desert was there to stay.

The Publication of the First Simun Shvilim Map

On June 8, 1963, Yossi Feldman led a group of about one hundred people out from the Field School and up a narrow footpath that ascended Mount Yishai and overlooked Nahal David.[103] The path was marked with red-and-white blazes, identical to the ones Birger had used in 1947. The group stopped at the top of a hill that projected from the mountain, just below the point where

Giora Barzilai was killed in 1960, and just above the hostel that memorialized Sarah Rabinovitch, who had fallen at Ras Feshkha in 1934. There, on the edge of Israeli territory, Feldman announced the publication of Israel's first simun shvilim map and distributed the first printed copies to the guests in attendance, all of whom had played a role in bringing the marked and mapped trail network to fruition. Hillel Birger, Yehuda Almog, and Tzion Sheetrug were there. Zev Vilnay, one of the founding fathers of Israel's culture of yedi'at ha-aretz, was there as well. During the celebration that followed, the detail-oriented Birger noticed that one of the trails was missing from the map; later in the evening, Sheetrug and some colleagues from the Survey of Israel used colored markers to carefully correct the maps by hand.[104]

Overall, though, the first simun shvilim map was a vast improvement over previously published maps of the Judean Desert. On the outside, the map was clearly a local product of Israel's community of hikers and yedi'at ha-aretz experts. When folded, the map bore a brown-tone illustration of an ibex—a wild mountain goat native to Ein Gedi and southern Israel. Behind the animal's horned head, white paths ascended into a rocky landscape. (See fig. 3.2.) The title, "Map of the Signing of the Trails of the Judean Desert," was hand-drawn along one edge of the illustration, and the words "Ein Gedi Field School" were written along another. On the inside, the map looked similar to other Israeli topographical maps produced at the time, and its descent from the Survey of Palestine's 1:100,000-scale series was obvious. However, whereas the original map data—showing the southern Dead Sea and the Israeli territory south of the Green Line—appeared almost completely in muted tans, browns, and blues, the trails were depicted in bright red, black, blue, and green. The trails were the map's central and most noticeable features. (See fig. 3.3.)

The simun shvilim map was the first to project Israeli presence so boldly and clearly into the Judean Desert. Beginning during the early pioneer era, Labor Zionists had become accustomed to rendering territory part of the national body through cultivation and development. The problem with the Judean Desert, and with the Negev as a whole, was that such transformations were impossible in the short term, given the limited resources of the newly established Jewish state. On the map, though, the marked trails were drawn to appear even more prominently than paved roads. What viewers saw as they looked at the map was a territory crisscrossed with bold lines, filled in with arteries of movement all the way to the country's borders. They saw a land that was not only known but built.

Figure 3.2. 1963 Judean Desert simun shvilim map cover. *From the author's collection.*

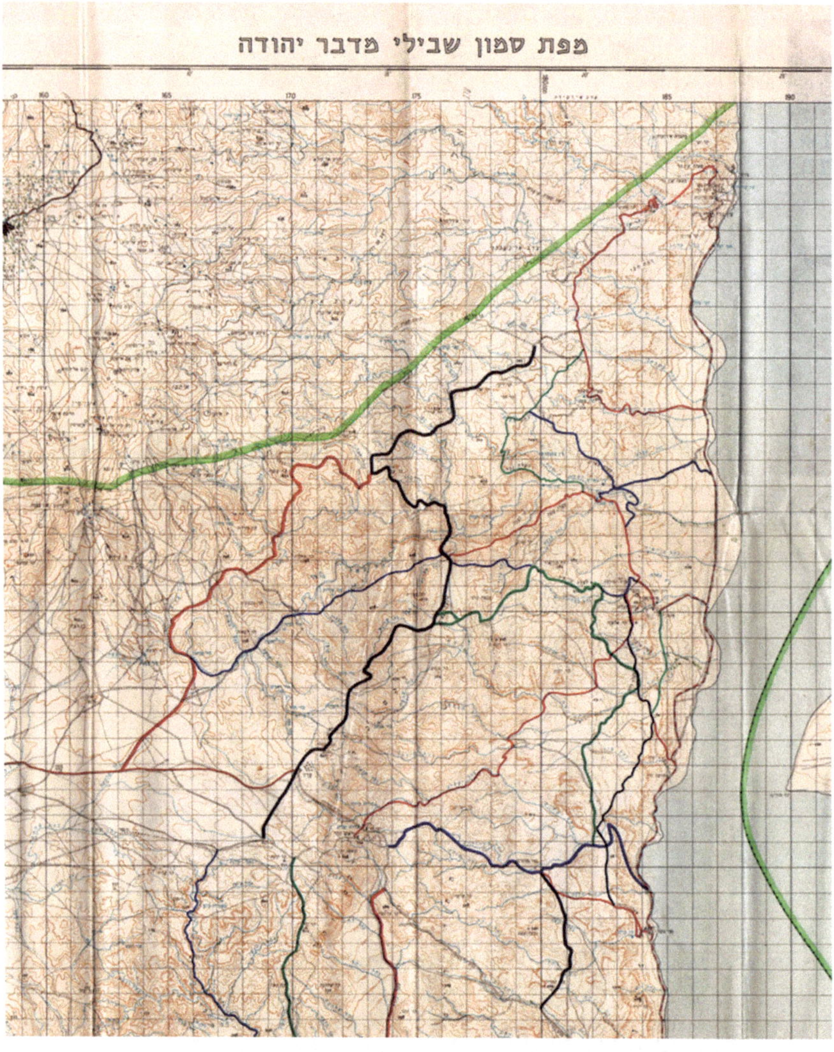

Figure 3.3. Detail of the 1963 Judean Desert simun shvilim map, depicting marked trails filling the area south of the Green Line. *From the author's collection.*

Conclusion: Effects of Marking and Mapping

People across the country viewed and used the first simun shvilim map. It was tremendously successful; decades later, it was described as an essential piece of equipment for all Israeli backpackers during the remainder of the 1960s.[105] The map not only made it possible for hikers to navigate safely while they were in the Judean Desert but also enabled them to explore the desert in absentia—to study the terrain, to learn about the routes that crossed it, and to plan hikes in advance. Once the map became available to all Israelis, the Judean Desert itself became available to all Israelis. Even for those who did not make the trip all the way out to Ein Gedi, the trail maps at least made going there theoretically possible; the desert was no longer an unknown blank space, but one that could be crossed and known if one wished. The map, then, projected a greater Israeli presence onto the desert, but it also projected the image of the desert onto the minds of Israelis. Both processes created the sense that the Judean Desert was truly a Jewish and Israeli space.

Those who did visit the Judean Desert, of course, found quickly that the impression of development created by the map was different from the reality on the ground. Simun shvilim represented only the most lightweight form of development. Thousands of markings had been painted onto the ground, but almost nothing had actually been built. Many of the older footpaths followed watercourses that had served humans as footpaths for thousands of years. Others, especially those that climbed westward out of the Dead Sea depression, had originally been improved by the Romans or even the ancient Israelites and for centuries had been used almost exclusively by Bedouins. Newly created trails generally ran across the relatively flat highlands to the west of the cliffs that overlooked the Dead Sea, where waymarking needed only to create footprints for hikers to follow and thus make a trail where there had been none. Simun shvilim was, as its name made clear, not a construction project, but a signing project.

The placement of *simanim*—signs, symbols, markers—along old paths transformed them into new things. Simun shvilim meant different things to different people, depending on how they understood and used trails and depending on the cultural lens through which they viewed markings upon the land. The different understandings, then, of the meaning of the thousands of markings across the desert, drove different people to react to the markings in different ways, just as they would when similar markings were placed around the country in the ensuing decades. Israelis who were not avid hikers and encountered the trail markings in the course of a guided hike organized by the Ein Gedi Field School might have given the markings little thought and viewed them as simply denoting the presence of a hiking trail. Those who had been steeped in the culture of hiking during the years immediately before and after the 1948–1949 war, however, would likely have seen multiple layers of meaning in the trail markings and could therefore choose which layer related most closely to their concerns.

Military and government officials who were more sensitive to the contested nature of the Judean Desert added another layer of meaning: they understood the signs as enabling Israeli movement and therefore heightening Israeli presence; the markings meant that Israelis had visited the area before and would continue to visit there in the future. Officials like Yehuda Almog, who were responsible for development, understood the way waymarking could be viewed as an extension of Zionist efforts to transform the desert and make it habitable. Environmentalists and outdoor educators like Azaria Alon, Yossi Feldman, and Ori Dvir, steeped as they were in a culture that had connected hiking with military reconnaissance, were not blind to any of these meanings, but added their own glosses: the profusion of trail markings in the desert represented a universe of possibilities for outdoor education.

Implicit within all of the Israeli views of waymarking was the idea that Israel, as the sovereign power in the country, had the right and perhaps even the duty to create safe lines of travel for Jewish Israelis. These meanings were not lost on Bedouin Arabs, who had their own system of route marking that they understood as a means of asserting claims over territory. For them, Israeli trail markings clashed with that system, enabled the incursion of interlopers onto their ancestral dwelling and grazing lands, and therefore constituted threats to Bedouin claims on the land. If simun shvilim was controversial in the beginning, it was only in the sense that it asserted Israeli claims and threatened Bedouin ones—which is to say that in Israeli society, it was not controversial at all.

After the completion of the trail network around Ein Gedi, Feldman turned over control of the Technical Committee to Ori Dvir, the tour guide who had founded Egged's department of yedi'at ha-aretz and who had joined Yehuda Almog in welcoming the first bus-borne Ein Gedi hikers in 1959. Dvir, whose biography will be discussed in the next chapter, was already a well-known personality in Israel. Like Feldman, he had a wide network of connections and a powerful desire to explore the Land of Israel. Unlike Feldman, however, he was passionate enough about waymarking to make it his life's work. It was Dvir who took waymarking out of the desert and into places and times in which painted blazes took on myriad and complex meanings. Interpretations of the meaning of trail markings no longer boiled down to Jewish claims versus Arab claims over land. As Israel's trail network spread across the country during the remainder of the 1960s, through the 1970s, and into the 1980s, different lands were marked and Israeli society changed.

4

The Foundations of the Countrywide Trail Network, 1963–1979

Marking and Mapping a Changing Israel

By the early 1960s, Jewish hiking had been taking place for more than sixty years in British Mandate Palestine and the State of Israel. Throughout most of that time, the precedents originally established by the Labor Zionist halutzim continued to shape the way Jews walked across the land they regarded as their homeland. The Sabra generation, of which Yossi Feldman and his contemporaries were a part, had inherited the legacy of the halutzim, and many of the original pioneers who had founded the Yishuv's central institutions still played leading roles in the Israeli government. On an official level, the state supported pioneering organizations like the Nahal youth settlement corps and encouraged youth movements to continue asserting Israeli presence in contested and unsettled areas. During every hiking season, thousands of young men and women still climbed to the summit of Masada and also explored farther-flung areas like the Southern Negev and the Eilat Mountains. The process of defining and articulating the body of the Land of Israel continued according to time-tested methods.

In the wake of the 1967 Six-Day War, Israeli society began to change, and the socialist values that had long charted a course for the Zionist movement started to give way to capitalist ideas.[1] The image of the Sabra scout began to fade as an ideal among Israeli youth. Fewer hikers aspired to follow in the footsteps of the Palmach by walking through the border areas where

Israel's first trail networks were marked, and more of them started venturing overseas. These changes gained momentum in the aftermath of the 1973 Yom Kippur War, which shook Israel's aura of invincibility and led to the repudiation of the Labor Zionist leadership that had controlled the state throughout its short history. With the large-scale erosion of Labor Zionist ideals, Israel's culture of hiking continued to evolve. Hikers were driven less by an ideologically based urge to know the distant corners of Eretz Israel and more by a general desire to encounter nature; instead of taking difficult desert treks, they took shorter hikes closer to home, sometimes alone, but often as families. These dynamics strengthened Israel's environmental movement, which revived the impulse to preserve nature and to spare undeveloped rural spaces from urbanization.

During the period of time dealt with in this chapter, one man stood at the helm of simun shvilim, and made most of the decisions that guided the project's growth and development. Ori Dvir inherited the waymarking mantle from Hillel Birger and Yossi Feldman in 1963, and he continued to influence simun shvilim not only throughout the 1970s but over the next two decades as well. Under Dvir's supervision, Israel's trail networks continued to grow, first in the country's farthest southern corner, then in newly conquered but mostly unsettled territories, and finally in the more densely populated interior; eventually, those networks grew together into a unified system that covered the territory within the old Mandate boundaries—which Dvir and the leaders of Israel's culture of hiking still regarded as the Land of Israel—from border to border. The process was not always smooth, however, and the expansion and contraction of Israeli territory during the growth of the marked and mapped hiking trail network helped give rise to fault lines, some of which continue to cause friction to this day.

This chapter will trace the way changes in Israeli society and in the dimensions of Israeli territory affected Israel's culture of hiking and how changes in the culture of hiking in turn affected the shape of Israel's trail network. The wars of 1967 and 1973, the crystallization of a culture of environmental activism, and new laws oriented toward nature preservation all had effects on the growth of the country's marked and mapped hiking trails and engendered a number of tensions regarding the way Israelis viewed the project of placing marks upon the Land. Those tensions, however, only came into full view after the 1979 peace agreement with Egypt and the subsequent Israeli withdrawal from the Sinai Peninsula.

Passing the Torch: Ori Dvir and the Public Committee for Waymarking

Ori Dvir was born in Tel Aviv in 1931 and began taking long treks (masa'ot) as a youth with his friends Micha Livne and Yehuda Ziv.[2] Livne, along with Shmaryahu Guttman and Ze'ev Meshel, became one of the notable Jewish explorers of Masada and the Judean Desert during the 1950s and helped turn the ancient Snake Path into a trail for modern hikers.[3] Ziv eventually served as a Palmach scout and, after statehood, became one of Israel's most prominent geographers.[4] Dvir thus became a member of the tight circle of Sabra youth who boldly explored the country during the pre-state era. By the time he joined Ha-Shomer ha-Tzair in high school, Dvir was well-versed in yedi'at ha-aretz, and soon afterward, he started guiding hikes. He met his wife-to-be, Chava, on a youth movement hike when they were both fifteen years old. At seventeen, just before the beginning of the 1948 War, Dvir was recruited into the Palmach; he fought in the war and remained in the IDF until 1950.[5]

After his release from the military, Dvir began working at the Egged transportation cooperative. Such jobs, which offered employment for life, were coveted and difficult to obtain, especially in the austere years of early statehood. Dvir's father had worked for Egged, however, and when he died, he left his share in the cooperative to his son. Dvir began as a tow truck driver and was sent all over the country to haul buses back to the main garages in Tel Aviv and Haifa. Eventually he got a bus driver's license and found himself shuttling children across Israel on school trips. Whenever he was in a remote location and had spare time, he sought to "know the Land" by exploring its lesser-known corners.[6] At the same time, he took classes in tour guiding at the Avshalom Institute and was part of its first graduating class.[7]

Dvir, as a family and career man based in Tel Aviv, lived a life that was much different from the solitary one Yossi Feldman lived in the desert, but the two men were engaged in similar pursuits during the early 1950s: walking the length and breadth of the country in an effort to know its spaces with a view toward developing a deeper knowledge in the future. Dvir felt a strong desire to know the parts of the Land that had just been incorporated into the body of Jewish territory and gathered knowledge wherever he could find it, especially regarding the Negev. In one of his later writings, Dvir describes a correspondence with Azaria Alon in which the latter sent him a poorly copied map with a note written in the margins: "I'm sending you a copy of the Negev map with no publisher name and no publication date (looks like 1944, from the settlements that are labeled, and from the ones that aren't shown). Watch out for what there is in the Negev, because many wadis are unnamed, and it's unclear where they come from and where they're going. . . . For your use."[8]

Having gathered a substantial amount of such information, Dvir believed there should be better ways of disseminating "knowledge of the Land" to youth than through informal correspondences and map exchanges. He proposed that Egged create a yedi'at ha-aretz department that could further educate students about the geography of Israel. The company approved, and Dvir became the department's head. He wrote educational booklets and created a yedi'at ha-aretz quiz that students could use to pass the time while riding buses. That quiz gave rise to a nationwide yedi'at ha-aretz contest, which took place annually in Tel Aviv before sold-out audiences. At the first contest in 1961, Dvir served as a judge alongside Azaria Alon, who had gone on to become one of the founders of the SPNI, and Yosef Braslavi, the famous writer whose books had guided youth across the country prior to statehood.[9] The following year, Dvir judged the contest with Zev Vilnay, the early Histadrut hiking guide and exponent of yedi'at ha-aretz, and Amotz Zahavi, another founder of the SPNI.[10] All of this was taking place at the same time Yossi Feldman was marking trails around Ein Gedi; through these connections and others, Dvir was part of the small circle of people who were familiar with the "technical committee" and its efforts toward simun shvilim.[11]

By the early 1960s, as a result of his tireless work ethic, Dvir was becoming known in the Israeli public for his knowledge of the country's landscapes and historical sites and for his skills as an educator. He wrote monthly articles for numerous Israeli periodicals and taught geography classes for children and adults. In 1962 he began hosting a long-running radio program called Le'an Netayel ha-Shavua, or "Where Will We Hike This Week?," that described short hikes for families based on the weekend trips he took with his own wife and children.[12] Government officials were familiar with him as well, not only from their encounters with him in the course of his frequent travels but also from his efforts alongside the Ministry of Tourism to create Israel's first formal accreditation program for tour guides in 1960.[13] With his knowledge, reputation, and network of connections across Israel, Dvir was an ideal candidate to serve as Feldman's successor as leader of the Public

Committee for Waymarking in Israel. He accepted the nonpaying position in 1963 and immediately started working to create marked and mapped trails in the Eilat Mountains between the Egyptian and Jordanian armistice lines at the extreme southern tip of Israeli territory.

Israel's Second Trail Network: The Eilat Mountains

Throughout the 1950s, the southern Negev was only tenuously linked with the rest of Israeli territory, both in terms of its status in the minds of Israelis and in terms of its transportation connections. In the discussions leading up to the 1919 Paris Peace Conference, the Negev south of Be'er Sheva was regarded by the British as a territory that linked the Sinai with the Hijaz in northwest Arabia, and it was therefore nearly excluded from the boundaries of Mandate Palestine.[14] After its inclusion, Jews in Palestine considered the Negev to be part of the Land of Israel, but its distant southern portions were out of sight and generally out of mind. The Southern Negev lay outside the traditional boundaries of Eretz Israel as articulated in the recurring biblical formulation "from Dan to Be'er Sheva." Eilat was mentioned in the Bible as one of the stops of the children of Israel during the exodus from Egypt and as an Israelite port city on the Red Sea during the reign of King Solomon.[15] During the Mandate period, however, more than two hundred kilometers of open desert separated the end of the paved road at Be'er Sheva from the Gulf of Aqaba. Even if it were practical for Jews to visit, the area offered little to see besides the Arab village of Umm Rashrash and the British police post that had stood there since 1906.[16]

After the 1948–1949 war, the situation changed, but very slowly. The southern reaches of the Negev were only incorporated into Israeli territory after the final campaign of the war in March 1949. Umm Rashrash and its police post were renamed Eilat, and a Jewish settlement with an Israeli Air Force landing strip was immediately established there. The old difficulties of reaching the area remained, though, and for most of the 1950s, military trucks and jeeps constituted the only overland vehicular traffic. Eilat became a development town where the Israeli government settled new immigrants, but it suffered from its isolation, its hot climate, and its proximity to the Jordanian and Egyptian armistice lines. As took place in other development towns, many Jews of European origin migrated to urban areas, leaving only Jews who had immigrated to Israel from Arab countries. Even after the completion of the paved road from Be'er Sheva in January 1958, Eilat remained a remote outpost, ethnically and geographically segregated from Israeli society.[17]

In 1962, the Israel Exploration Society (IES)—a Zionist cultural institution devoted to studying the history and geography of Eretz Israel—held its annual meeting in Eilat in an effort to draw attention to the southern Negev and strengthen its links to the rest of the country. Eilat was interesting to devotees of yedi'at ha-aretz because of its biblical provenance and because of nearby archaeological sites, which included some of the oldest copper mines in the world. Equally interesting was the list of speakers; every year, government officials like David Ben-Gurion, Yitzhak Ben-Zvi, and Moshe Dayan discussed yedi'at ha-aretz alongside renowned professional scholars. IES conferences thus drew large numbers of visitors from all over Israel and served to tie the country's peripheries to its center. At the 1962 conference in Eilat, Yigael Yadin said in his final remarks, "We shall leave as ambassadors of Eilat and the Negev, and that will be the benefit of this meeting."[18]

For youth movement hikers who still held pioneer ideals in high regard, the southern Negev around Eilat was a part of Eretz Israel that was still wild, natural, and unknown. Palmach hikes during the pre-state era had spilled out of the Judean Desert some distance into the Negev and had established a route that linked Sdom with Revivim via the Large Crater and the Small Crater. After statehood, youth movement hikers began using that route again, and Revivim became a base for exploration further to the south—generally to the great crater of Makhtesh Ramon with its thousand-foot cliffs. Yossi Feldman, Meir Har-Tzion, and Rachel Savorai were some of the exceptional few during the 1950s who ventured extensively south of the crater, to the edges of the country, and beyond. It was not until the completion of the Be'er Sheva-Eilat road in 1958 that youth movements began organizing large-scale hikes in the Eilat Mountains.

Hikers who made it to the Eilat Mountains encountered landscapes that were entirely different from those that could be found elsewhere in Israel. Most of the mountains in the Negev were composed of limestone and were tan or brown in color. The mountains near the Red Sea, however, were essentially a continuation of the volcanic formations that stretched across the Sinai Peninsula. In the Southern Negev, then, granite peaks thrust up through the middle of sedimentary rock formations, creating areas where purple and black volcanic rock stood in sharp contrast with brilliant red sandstone and bright yellow and white limestone. Deep and narrow canyons, strange rock formations, and elevated moonscapes were only a few of

Figure 4.1. Egged tour bus at "Solomon's Pillars," Eilat Mountains, 1964. *Photo by Fritz Cohen, courtesy Government Press Office.*

the natural features that drew hikers to the area. It was also possible in the Eilat Mountains to gain a sense of the shape of Eretz Israel; in the course of a single hike, hikers could see the country's boundaries—the Arava Valley, the mountains of Sinai, and the Red Sea coastline—to the east, west, and south.

The dangers of the Eilat Mountains were similar to those of the Judean Desert. The mountainous terrain and the general lack of water sources meant that established trails were lifelines from which hikers departed at their own peril. The proximity of international boundaries was also a problem for hikers. While the armistice line with Jordan ran through the wide Arava Valley, and was therefore somewhat discernible even when it was not marked, the boundary between the Negev and the Sinai had been drawn by the British in 1906 with little regard for the terrain it crossed.[19] Hikers therefore had to be careful when using the most natural transportation routes—wadis and canyons—because they sometimes led across the armistice line into enemy territory.[20]

In the fall of 1958, on the heels of the completion of the paved road, a youth hostel opened in Eilat, providing the same type of infrastructure that had enabled hiking to flourish around Sdom, Masada, and Ein Gedi.[21] By the spring of 1960, demand for hiking, primarily by large youth movement groups, had outstripped the town's facilities for camping and lodging.[22] As youth hiking continued to grow in popularity in the Southern Negev, accidents of all sorts became more common. From the standpoint of Feldman, Hillel Birger, and others interested in simun shvilim, the Judean Desert remained the top priority for waymarking at that time because it drew much greater numbers of hikers. After the trail network between Ein Gedi and Masada was completed, though, the Southern Negev was the next logical place for marking and mapping trails.

Dvir began by enlisting help wherever he could find it. He approached Egged for support, which made sense since the transportation cooperative had an interest in creating new markets for Israeli travelers.[23] He also sought assistance from the IDF, which remained, in Moshe Dayan's words, "the broad-shouldered body" to which Israelis turned when undertaking any endeavor in the Negev.[24] Dvir also approached local business and government officials. In the end, Egged and the Timna Copper Works agreed to donate signage; the Eilat Municipality and the Eilot Regional Council agreed to provide funding for equipment; the military agreed to provide security and logistical support; and Dvir's friends—tour guides and youth movement leaders—agreed to spend a week working in the desert as volunteers.[25] Other local volunteers and supporters included Ezra Cohen and Giora Ilani, both of whom were later instrumental in the creation of the Eilat Field School. A more unusual form of assistance came from Major General Avraham Yoffe, who was then head of IDF Southern Command and a staunch supporter of the SPNI. On two occasions, Yoffe made sure Dvir's military reserve duty was fulfilled in the course of his waymarking activities, and he even sent soldiers to help in the field.[26]

Israel's second waymarking initiative began on the morning of August 26, 1963. Overall, the organizational methods Dvir employed were similar to those Feldman had used in the Judean Desert. Twenty-eight volunteers fanned out across an area bounded by the settlement of Yotvata on the north, the Red Sea on the south, Jordan on the east, and Sinai on the west, and they spent a week painting markings on the granite and sandstone mountains.[27] Again, the marking system was based on Birger's; each rectangular blaze was composed of two horizontal white stripes with a colored stripe in between and placed alongside the trail so that it would be visible to hikers in both directions. The system of coloring the trails seems to have been slightly more intentional than it had been in the Judean Desert, and it was also slightly different. Red markings were used for long trails, and blue and green markings were used for shorter secondary trails. Instead of black markings, though, as had been used in Feldman's network, Dvir's volunteers used yellow markings, which appeared along smaller "connecting" trails.[28]

Marking trails in the Eilat Mountains was not like marking trails anywhere else in the world. Dvir describes the paths of the Southern Negev as highways for Bedouin smugglers who moved freely between Egypt and Jordan across Israel's unsecured borders during the early 1960s. Given the tenuous security situation for waymarking crews, General Yoffe had given Dvir a Piper Cub airplane and a pilot, Rina Levinson, to assist in checking the safety and whereabouts of personnel in the field since the communication equipment available at the time could not cover the long distances involved. On numerous occasions, when Dvir and Levinson saw a group of people walking through the desert or resting under a shady tree, they flew in to take a closer look only to discover that they had happened upon a convoy of smugglers, who would then fire at the plane with automatic rifles. Such incidents underscored the dangers inherent in hiking in Israel and, for Dvir, underscored the importance of marking trails in order to keep hikers safe.[29]

By the end of 1965, most of the marked network on the ground had been completed, with a total investment of twenty thousand Israeli lirot. Mordechai Edelstein, the coordinator of the SPNI during the mid-1960s and one of the supervisors of the waymarking project, wrote afterward that more than five hundred kilometers of trails had been marked across the triangle of desert between the Ovda Valley and Eilat. Overall, the effort seems to have benefited from the lessons learned in the Judean Desert. During a comparable period of time, a considerably larger area—about eight hundred square kilometers—was marked on the ground. It also incorporated some new elements; at every roadside trailhead, large signs were erected explaining simun shvilim and the destinations of the trails, and at every trail intersection, small signs were posted for orientation purposes. Such signs appear to have been necessary at that point because a trail map had not yet been published. According to Edelstein, the signs were the first victims of sabotage along Israel's trail network; already by 1966, many of them had been used "by destructive people of various sorts" for target practice.[30] Dvir later wrote that "extremists" had destroyed the signs not because of politics but because they read, "Donated by Egged."[31]

Hiking Trails and Israel's Nascent Environmental Movement

Whatever the reasons for the signs' destruction, the trails and their markings were emblematic of larger tensions that were simmering within Israel and its environmental movement. As noted earlier, Labor Zionism had a dichotomous view of the Jewish relationship with the Land of Israel; on one extreme was veneration for pure nature and on the other was the concrete-and-steel developmental ethos. After statehood, however, the use of land was not an either/or proposition; even when people could agree that a given space should remain free from urban and industrial development, they disagreed on whether the area should be conserved for responsible human use or left completely untouched by people. As early as 1949, the Israeli government acknowledged the need to protect special areas, and the Planning Department of the Ministry of the Interior began working on proposals for national parks, but no comprehensive policies were enacted.[32] Sites like Shivta in the Negev were set aside and developed as tourist destinations by the Department for Landscape Improvement throughout the 1950s. State-owned rural lands were largely administered by the Jewish National Fund (JNF), which often blocked urban development but by no means left nature to work on its own; it was famous for "improving the Land" by means of pine seedlings and bulldozers.

By the 1960s, the preservation-oriented SPNI had gained strength as a counterpoint to the JNF, and Israeli society was becoming aware of the need to protect the country's sensitive environmental areas. On June 12, 1962, Member of Knesset Yizhar Smilansky delivered a speech that spurred the Israeli government to action. Smilansky was a scion of prominent Labor Zionist pioneer families who had been profoundly influenced by the methods of Epstein and Wilkomitz—the educators who had written hiking into the national school curriculum in 1903.[33] Under the pen name S. Yizhar, Smilansky was also one of Israel's greatest literary figures; his writing was full of evocative descriptions of the Land and its features. Using language that hearkened back to A. D. Gordon, Smilansky argued passionately before the Knesset that while national parks were important, nature reserves were important as well. Zionism's developmental ethos, he said, had run amok and now threatened to destroy not only Israel's natural spaces but the very humanity of its citizens:

> It is possible that the question that I ask may appear excessively naïve or extremely peripheral. And in spite of this, it appears to me to be the most

> essential. What will the landscape where humans live look like? What will a man see when he opens his windows in the morning? Will there be a sea breeze blowing on his face? What will be the measure of "the green" in his habitat? What will be his sense of freedom to move and to absorb, as he seeks the ultimate, uninterrupted connection? Where will he be able to seek refuge, when life in the closed city has consumed everything? In short: what should the leaders of the nation do if they want the people of this land to love their land?[34]

The speech inspired Ben-Gurion, and when the prime minister submitted a bill on national parks and nature reserves to the Knesset in December 1962, he quoted Smilansky extensively.[35] The ensuing discussion resulted in the enactment of the Nature Reserves and National Parks Law in 1963, which created one agency oriented toward developing tourist sites and one oriented toward preserving nature. According to Israeli environmental historian Alon Tal, the law had the long-term effect of restoring the balance between the two sides of the Zionist relationship with the Land of Israel.

> Rather than establish a single National Park Service, the Smilansky compromise created the parallel frameworks of a National Parks Authority and a Nature Protection Authority. National Parks were to be landmarks, largely of historical significance, where human presence was allowed and honored. Nature reserves were to be sanctuaries where people were the guests and development was eschewed. The dichotomy was described as analogous to the book of Genesis's call "to work and to preserve" the Garden of Eden. National Parks were to be worked, Nature Reserves preserved. In retrospect, this prescient, seemingly bureaucratic, distinction was responsible for saving dozens of ecologically precious corners of the Land of the Bible.[36]

The waymarking project in the Eilat Mountains took place immediately in the wake of these developments, so one can imagine why signs in the desert bearing the name of Israel's largest transportation cooperative could be offensive to environmentalists—perhaps from the ranks of passionate SPNI-affiliated youth who had begun to range across the country in the hopes of protecting its wild places.[37] Nevertheless, trails were viewed at the time by the SPNI and by the Israeli government as useful tools for nature preservation. Just as the trail network was nearing completion in December 1965, a large section of the Southern Negev, including the Eilat Mountains, was declared a nature reserve. The intention of the National Parks and Nature Reserves Law had been to block development in such areas, but the thousands of painted trail markings Dvir and his volunteer crews had placed were not erased. On the contrary, the network was allowed to grow to completion, and its structure was incorporated into that of the nature reserve. Ahead of the Hanukkah hiking season, the nascent Nature Reserves Authority, in cooperation with the SPNI and the IDF Southern Command, deployed personnel across the Negev so that the unprecedented numbers of youth movement hikers would not destroy sensitive sites.[38]

Different opinions exist in environmental movements worldwide about the best ways to navigate the tension between allowing public access to nature reserves and blocking that access entirely. Blocking access and leaving reserves wholly undeveloped may seem like an attractive option for purists but doing so is usually impossible, and human movement goes unchecked and uncontained. Hiking trails and even vehicle roads are compromises that damage nature but ultimately concentrate all human impact on the environment—erosion, litter, noise, and so on—into defined corridors of movement. Allowing hiking trails in the Ein Gedi and Eilat Mountains nature reserves was a pragmatic decision aimed at navigating this tension; if there were no trails, Israeli hikers would hike there anyway but would roam freely and cause a wider impact on the environment.[39]

The question few people seemed to be asking in 1965 was where the boundaries lay for the trail markers themselves. Feldman seems to have had few qualms about leaving his own mark on the Land. He had fought the destruction of the ancient ruins at Shivta during the late 1950s but had later dug up the remainder of those ruins and rebuilt them on a large scale with an immigrant work crew. He had gone to Ein Gedi and fallen in love with the remote desert oasis but had then built a school there and started leading large groups of people into the once seemingly empty space. Like the early Zionist pioneers, Feldman loved the Land, and in working to beautify it, he always managed to leave transformation in his wake. Unlike the pioneers, though, he left his mark on footpaths as well. Under his watch, the paths to yedi'at ha-aretz remained unpaved, but they became marked with the evidence of someone else's passing. His motto in the Judean Desert was, "Wherever it is possible to walk, there will be a trail."[40]

Dvir had a similar outlook; regarding the work of the waymarking committee Dvir headed, his daughter later wrote, "Its goal was to mark all the hiking trails in the Land, short and long, to make it possible for everyone to go out and travel."[41] Dvir himself wrote later that the Eilat Mountains trail network did not simply satisfy demand for hiking; rather, it generated new demand for hiking. Perhaps more accurately, the network did not merely satisfy the demands of the hikers who were already visiting; it satisfied the demands of large numbers of Israelis who had been raised in Labor Zionist institutions, who had taken annual school hikes, and who had been taught the value of exploring the Land but lacked the knowledge, skills, and resources to visit the Land's farthest corners on their own. By creating a marked trail network in the Eilat Mountains, Dvir created lines of movement along which a wide segment of Israeli society could articulate its desire for the Land. He did not create just a few such lines; he created thirty-five of them that totaled five hundred kilometers in length.[42]

In any case, the decision to allow marked trails through Israel's nature reserves was a boon to the simun shvilim project. As the head of the Public Committee for Waymarking, Dvir became the de facto manager of walking paths through Israel's nature reserves. From his point of view, the unprecedented number of hikers visiting the Eilat Mountains during Hanukkah 1965 was not a problem at all—it was a good thing, and it had been aided by the presence of the newly marked trails. Dvir's whole life—his job at Egged, his work as a radio host, his efforts to train tour guides, his recreational activities with his family—was completely oriented toward getting Israelis out of cities and into beautiful and lesser-known places. He approached his waymarking work no differently. He had no desire to harm nature, but he believed the benefits of simun shvilim far outweighed the costs.

The simun shvilim map covering the Eilat Mountains was published by the Survey of Israel in March 1967 at a scale of 1:100,000. Once again, Tzion Sheetrug oversaw the process of gathering data on trail routes and correlating them with existing topographic data. The map was similar in appearance to the Judean Desert simun shvilim map. When folded, its outside panel bore a monochrome brown image of waving palm trees, the title "Simun Shvilim Map of the Eilat Region," and the caption "Printing of the map made possible by Egged," with the Egged logo in the lower-left corner. (See fig. 4.2.)[43] More importantly, it performed the same function as the Judean Desert map had: it covered an area of the country in which very little human development was visible on the ground and depicted it as crisscrossed with bold and bright-colored lines. (See fig. 4.3.) Anyone looking at the map would see a territory charted and bounded by lines of Israeli movement. It helped create a deeper sense among Israelis that the Eilat Mountains and Southern Negev were indeed parts of Israeli territory. It also helped create new realities: as hikers moved along the lines marked on the map and on the ground, Israeli society was able to increase its human presence there as well.

Figure 4.2. 1967 Eilat Mountains simun shvilim map cover. *From the author's collection.*

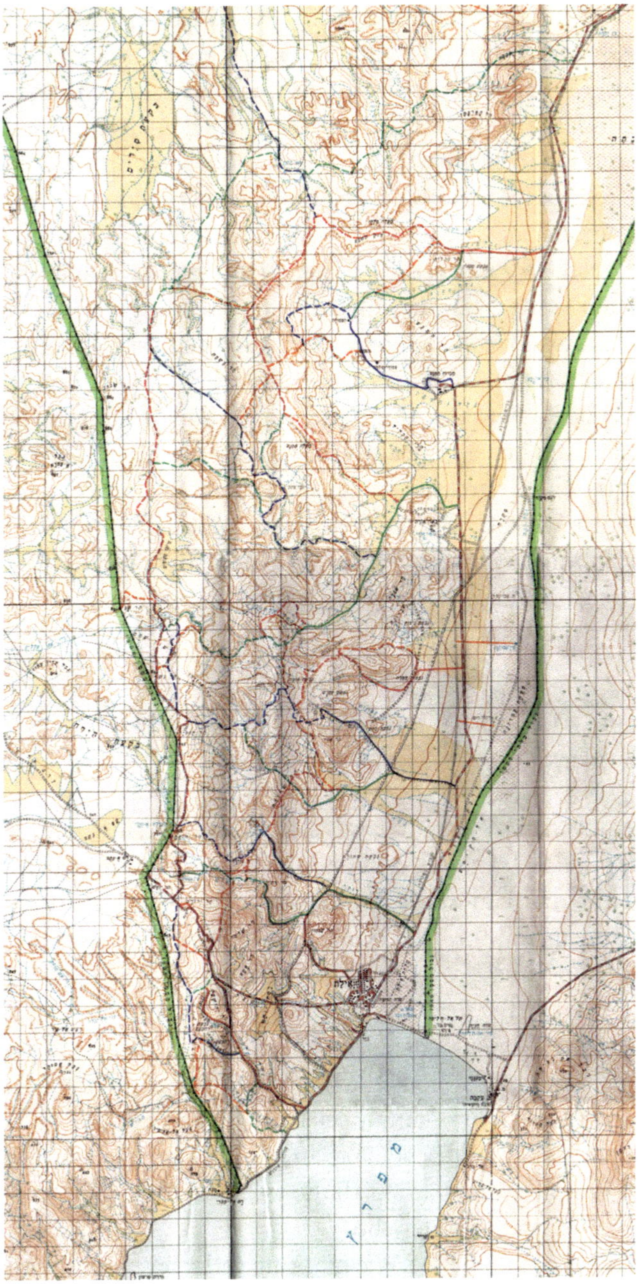

Figure 4.3. Detail of the 1967 Eilat Mountains simun shvilim map, depicting marked trails filling the area between the Egyptian and Jordanian borders. *From the author's collection.*

Meanwhile, the trail network in the Judean Desert had continued to develop. A second edition of the 1:100,000-scale simun shvilim map was published in March 1966 to reflect significant changes that had taken place on the ground. Many of the trails originally marked by Yossi Feldman and his companions had been dual-use routes, suitable for hikers or for off-road vehicles. Between 1963 and 1966, personnel from the Ein Gedi Field School marked a number of new trails, most of them single-track footpaths too narrow and steep for any vehicle to negotiate. In 1964, Feldman and Eitan Golan created four new trails with the help of a large group of youth movement volunteers; one was a brand-new route that ascended the northern wall of Nahal Arugot, inspired by the effort of Palmach Company Gimel in 1944 to create a new ascent into the mountains west of the Dead Sea.[44] The new trails did not significantly expand the breadth of the network; for the most part, they increased its density, primarily between Ein Gedi and Masada. One new trail near the Field School, though, pushed the network northward, going so close to the Green Line that its distance from Jordanian territory—perhaps only tens of meters—appears almost immeasurably small on the map.[45]

The June 1967 War and the Expansion of the Judean Desert Network

Israel's territorial expansion during the course of the June 1967 war immediately affected the trail networks and the simun shvilim maps, first in the Judean Desert and then in the Eilat Mountains. Right after the Israeli capture of Jerusalem and the West Bank, Yossi Feldman contacted Yigal Allon and requested permission to mark trails in the newly conquered northern Judean Desert. For the first time in nearly twenty years, it was possible to hike north from Ein Gedi, not just south, and to retrace the old youth movement and Palmach routes along the Dead Sea's western shore. Allon gave his blessing, and in July 1967—only weeks after the end of the war—Feldman and a group from the field school began marking trails across the northern desert. The new network reached all the way to Wadi Qelt, the deep canyon that ran from Jerusalem to Jericho.

The Public Committee for Waymarking in Israel moved with unprecedented speed. Working alongside the SPNI, and with the support of the IDF, it made its presence felt across the West Bank faster than any other Israeli civilian institution. Within the span of just a few months, Feldman and his

Map 4.1. Israel and the occupied territories, July 1967.

waymarking crews spread out across the northern Judean Desert and created more than two hundred forty kilometers of new trails, many of which joined seamlessly with existing trails south of the Green Line. Sheetrug and his colleagues immediately gathered data on all of the routes and updated the pre-1948 topographic surveys. By December 1967—six months after the war—a new 1:100,000-scale simun shvilim map was published, depicting a unified Judean Desert knitted together with colored lines and no sign that the Green Line had ever existed.

The work, carried out as it was in the immediate aftermath of the war, appears to have been quick and dirty. Most of the marked trails that appear on the 1967 Judean Desert simun shvilim map follow jeep roads, which were easy to find and required fewer blazes because their routes were so clear. Many of the newly marked paths followed lines of movement that had been well-known by the Palmach and the youth movements before the 1948–1949 war. For example, a blue-blazed trail ran south from Bethlehem to Tekoa and then connected with a red-blazed trail that ran from Tekoa to Ein Gedi; together, the trails reestablished one of the Palmach's old trekking routes. Trails through Wadi Qelt and Wadi Muraba'at (soon renamed Nahal Darga by the Israelis) made it possible to hike to Jericho and the Dead Sea, respectively, from Jerusalem. Some of the major ancient ascents toward Jerusalem from the Dead Sea were also marked, including those that began at Qumran and at Ain Feshkha.

Along the ascent from Ain Feshkha to Ras Feshkha, waymarking crews were greeted by the familiar sight of white-red-white blazes. After nearly two decades, the markings Hillel Birger and his detachment of Palmach scouts had painted in November 1947 were still in place, high up on the rocks. The rediscovery of the blazes was perhaps the ultimate confirmation that simun shvilim was sustainable and effective; the markings had been abandoned for twenty years to time, the elements, the Bedouin, and the Jordanian military, yet they still pointed a safe way up the treacherous ascent.[46]

Ironically, Birger's numbered blazes were erased in the end by the trail markers themselves, who were operating according to principles Birger had established in the intervening years. In the Eilat Mountains, Dvir had used red blazes for marking long trails, and this system appears to have been in place in the northern Judean Desert as well. The main artery through the area was a red trail that began at Nebi Musa, halfway between Jerusalem and Jericho on the main highway, and ran south-southwest through the Hyrcania Valley, just above the line of cliffs that overlooked the Dead Sea.[47]

From that central trail, branches extended downward and eastward toward the shore, alternating in color: blue, green, black; blue, green, black. This pattern ensured that two trails of the same color would not intersect each other, which was the whole point of the four-color scheme Birger had originally put forth in 1957. Black was the color that fell to the Ain Feshkha-Ras Feshkha ascent, and the large red blazes that had stood the test of time were unceremoniously erased and replaced.[48]

By 1967, organized hiking had been taking place among Zionists in the land they knew as Eretz Israel for more than half a century. Throughout that time, movement across the country on foot had been an important means by which Jews established connections with the Land, fulfilled their desire for contact with it, asserted their right to live and dwell in it, and articulated their own identity in relation to the body of national territory. Simun shvilim had concretized the relationship between Jews and the Land that had long been practiced along unpaved paths; it had given form and shape to spaces on the ground that were viewed as empty and undefined and which had been depicted as such on paper. It had turned those areas into known places and marked them on the ground and on maps as integral parts of the body of Jewish-Israeli territory. The expansion of the Israeli trail network into the northern Judean Desert was no departure from established practice. It occurred on the heels of Israel's military conquest of the West Bank and established the first large-scale Israeli civilian presence there. Long before the settlement movement crystallized into a means of integrating the occupied Palestinian territories into the body of Jewish national territory, simun shvilim transformed about one thousand square kilometers of the southern West Bank into Israeli space.

The trail network's expansion across the northern Judean Desert was the beginning of a complicated relationship between the simun shvilim project and the occupied territories. It took place during the lingering euphoria of the war's aftermath, during a time when Israelis were rushing to visit East Jerusalem, Hebron, and other sites in the West Bank. There was no ambivalence about the need for the network to expand to the north because there was no question that Israeli hikers themselves would move in that direction. Before the 1948–1949 war, the Judean Desert had been viewed by Jews in the Yishuv, and particularly by hikers, as a single territorial unit whose historic Jewish provenance was undisputed. Explorers of the Land, youth movement hikers, and devotees of yedi'at ha-aretz would do as they had always done and would journey as far as they could across the territory they understood to constitute Eretz Israel. The Public Committee for Waymarking in Israel had a mandate to keep hikers safe, and keeping hikers safe meant marking trails in desert areas.

Wadi Qelt, therefore, represented the northernmost limit of the expanded network. The deep gorge, which began northeast of Jerusalem and ran almost straight eastward to the Jordan River valley, was the geographic feature most commonly understood as the Judean Desert's northern boundary. Beyond it lay the land described in the Bible as Samaria—the mountainous and relatively well-watered northern part of the West Bank where the largest numbers of Palestinian Arabs lived. As a means of asserting Jewish presence in contested territory within Eretz Israel, simun shvilim would have functioned there as it had elsewhere; through the placement of markings on the ground and the projection of lines onto maps, a trail network would have helped turn the West Bank into Jewish Samaria. However, any dangers Israeli travelers may have faced there were not the type best addressed by simun shvilim, and there appears never to have been a push by Feldman, Dvir, or anyone else in the Public Committee or the SPNI to move farther into the West Bank.

Simun shvilim had limits, then; it was not reckless in its expansion. There were other reasons to limit waymarking in the West Bank. From the viewpoint of Israeli government officials, and particularly that of Yigal Allon, to whom Feldman turned for permission to expand the network, the Judean Desert was one of the sparsely populated territories into which Israel immediately needed to extend its presence in order to create defensible long-term boundaries. The famous "Allon Plan" called for Israel to stay out of the highlands of Judea and Samaria—the portion of the West Bank heavily populated by Palestinian Arabs—and to limit itself to establishing a series of bases in the Jordan River valley and the northern Judean Desert that could function as a "tripwire" against future attacks from the east.[49] The expansion of the trail network into the Judean Desert was in line with these efforts, but the trails' relationship with the settlement movement in the West Bank, which developed later, was more complicated.

Different dynamics were at play in Israel's far south. The Eilat Mountains trail network never expanded westward into the Sinai Peninsula, even though such an expansion would have made sense for several reasons. Like the Judean Desert and the Southern Negev, the Sinai had hot weather, mountainous terrain, and few water sources. Its large size—about four times the size Israeli-controlled territory had been before 1967—meant that anyone who wanted to explore it had to cover great distances. The Sinai Peninsula's association with the biblical mountain where God had given the Torah to the children of Israel in the book of Exodus had given it a special place in Jewish collective memory. In anticipation of the great Israeli demand to visit the Sinai, the SPNI quickly established a field school near Saint Catherine's Monastery from which guides organized hikes and jeep tours. Despite the demand that could have justified simun shvilim and the infrastructure that could have established it, marked hiking trails hardly penetrated the Sinai Peninsula during all the years it was under Israeli occupation.

Instead, the trail network in the Southern Negev grew inward and northward, increasing in density by filling more of the spaces between existing trails and increasing in size by filling more of pre-1967 Israel. The second edition of the Eilat Mountains simun shvilim map was published in 1970, and it depicted a trail network that was no longer hemmed in by an international boundary. Like the Green Line on the 1967 Judean Desert map, the 1906 boundary between the Negev and the Sinai had been erased. The shape of Eretz Israel, though, as it had come to be defined since the early days of the British Mandate, was not only visible, but rendered visible by the trail system. Trail routes, depicted as colored lines across the map, spread to the farthest edges of Israeli territory, filling its open spaces in a way nothing else could have. Eilat was still a small collection of buildings on the Red Sea shoreline, and Israel's transportation network in the southern Negev still consisted of a few thin lines running up the Arava Valley. If the trails had been erased from the map, nothing would have differentiated Eretz Israel from the Sinai Peninsula. As it was, though, the form of the Land of Israel was separated from the void of the empty desert in the same way the outlines of the human body are clearly visible on a map of the circulatory system.

Ori Dvir's extensive writings offer no reasons why Israel's trail network never moved into the Sinai Peninsula, and no one seems ever to have raised the question. Perhaps since the Sinai Peninsula had a questionable territorial status and was never regarded by a large segment of Israelis as part of the Jewish homeland, Dvir and other members of the Public Committee simply saw trails in the Sinai Peninsula as an unworthy investment. Waymarking there was not utterly out of the question; the 1975 Eilat Mountains simun shvilim map does show a few trails extending across the old boundary, but they were continuations of trails that began on the Israeli side and naturally followed canyons and watercourses westward. For the most part, the SPNI and other Israeli civilian organizations operating in the occupied

Sinai Peninsula seem to have been content with leaving travel routes unmarked, save for the Bedouin rujum, or "stone-cairns," that designated important landmarks.

There was, however, one notable exception. In a 1978 article, written just prior to the peace talks that culminated in the Israeli withdrawal from Sinai, Dvir mentions that waymarking was underway in the area around the town of Saint Catherine. That was the area that lay around Jebel Katerina and Jebel Musa—respectively, the highest mountain peak in Sinai and the nearby mountain traditionally recognized as the biblical Mount Sinai. Dvir writes that a map of that area—separate from the main simun shvilim series—would soon be published at a scale of 1:25,000.[50] Besides this brief mention, Dvir writes nothing else about the abortive project, which was abandoned when the Israeli-Egyptian peace agreement was finalized. It merits further examination, however, and is mentioned in more detail in the conclusion of this chapter.

Change in the Air: The Hiatus between 1967 and 1973

After the expansion of the Judean Desert network in 1967, Israel's existing trail networks were deepened, and their marks were continually renewed, but several years passed before simun shvilim spread into any new areas. During that time, Dvir was occupied with all sorts of other pursuits. In 1969, he started earning his bachelor's degree in geography from Tel Aviv University. He graduated in 1971 but worked throughout the next year on his first book, *Where Will We Hike This Week*—a travel guide based on the weekly radio program he had hosted since 1960. The book, published in 1972, was popular across Israel and turned Dvir into a household name. Throughout all this, Dvir had been working full-time since 1960 as the head of Egged's yedi'at ha-aretz department. He was able to retire from Egged with a pension in 1972, but that year he began two new pursuits: first, he became a college student again and began working toward his master's degree in geography, again from Tel Aviv University; second, he became a college teacher and established the Department of Land of Israel Studies at Beit Berl.

Everything Dvir did reflected his desire for the Land. He had four children, and he named all of them after different parts of Eretz Israel: Carmel, Kinneret, Sharon, and Eilat. On weekends, he and his wife Chava continued to take the children on hikes, and the hikes continued to be featured on radio programs and in magazine and newspaper articles. Carmel, Dvir's oldest daughter, accompanied him on waymarking projects. Exploring the Land and communicating yedi'at ha-aretz was woven deeply into the fabric of his life. Not all of the "perfect Sabras" of Dvir's generation had maintained such strong connections with the Land, nor could they have; the men and women who had been active in the Palmach and the pre-statehood youth movements were older, and many of them had key roles in the government, where the Labor Party was still dominant. For those who could no longer explore the Land to their hearts' content, Dvir served as a mediator. He fulfilled this role as a radio voice, as a writer, and also as a trailblazer—a man who left signs upon the Land for others to follow.

Things were changing in Israel, though. A new era of prosperity had started after the June 1967 war. Coca-Cola, which arrived in Israel in 1968, was just one indicator of Israel's increasing Western orientation and of the beginning of the country's shift away from socialism and toward capitalism. A new generation of youth was coming of age, too—a generation of native-born men and women who were less indoctrinated with Labor Zionist pioneering ideals than their parents had been. While they still hiked on their own and with school trips, they associated hiking less with nationalism and more with recreation. Masada began declining in importance as a civil-religious pilgrimage site.[51] Many young Israelis were affected and inspired by the global counterculture movement, and a few of them began traveling overseas in the late 1960s and early 1970s to do a different sort of backpacking in South America.[52]

By 1973, having retired from Egged, and despite all of his other yedi'at ha-aretz-related pursuits, Dvir was ready to devote himself more fully to the simun shvilim project. After the renewal of the Eilat Mountains network—which involved revisiting marked trails, making sure blazes were still clearly visible, and repainting those that had become worn or faded—IDF Northern Command requested that Dvir and the Public Committee organize a new waymarking initiative.[53] For the first time, trail markings would be painted outside of Israel's deserts, in the relatively cool and well-watered Golan Heights, where the biggest dangers to hikers were not terrain and climate but man-made weapons buried in the ground.

Israel's Third Trail Network: The Golan Heights

The elevated, windswept volcanic plateau of the Golan Heights was bounded by the snowcapped Mount Hermon on the north, the Yarmuk River on the south, the UN demilitarized zone on the east, and the steep drop to the upper Jordan River valley and the Sea of Galilee on the west. Like the Judean Desert and Southern Negev, Ramat ha-Golan was a sensitive and sparsely settled border area where Israeli control was contested but where Israelis nevertheless liked to go and hike. Much of the Golan was flat; its central and eastern portions consisted of wide, open spaces punctuated with a few extinct volcanic cones. Rudimentary walls of black basalt stones, piled up after having been removed from plowed fields, ran along the edges of farms and unpaved roads. In the far north, the foothills and southern slopes of Mount Hermon were covered in forests and broken with deep valleys and gorges. The terrain was also rugged along the Golan's southern and western edges, where the land descended to the Yarmuk and Jordan River valleys.

Israelis were interested in hiking across the Golan Heights for several reasons. First, they wanted to hike there simply because they could; Israel's culture of hiking had always been about possibilities and exploration, and with the addition of the formerly Syrian lands to the territory of their small country, there was no stopping hikers from going there. Second, it was a great place to hike; the Golan was largely open and rural and offered landscapes that could not be found in pre-1967 Israel. Third, the area had strong connections with Eretz Israel and was considered by many to constitute a part of the body of the Land. True, it had not been included in Palestine during the Mandate nor did it fall within the traditional formulation of the Land's boundaries as stretching "from Dan to Be'er Sheva." However, the waters that poured forth from Dan at the beginning of the Jordan River—the lifeblood of the country—began in the Golan as snowmelt from Mount Hermon. Other important tributaries of the Jordan began in the Golan as well, including Nahal Senir—known in Lebanon as the Hasbani—and the Banias springs. Jewish communities were known to have existed in the Golan in ancient times; many of them took part in the Great Revolt against Rome described by Josephus. Moreover, the territory was known in the Hebrew Bible as Bashan and was described as being part of the Israelite kingdom under Solomon.

There was also a strong likelihood that Israel would retain long-term control over the Golan Heights. On June 19, 1967—nine days after the end of the war—Israel proposed negotiations with Egypt and Syria based on the land-for-peace principle. In short, Israel would return the Sinai Peninsula and the Golan Heights in exchange for peace treaties with Egypt and Syria. Israel sought border agreements based on the boundaries originally established with the British Mandate and also sought certain security guarantees from both countries. The commitments Israel sought from Syria were, first, complete demilitarization of the Golan Heights; and second, the non-obstruction of water flow from the sources of the Jordan River into Israel. Syria and Egypt both rejected Israel's overtures, however, and at the Khartoum Conference in September 1967, Arab countries formed a united front that opposed any negotiations with Israel.

On November 22, 1967—the twenty-year anniversary of Hillel Birger's waymarking effort at Ain Feshkha—the UN passed Resolution 242, which enshrined land-for-peace as the principle on which future negotiations would be based. The document did not specify the time or extent of Israeli withdrawals from territories occupied during the war, but it affirmed the right of every country "to live in peace within secure and recognized boundaries free from threats or acts of force."[54] Within this framework, Israel saw its occupation of the Golan Heights as necessary and legitimate, since Syria had used the territory since 1948 as a platform for shelling Jewish settlements in the valleys below and was now unwilling to offer guarantees that similar attacks would not plague Israel in the future. Even David Ben-Gurion, who immediately after the war was able to see through the messianic haze and acknowledge that a long-term occupation of the West Bank would be problematic for Israel and a provocation to the Arab world, believed Israel should keep the Golan Heights for strategic reasons. Its non-Jewish population who remained there after the war—six thousand inhabitants, mostly Druze—did not offer the same challenges to Israeli occupation, and even annexation, that the large Arab populations of the West Bank and Gaza did.

As time passed and negotiations became less and less likely, Israel entrenched its presence in the Golan Heights, as it did in the other occupied territories, and established its own settlements there. By 1973, nineteen new Israeli settlements had been established on the Golan, but the largest population center remained the Druze village of Majdal Shams on the slopes of Mount Hermon near the Syrian border. The town of Katzrin, which later became the seat of the Golan Heights Regional Council and is today known as "the capital of the Golan," did not yet exist.[55]

Why did the IDF Northern Command get involved in choosing the site of Israel's next trail network? Until 1973, the military had played a key supportive role in simun shvilim, but the marking and mapping efforts had always been initiated by civilians. Men like Birger, Feldman, and Dvir had all served in the military, but they were hikers first and foremost and were concerned with keeping Israeli youth safe. For them, climate, terrain, borders, and bullets were the key dangers that faced Israeli hikers, and the worst combinations of those were found in the south. For the most part, hiking in the Golan Heights was similar to hiking in the Galilee, where simun shvilim had never been considered necessary for safe hiking. Its proximity to Syrian and Lebanese territory might have been a concern, but hikers were blocked from the armistice lines by the heavy presence of the IDF across the Golan, the UN forces manning the demilitarized zone to the east, and the high wall of Mount Hermon to the north.

Landmines—hundreds of thousands of them—were the danger that set the Golan Heights apart from the main body of Israeli-controlled territory. Before 1967, the Jaulan, as it was known in Arabic, had been part of the Damascene hinterland. The plateau's high walls were the only serious geographic obstacle between Israeli territory and the Syrian capital. The Syrians had therefore studded the whole escarpment with fortifications, including bases, pillboxes, trenches, gun emplacements, and minefields. Much of the larger military infrastructure was reduced to ruins during the Six-Day War and its immediate aftermath, but the locations of the minefields—and the thousands of antitank and antipersonnel mines buried within them—were mostly unknown. IDF patrols frequently encountered mines in the early days after the war, and by July 1967, the IDF engineering corps was working to locate mines and other unexploded ordnance.[56]

Hiking accidents soon followed. In April 1968, a woman from Kibbutz Tel Geva stepped on a mine while helping lead a group of twenty-five children on a hike; she and one of the children were severely injured.[57] In July of that year, two eleventh-graders—members of the religious Bnei Akiva youth movement—innocently climbed a fence while hiking and realized they had entered a minefield only after they were both hit with shrapnel.[58] IDF engineers estimated at that time that somewhere between two hundred thousand and half a million landmines remained scattered across the Golan, mostly within fenced areas, but large areas were still suspected to be dangerous.[59] Minefields seriously limited movement in general upon the plateau and made life difficult for everyone who lived there. Fields had to be carefully checked before they were plowed. When wildfires swept across minefields, nearby areas had to be evacuated, and then firefighters had to deal with spontaneous explosions.[60] Accidents involving soldiers, sappers, and hikers continued to take place throughout the remainder of the 1960s and into the early 1970s. Terrorist attacks, too, continually plagued the Golan Heights; nevertheless, during every school break, thousands of Israelis went there to hike.[61]

As far as Dvir was concerned, the specific dangers to hikers in the Golan Heights may have been different from the ones in Israel's southern deserts, but the goal of marking trails in that territory was in line with the main idea behind simun shvilim: to enable people to hike safely. Since simun shvilim was oriented toward marking existing paths, not creating new ones, the mechanics of waymarking in the Golan Heights stood to be little different than they had been elsewhere. Dvir agreed to supervise the project and employed methods that would serve him well in years to come as he built trail networks across the rest of the country.

First, he built on the precedent Yossi Feldman had originally established and used SPNI field schools—which now existed all across Israel—as spatial and organizational hubs for new waymarking initiatives. This made sense because field schools led hikes regardless of whether marked and mapped trails yet existed; in the course of their everyday activities, their guides and students explored the surrounding areas and found the routes best suited for group excursions. Field school personnel, then, were ideal consultants for converting existing paths into new hiking trails, and the schools themselves could supply volunteer manpower for the projects.

Second, Dvir diverted resources from his other yedi'at ha-aretz-related projects into simun shvilim. While the Israel Trails Committee (ITC) formally operated under the auspices of the SPNI, very little money was ever allocated for trail marking and maintenance. In fact, while working in other capacities for the SPNI, Dvir states in a 1977 article that his position as Chairman of the ITC was unpaid. The only person who drew a salary from simun shvilim was the ITC's Coordinator of Waymarking, who was responsible for organizing efforts on the ground; at that time, David Einav had just left that position, and Uzi Chaplin had just started.[62] Operating on a shoestring budget, then, Dvir used his status as an educator and a public figure to generate interest in simun shvilim and to gather necessary resources. He talked about trails on his weekly radio shows, in his monthly magazine columns, and at his frequent public engagements. He required his students in the yedi'at ha-aretz and tour-guiding programs at Beit Berl to help mark trails as part of their education.[63] Perhaps most importantly, he used the contacts he gleaned from his frequent cross-country travels to curry favor and secure assistance from government bodies.

When Dvir started marking trails in the Golan Heights on March 25, 1973, he used the SPNI's Golan Field School near present-day Katzrin as his headquarters. Workers from the field school also participated in the waymarking work, as did workers from the Nature Reserve Authority, students from Beit Berl, and a detachment of IDF soldiers. Over a period of less than one week, Dvir and his team marked a network of fifteen important trails across the central and southern Golan Heights, including two trails that are now regarded as iconic Israeli hikes—Nahal Meshushim, in which water flows into a deep pool bounded by natural hexagonal columns of black basalt, and Nahal Zavitan, the gorge that descends in a series of cliffs and waterfalls from the high escarpment to the Jordan River valley. Dvir and his workers finished on March 30 and returned home; the next phase of waymarking was slated to take place on October 31, 1973.[64]

On October 6, however, the Yom Kippur War began, and for a period of about twenty days, the Golan Heights once again became the scene of fierce fighting between Israel and Syria. The waymarking project was postponed, of course, and picked back up after the war. One of the initial goals of the Golan Heights waymarking project had been to publish a simun shvilim map of the area along the lines of the Judean Desert and Eilat Mountains maps.[65] That did not happen immediately, though. In fact, about a decade passed before a real effort was made to create a simun shvilim map of the Golan Heights. One reason for this may be that in 1971, a 1:100,000-scale topographical map of the territory was published by the Survey of Israel in partnership with the SPNI's Golan Field School.[66] The map looked basically identical to the Judean Desert and Eilat Mountains maps, but it showed no marked trails. Hikers did not have a simun shvilim map for the Golan, then, but they had an accurate topographical map, a marked trail network, and an SPNI field school with knowledgeable and helpful personnel. In any case, adding marked routes to the Golan map was not a high priority after the Yom Kippur War. Dvir's priorities, and the priorities of most Israelis, had suddenly changed.

The Turn Inward: The Mount Carmel Trail Network, 1976

The massive internal crisis engendered in Israeli society after October 1973 had an effect on Israel's culture of hiking, which until that point had been largely defined by the pioneering ideals of Labor Zionism. After the war, Israelis still wanted to hike, and loved exploring Eretz Israel, but were through with the Labor Zionist leaders who had been in power since the establishment of the Jewish state. The global counterculture movement and the prosperity of the late 1960s and early 1970s had already taken their toll on Labor

Zionist culture in Israel and its associated symbols. The Scouting and youth movements sustained steep declines in membership. Masada ceased to be a popular civil-religious pilgrimage destination, and instead became a tourist attraction with a cable car. Fewer Israelis sought to embody the image of the Sabra scout who walked bravely along the country's frontiers.

Given the Labor Zionist roots of modern hiking in Israel, one might expect that the erosion of Labor Zionist ideals and the repudiation of Labor Zionist leadership might have led to an overall decline in hiking, and perhaps even the end of simun shvilim. That was not the case, though. Much has been made of the phenomenon of Israeli backpacking that became popular during the mid-1970s, and which continued to grow during the 1980s. In reality, though, the months-long overseas trips, during which youth rambled across the Far East or South America after their release from military service, were expensive, and were undertaken only by those who could afford it. Most Israelis still loved walking the Land, even if fewer of them did it in the framework of youth movements like Ha-Shomer ha-Tzair or Ha-Machanot ha-Olim. It was still a part of the school curriculum, and was as enjoyable, relaxing, and cheap as it had always been. In fact, demand for hiking grew as more and more people associated it with nature and environmentalism.

Israel's trail networks, however, were not suited to meet this demand. The long, one-way routes that ran along borders and through deserts were ideal for challenging masa'ot and youth movement hikes, or for organized field trips led by schools and the military. They had not been designed with everyday Israelis in mind, and did not enable them to take walks near the places where they lived. Residents of Haifa, Tel Aviv, and Jerusalem all lived in close proximity to open spaces, and could access them quickly via public transportation. However, because those spaces did not have marked and mapped hiking trails, people had to either find their own way along unmarked paths, or walk with guides who could lead them. The family-oriented guidebook Dvir published in 1972, Where Will We Hike This Week, is a good example of the type of resource available to people who hiked in Israel's more central areas. The book abounds with verbal descriptions of trails, notations of landmarks and the distances between them, photographs, and hand-drawn maps.[67] It rarely mentions marked trails, though, because families taking afternoon walks and short weekend trips close to home were not likely to encounter them.

Dvir realized that simun shvilim had the potential not only to keep Israelis safe in dangerous areas, but also to encourage greater numbers of

Israelis to go hiking in relatively safe areas. If trails were marked closer to Israel's settled areas, hiking could become an everyday activity for everyday people—the individuals and families who enjoyed being outdoors, and who went to parks and nature reserves on weekends.[68] Dvir describes the thought process that gave rise to a new approach to waymarking:

> For many years, scouts and landscape enthusiasts hiked the country's trails; regular hikers, families, and solo hikers were often prevented from going out on hikes in the Galilee by difficulties in navigation and movement in the field. Simun shvilim was designed for hikers in the first category. For them, we marked long trails and gave them preference. But some years ago, our approach changed. No longer was waymarking only for fit walkers in desolate areas (people like these already knew how to manage, sometimes, without marking); now, simun shvilim and the information we gave were also for hikes within reach of every person—for families and individual hikers.[69]

In 1976, Dvir announced that the country's next trail network would be marked and mapped on Mount Carmel, the ridge that begins as a headland on the Mediterranean Sea and divides the coastal plain from the Jezreel Valley as it runs southeast toward Jenin.[70] The area was perfect for creating the new type of trail network Dvir envisioned because it offered a unique mixture of settled areas and wild spaces. On the ridge's northwestern extremity, the city of Haifa was built upon steep mountainsides overlooking the bay and harbor and upon the wide plain below. Jewish, Druze, and Arab towns and villages were scattered all along the Carmel's heights and flanks. Within reach of all these settlements, as well as those along the northern coast and in the Jezreel Valley, were the rugged and heavily forested areas of the mountain that had never been developed. The ridge was a patchwork of built areas and green spaces, and the watercourses that ran down its sides and along its base were perfect corridors for foot travel. For these reasons, the area around the Carmel had hosted some of the earliest Jewish hikes in the Yishuv and had continued to serve over the decades as a popular hiking destination for Israelis.

The creation of the marked network on the ground went quickly. The National Parks Authority and the Nature Reserves Authority both supported the project, and the staff of the SPNI's Carmel Field School immediately began surveying the area for appropriate trails. The first network near Israel's populated centers was characterized by loop trails, short routes to interesting natural and historical sites, and hikes that began and ended at trailheads and road junctions so that it would be possible for people to access trails by car or bus and then return the same day by similar means.[71] For people who wanted to take longer hikes, or even to spend the night in the field, it was possible to connect a number of shorter trails and thereby hike up and over the mountain from the coastal plain to the Jezreel Valley or walk the length of the Carmel ridge for views across the fields to the east and the Mediterranean Sea to the west. By the end of 1976, several trails were already marked, and the bulk of the work was finished by the end of 1977. In the fall of 1978, Dvir announced that the marked network on the Carmel was complete and that a new simun shvilim map would soon be published.[72]

Along with the new approach to the waymarking project came a new type of simun shvilim map. When the Director of the Survey of Israel, Joseph Elster, promised Yossi Feldman during the early 1960s that the Survey would create a special map depicting trails in the Judean Desert, he made it clear that the scale could only be 1:100,000 because at the time it was illegal to create higher-resolution topographic maps of the country. By the late 1970s, however, this had changed, and it was now possible to print maps at a much larger scale of 1:50,000. At the same time Dvir decided to aim the simun shvilim project at Israel's settled centers, he also opted to update the entire simun shvilim map series to this higher resolution and to offer additional information on the back of each map that reflected the needs of less-experienced hikers and yedi'at ha-aretz enthusiasts. Uzi Chaplin, who had been involved with waymarking since the creation of the Eilat Mountains network, had started handling the practical side of marking and mapping in 1977 and now started working to create useful small maps, charts, and illustrations that could fill the back of the map.[73] As a result, the Carmel simun shvilim map, which was being created from scratch, took some time to produce.

The Eilat Mountains trail network, however, had been continually updated during the 1970s, and the Survey of Israel already had the data necessary to begin preparing a new map for publication. Immediately following Dvir's decision to increase the map scale in 1976, the Survey started working on the new Eilat Mountains map. It was the first to be published on the new 1:50,000 scale, and it represented a marked improvement over previous simun shvilim maps. On the old scale, one centimeter on the map represented one kilometer on the ground; on the new scale, two centimeters represented one kilometer, making each square kilometer on the new map appear four times as large as on previous maps. This meant that for any given location, much larger amounts of data were available. The contour lines that showed the shapes and slopes of hills and mountains had appeared on the old maps at intervals of twenty-five meters; the new maps had a contour interval of only ten meters, allowing the country to be shown in much greater detail.

The new map of trails in the Eilat region was published in January 1979, but did not represent the revolution in simun shvilim maps that Dvir envisioned. Aside from the scale, little about it was new. In fact, the map appears to have been built quickly upon an existing 1:50,000-scale geological base map because it has colored areas showing different types of soil and stone composition, which do not appear on any subsequent simun shvilim maps.[74] Only in 1981 was the Carmel map finally published—with its emergency information, tables of places and names, illustrations of plants and animals, and so on printed across its back—and the shift in the waymarking project complete.

Conclusion: Returning from Sinai

The 1979 Eilat Mountains map was notable in the sense that it was one of the last widely published Israeli maps to depict the country without a border between the Negev and the Sinai. As mentioned previously, a few marked trails had extended westward since 1967, but nearly twelve years after the Six-Day War, the shape of the body of the Land of Israel was still clearly defined on the map by its circulatory system of red, blue, green, and black lines. Even though the Negev and the Sinai were depicted as a single territory on the map, then, the invisible 1906 boundary line originally established between the British and the Ottomans was still apparent.

The presence of trails within Israel's Mandate-era boundaries, and the lack of them outside of those boundaries, also illustrated the different cultures of hiking that existed in the Negev and the Sinai. In the wake of the Six-Day War, the SPNI was one of the first Israeli civilian institutions in the Sinai Peninsula, just as it had been in the northern Judean Desert. It had moved quickly to establish field schools there—first, near Saint Catherine's and the traditional holy mountain; and later, at the Israeli settlement of Yamit in the north and the resort town known today as Sharm el-Sheikh in the south. Even as it brought Israeli presence into newly occupied territory, though, it did not immediately attempt to do so through waymarking. On the contrary, the personnel at the SPNI field schools in the Sinai were known for exploring the desert the old-fashioned way—by following the unmarked and unpaved ancient paths that followed watercourses through the mountains and by using Bedouin-style stone cairns to mark important landmarks and junctions.

Since its appearance during the 1950s, Israel's leading environmental organization had formed its own internal culture, and within the long-standing Zionist tension between the impulses to develop the Land and to venerate nature, the rank and file of the SPNI embodied the latter. For the hiking guides most zealous about encountering pure nature, the Sinai became a home away from home. Avraham Shaked, a veteran hiker who had been involved with the SPNI since its early days and had even helped Yossi Feldman mark the trail network around Ein Gedi in the early 1960s, was one such guide. Like Feldman and other hikers during the 1950s, Shaked felt stifled by Israel's new boundaries, particularly the Green Line, and lamented the fact that the old desert treks that had run in the pre-statehood period from Jerusalem, Bethlehem, and Tekoa to the Dead Sea by way of the old Arabic-named wadis had become impossible. After 1967, he had returned to the Judean Desert to help resurrect those routes but eventually made his way to Sinai where there was more to explore.[75]

By the late 1970s, Shaked had become the head of the Tsukei David Field School at Saint Catherine's in the Sinai, and like many Israelis, he was shocked by the announcement of the Camp David Accords between Egyptian President Anwar Sadat and Israeli Prime Minister Menachem Begin in September 1978. With the signing of the Israeli-Egyptian peace agreement, the way was paved toward Israel's withdrawal from the Sinai Peninsula, the uprooting of Israeli settlements, and the closing of the SPNI's field schools. The 1978 simun shvilim map that showed no border between the desert territories would become a historical relic before it even became available in stores. The few Israeli trail markings that existed in the Sinai would presumably be left to the Egyptian authorities and to the Jabaliya Bedouins who lived in the high mountains around Saint Catherine's. Nevertheless, Shaked realized that for him, the Sinai was more than a home away from home. It had become, quite simply, home. Shaked, therefore, pressed on with the waymarking project.

The very existence of the Sinai waymarking project might appear to defy the logic that simun shvilim was a way of concretizing and making visible the connection Israelis wanted to create with the Land of Israel. After all, the Sinai lay outside the boundaries of the Land, even in the minds of Zionists who wanted Israel to maintain control there. In fact, the Sinai waymarking project was the exception that proved the rule. Waymarking in the Sinai was initiated by Shaked and the other staff members at the Tsukei David

Field School. Shaked and his colleagues had grown up in Israel's culture of hiking and yedi'at ha-aretz with all of the mechanisms it employed for creating a sense of connection between people and land. In June 1967, when the SPNI entered the Sinai Peninsula on the heels of the IDF, its personnel immediately began studying the newly occupied territory in the ways they had been taught to study the Land of Israel.

The result was an unexpected outcome of the Zionist nation-building project: Shaked and the Tsukei David guides began to feel that the Sinai was home and, eventually, tried to do whatever they could to realize that connection and make it permanent. The waymarking project, which Shaked justified (and which Dvir approved) on the grounds that it would help keep hikers safe, was a part of the process of strengthening that connection and colonizing territory in the same way the Zionist movement had done through hiking and waymarking in Mandate Palestine, the early State of Israel, and parts of the West Bank after 1967. The Sinai, however, was territory that Israel did not seek to permanently colonize; in the end, Israel used the peninsula strategically as a bargaining chip for peace with Egypt.

Not surprisingly, Shaked continued the waymarking effort even as it became likely that Israeli-Egyptian peace talks would result in the return of the Sinai Peninsula to Egypt. Finally, when the eventual Israeli withdrawal from Sinai became a fait accompli, Shaked enlisted help from the radical American environmental activist Edward Abbey in the hope that the Israelis at the Tsukei David Field School could continue their labor of love, which they framed as environmental protection. It is worth noting that while Shaked's love for the Sinai appears to have been born from Zionist practices of "knowing" land, his motives, like those of the halutzim, were deeper than politics. Shaked's ultimate hope was to keep fighting for the Sinai itself, regardless of which government controlled it. In Abbey's handwritten response to Shaked, dated August 9, 1979, Abbey responded that he would not be able to visit the Sinai and support Shaked's cause, but that as a lover of nature in his own country, he could sympathize with it: "I have always hoped to visit the Sinai someday and can well understand the love that you feel for it. It is indeed a tragedy that this beautiful region should have become a battleground in international politics. Ideally, the entire Sinai peninsula [*sic*] should have been set aside as an International Wilderness Park, open to all as visitors but with only the Bedouin as residents. Perhaps, as your letter suggests, the Sinai will survive better under Egyptian inefficiency and neglect than under Israeli rule. Perhaps. We can only hope, and wait, and see."[76]

In the end, Shaked was forced to either return to Israel or seek adventure elsewhere. Shaked, in "closing the chapter" on his life in the Sinai and upon handing the keys of the Tzukei David Field School building to employees of Ismailiyya University, chose the latter and spent years afterward traveling in a self-described effort to find himself.[77] Other young Israelis did the same. Israeli youth had already begun backpacking overseas during the 1960s and the 1970s, and after the withdrawal from Sinai, new waves of Israelis would travel to South America and the Far East. Those who returned to Israel, either immediately after the withdrawal or after their travels overseas, encountered a country whose desert territories seemed even smaller than they had been before 1967. During the years of the Sinai occupation, Israel had moved much of its military infrastructure into the peninsula, leaving the Negev relatively open. Now the IDF needed space, and vast tracts of Israel's southern desert became closed to civilians.

Many of the remaining spaces across the country that were not yet touched by urban development or the presence of the IDF had become incorporated into Israel's system of national parks and nature reserves. The original idea put forth by Smilansky in the Knesset, and subsequently supported by Ben-Gurion, enabled Israel's environmental movement to make significant gains during the 1960s and 1970s as large areas of the country were set aside for preservation. Within such lands, however, travelers on foot could not simply roam freely over hill and dale—or cliff and canyon, as the case may have been—because hikers themselves could constitute a danger to sensitive environmental areas. Marked trails were viewed as the best way to contain the damage hikers might otherwise cause by trampling vegetation and disturbing animal habitats.

Just as Israel was preparing to withdraw from the Sinai Peninsula in 1979, then, the activities of hikers in Israel became further curtailed with the passing of new regulations for nature reserves that restricted all movement to marked hiking trails. Article Ten, the "Walking Prohibition," reads, "No person shall walk within the Reserve, nor be found within it, except on roads and paths marked by the Authority and designated for pedestrians."[78] The regulations did not specify the Public Committee for Waymarking or the SPNI as the only legal parties who could mark trails; indeed, the JNF created roads and paths within the portions of its forests that fell within nature reserves. For the most part, though, the Public Committee became the de facto organization that controlled all movement in Israel's most wild and far-flung spaces, and Dvir was the de facto decision-maker within that body.

During the 1960s and 1970s, then, simun shvilim had already taken root in Israel's border areas and had begun to appear more noticeably in its settled areas. During the 1980s, with a mandate to mark trails in nature reserves, Dvir expanded Israel's trail networks on every front until they grew together to constitute a single, unified system. Suddenly, complete coverage of the country by trails and maps was within reach.

The next chapter will examine the problems and possibilities associated with simun shvilim that revealed themselves as Israeli hikers found that many of the country's landscapes had become transformed through the appearance of thousands of trail markings. For the first time, principled opposition to the simun shvilim project arose from the historic tension between the impulses to develop the Land and to preserve the Land. As the reach of simun shvilim extended into every part of the country, some hikers—particularly those who had become accustomed to the vast, unmarked spaces of the Sinai—began to view waymarking as an activity that put a blight on the landscape, enabled movement in areas where hikers did not need to go, and limited movement in areas where hikers did not constitute a significant threat to nature. Despite this opposition in the 1990s—much of which came from within the SPNI—Israel's trail network continued to grow and eventually gave rise to a form of walking the Land that revitalized the country's culture of hiking: the long-distance, border-to-border Shvil Israel, or the "Israel National Trail."

5

Completing the Network and Creating a National Trail, 1980–2001

Revitalizing a Stagnant Culture of Hiking: The Israel National Trail

By the early 1980s, Ori Dvir was a celebrity in Israel. Not only did he continue to lead tours, teach guides, broadcast a weekly radio program, and write multiple monthly columns for yedi'at ha-aretz magazines and journals, but starting in 1975, he also hosted a television show that brought the landscapes of Israel and the West Bank into thousands of homes across the country. Israel's culture of hiking had come a long way since the days of the halutzim when Palestine was largely unmapped and unexplored by Jews and when Jewish hikers had to search for every scrap of information they could find about a given location before attempting to walk there. If anything, Dvir now faced the opposite problem: the land he still knew as Eretz Israel, having endured for decades under the lens of yedi'at ha-aretz, had become like a liturgical text that had once been redemptive and salvific but had now been studied and memorized to the point that many people found it meaningless. Dvir's great task, reflected in all of his writings, radio broadcasts, and television shows, was to revisit the old text of the Land of Israel and to infuse it with new meaning.

The challenge he faced as a yedi'at ha-aretz educator mirrored a larger challenge that existed within Israel's culture of hiking. Since the late 1960s and the early 1970s, the image of the Sabra scout had declined, and nothing had arisen to take its place. Hiking continued on a large scale across the country, but it lacked the glamour and excitement that had characterized it in the Yishuv and the early days of statehood. During the mid-1970s, Dvir had tried to address the problem by aiming the simun shvilim project at Israel's populated centers and, in doing so, had set in motion the project of covering the whole country with marked and mapped trail networks. That kept Dvir occupied, and it began to address an important need by opening hiking up to families and city-dwellers, but the endeavor ultimately failed to electrify Dvir or the Israeli hiking community. Nevertheless, as one of the great mediators in the relationship between Israelis and the Land of Israel during the 1980s, Dvir was in a unique position to revitalize the country's culture of hiking and again render the exploration of the Land an activity that resonated among Israeli youth.

In 1984, Dvir developed a plan to create something that existed in Europe and the United States but which had never before been built in the Middle East: a long-distance hiking trail that crossed an entire country. Dvir hoped to offer Israeli adventurers a challenge that rivaled the famous desert treks of the pioneer and Palmach eras. However, Shvil Israel, or the "Israel National Trail," was not merely an attempt to resurrect old tropes from an antiquated and irrelevant culture of hiking. It was a product of its time, and in many ways, it represented a departure from the direction Israel's culture of yedi'at ha-aretz had begun to take under the influence of the settlement movement. Remarkably, even as national-religious Jewish youth marched through the West Bank in an effort to conquer territory with their feet, Dvir created a national trail that did not visit the occupied territories, Jerusalem, or even Masada, but one that did highlight Israel's ethnic and religious diversity.

This chapter will focus on the completion of what Ori Dvir considered his most important projects: Israel's countrywide network of marked and mapped hiking trails, and Shvil Israel, the long-distance footpath that Dvir later described as "the pinnacle of the hiking and scouting story of modern Israel."[1] Neither project was accomplished easily. In the wake of the Israeli withdrawal from the Sinai Peninsula, the countrywide trail network faced opposition from parties within Israel's environmental movement who felt that marked trails blighted the landscape and destroyed any chance for pure encounters with the Land. Against a background of violent uprisings, public demonstrations, and impassioned debates over the right of Israelis to settle in the West Bank and Gaza, Dvir faced attacks from both the left and the right over the decisions he made regarding the route of Shvil Israel.

Nevertheless, both endeavors were successful in the end, precisely because Israeli hikers did not recognize Dvir's efforts as politically motivated. Instead, most Israelis saw Dvir's projects as being rooted in the deep love for the Land that had driven Israeli hiking since its early days and which was still shared by Israelis across the political spectrum. Dvir's imperative, like that of the Labor Zionist halutzim, was to walk in search of encounters with the Land of Israel wherever and whenever possible.

Motives notwithstanding, Dvir's decisions did have high-stakes political implications for Israelis and Palestinians. The meaning of Shvil Israel in English is simply "Israel Trail," but its more commonly used English translation is "Israel National Trail." The accuracy of that translation is rarely contested. The debates that took place around the time of the trail's creation, as well as discussions regarding its ongoing development, illustrate that trails and waymarking in Israel have never become disentangled from nationalism. Hiking remains an act most Jewish Israelis understand in terms of blood and soil, people and homeland.

The End of Simun Shvilim

At the beginning of the 1980s, Israeli hiking was experiencing an identity crisis. As mentioned earlier, Israeli youth no longer looked to the mythic pioneering scout as a role model. The values of Israeli society had changed and so had the physical character of the country. The population of the land between the Jordan River and the Mediterranean Sea had grown many times over since the days of the halutzim. Even the Judean Desert and the farthest reaches of the Negev had been penetrated by paved roads. Even though Dvir and other leaders of Israel's culture of hiking still understood the original territorial unit of Mandate Palestine as the Land of Israel, they could not regard the country as an undivided whole. Israel's occupation of the West Bank and Gaza Strip was now in its second decade, and even the most stalwart Zionist hikers were beginning to acknowledge that the Palestinian connection with land was steadfast and real. Within Israel proper, traditional hikers had the sense that there was little left to explore within the small and extensively researched country. For these reasons and others, Israeli youth increasingly traveled overseas after their military service to seek adventures in other countries.

Nevertheless, Dvir was busier with the simun shvilim project than he had ever been. The annual hike still represented an important component of the national school curriculum, and the SPNI field schools still guided large numbers of Israeli youth along the country's paths and trails every year. Marked trails had also become identified with nature preservation; just as Israel's environmental movement fulfilled Yizhar Smilansky's demand that "no man shall pick a flower without pangs of regret" by organizing a campaign to preserve wildflowers, the SPNI also made adherence to established backcountry trails a moral imperative.[2] It was also a legal imperative: as a result of the 1979 law that prohibited visitors in nature reserves from departing from official trails, more and more hiking guides were forced to rely on waymarking when leading tours through undeveloped areas. In the Negev, marked trails became increasingly necessary even outside the boundaries of nature reserves, due to the fact that the IDF, having withdrawn from Sinai, now used large parts of the desert as training areas and the boundaries of firing zones were not always visible. The early 1980s may have marked a low point for Israeli hiking, but they marked a high point for simun shvilim.

Using the network of SPNI field schools that now dotted the country, Dvir began putting irons in the fire for the creation of new trail networks. He organized a system in which field guides and instructors at the schools compiled lists of nearby paths and submitted them to Dvir and the Israel Trails Committee (ITC).[3] Dvir reviewed the lists, visited the areas the proposed trails traversed, made his own route adjustments when necessary, and created plans for how the areas should be marked. He contacted personnel from the various agencies in charge of land administration—such as the Jewish National Fund, the National Parks Authority, the Nature Reserves Authority, and the IDF—and secured all of the necessary permissions for marking trails on the ground.[4]

After that, Uzi Chaplin, the ITC's coordinator who carried out much of the actual fieldwork, organized a multi-day push to mark a series of trails in a given area, enlisting the help of students from the tour-guiding courses Dvir taught at Beit Berl.[5] Eventually, leaders at the SPNI field schools became experienced in waymarking methods and could go out on their own to finish off the tail ends of any trails the volunteer groups had not been able to complete. Once an area was completely marked on the ground, the Survey of Israel would send its own personnel to gather the necessary data for the creation of a new simun shvilim map.

Dvir writes that the process of building a marked and mapped trail network from the ground up typically lasted between four and seven years.[6] That meant that on the eve of the final withdrawal from Sinai, despite all the work that had been taking place within the simun shvilim project, Israel's trail network did not yet appear very impressive. The new 1:50,000 map series would require twenty sheets to cover the entirety of Eretz Israel, including the Golan Heights, the West Bank, and the Gaza Strip. So far, only four had been published: the Eilat Mountains map, the Carmel map, and the two maps that covered the Northern and Southern Judean Desert, which were both released in 1982.[7] However, Dvir knew that the seeds he had planted all over the country during the preceding years were about to begin bearing fruit in rapid succession.

As of 1982, the old Golan Heights network, originally marked at the behest of IDF Northern Command just before and after the 1973 Yom Kippur War, had been updated and was finally being mapped. A new trail network in the Upper Galilee was nearly complete as well and was in the surveying process. Routes through the western corridor to Jerusalem had been submitted to the ITC and had been approved for marking. Finally, another network had been partially marked in the northeastern Negev near the Dead Sea, and it too would soon be completed, surveyed, and mapped.[8] Overall, Dvir's system was poised to begin producing simun shvilim maps at an average rate of one per year, so that half of the country would be completely marked and mapped by 1989, with several more networks in various stages of completion.[9]

As irons came out of the fire, Dvir kept putting more in, and he populated each developing trail network by reporting on his progress in the pages of yedi'at ha-aretz publications like the tour guide magazine *Moreshet Derekh* and the SPNI magazine *Teva va-Aretz*. Hikers who read about new trails went out to visit them, and field school guides began leading groups of students along them. The public became increasingly familiar with the trail network as well, in large part through Dvir's continuing activities as a broadcast media personality. Dvir hosted a television program called *Nekudat Chen*, which meant "beauty mark" and referred, once again, to the pioneer myth of the feminine body-of-the-Land-of-Israel, whose attractive features were to be discovered and explored. In the show, Dvir guided Israelis to sites across the country that he found beautiful or interesting, and when relevant, he showed them how to access such places by way of marked and mapped trails. The series, with its ten-minute episodes, ran for sixteen years on Israel's sole television channel and had an enormous viewership because it aired right before the staple news program *Mabat la-Chadashot* ("A Look at the News").[10] In 1983, Dvir published a Hebrew-language book based on the show, and it became a best-seller in Israel before being translated into four other languages.[11] Both the books and the shows helped Dvir build momentum for marking more walking routes for individuals and families.[12]

By the middle of the 1980s, the countrywide trail network was far from finished, but its eventual coverage of Israel, along with the Golan Heights and parts of the West Bank, was practically a foregone conclusion. No clear path lay ahead, either for the waymarking project or for Israeli hiking in general. Simun shvilim had made hiking easier for Israelis, but it had done nothing to address the larger identity crisis that plagued the country's culture of hiking. The image of the Sabra scout as an inspiration for hikers had mostly disappeared; Masada had become a tourist attraction with a cable car; and upon the completion of the Israeli withdrawal from Sinai's vast desert spaces, the domestication of Israeli hiking was almost complete. It was no longer a boundary-blurring endeavor in the way it had been for the halutzim, nor could it be; all sorts of barriers to movement, visible and invisible, were now inscribed upon the Land in the forms of cities, highways, nature reserves, firing zones, and fences. Simun shvilim could enable hikers to travel somewhat freely across certain parts of the Land—especially nature reserves, in which it was illegal to depart from marked trails—but on the other hand, it was part of the problem. Painted blazes constantly reminded hikers that someone had been there before and that yedi'at ha-aretz in its original, eroticized sense was no longer possible.

As a public figure whose capacity as a writer, a radio host, and a television personality rendered him an important mediator in the relationship between Israelis and the Land, Dvir was uniquely positioned to shape Israel's culture of hiking. As the leading figure behind the country's waymarking project, Dvir also possessed a tool that could channel the flow of Israelis as they traveled on foot across the Land. Up until that point, though, the simun shvilim project had generally developed in response to changes within Israel's hiking culture and had never sought to actively shape it. Now, with the end of simun shvilim visible on the horizon, Dvir began looking for ways to breathe new life into Israeli hiking and into the project of marking and mapping the Land.

The Beginning of Shvil Israel

The idea that eventually gave rise to Shvil Israel was born in 1973, when the veteran hiker and journalist Avraham Tamir wrote an article for the children's edition of the *Davar* newspaper entitled "Eighty-Year-Old Grandmother Walks Three Thousand Kilometers on the Appalachian Trail."[13]

Tamir had noted the growing number of Israelis who did not identify with the traditional symbols of Labor Zionism and who sought new possibilities outside the borders of the country during the late 1960s and early 1970s. His own travels had taken him to the United States, where he had hiked from Georgia to Maine on the Appalachian Trail. Upon his return to Israel, he shared his experience with young men and women, and in his newspaper article about America's "national trail," he wrote, "When will a person or an organization arise to initiate also in our Land a long hiking trail, of hundreds of kilometers, from Dan to Be'er Sheva, or from Metulla to Eilat?"[14]

More than a decade later, Tamir looked back and realized that the children for whom he had written his original article had become adults, some with families of their own, and there was still no Appalachian Trail in the Middle East. In 1984, at the age of seventy-eight, Tamir contacted Yoav Sagi, who had succeeded Azaria Alon as the general secretary of the SPNI five years earlier, and he outlined the idea for a border-to-border footpath.[15] Sagi was interested and put Tamir in touch with Dvir.

Dvir was immediately taken with the idea. For him, it represented a potential solution to the identity crisis that afflicted Israeli hiking and also an endeavor that could infuse the waymarking project with new life. Sagi made it clear to Dvir, though, that the SPNI had no additional funds in its budget for simun shvilim. If Dvir wanted to embark on a new waymarking endeavor, he was free to continue using SPNI field schools and personnel, and to use existing funds to support the project, but if he needed anything extra, he would have to come up with it himself.[16] Then as now, the simun shvilim project was funded primarily by the sale of maps, of which few had yet been published. Since the map series was growing, though, and was spreading to cover more populated areas in which there was a high demand for hiking, Dvir knew he could expect an overall increase in funds. He decided to begin exploring the possibility of a trans-Israel trail. He and Tamir pitched the idea to the ITC, and the project was formally approved.[17] Shortly thereafter, Dvir went to the United States and visited the Appalachian Trail because he wanted to see for himself the long route that had inspired Tamir.

Visiting America's de facto national trail gave Dvir a vision for the future direction of Israeli hiking. The success and popularity of the long-distance footpath had given rise to a whole infrastructure for hikers along the East Coast, including stores, inns, and shuttle services in the towns and cities that lay near the trail's route and were easily accessed via specially marked side trails. Almost the entire corridor of the trail itself was formally designated as a right-of-way for travelers on foot or had been purchased outright by the

United States government, so it was protected from development and offered hikers the opportunity to camp out in the forest if they so desired. For those who preferred to have a roof over their heads, hiking clubs had constructed a series of huts that were spaced about a day's walk apart from one another and offered cheap or free lodging options. It was therefore possible to walk somewhat comfortably for more than three thousand kilometers across the eastern United States and to choose one's degree of interaction with nature on the one hand and civilization on the other. Moreover, there was no ideal image of how an Appalachian Trail hiker had to look or behave or what the goal of his or her travels should be; there was only the trail. "Hike your own hike" was the watchword.[18]

Dvir realized that there would be challenges in applying the Appalachian Trail model to a long-distance footpath across Israel. Upon his return to Israel, he looked into the possibility of acquiring a dedicated corridor for a north-south trail and found that without formal government funding and support, such a goal would be nearly impossible. Instead, with his limited resources, he would have to seek permission to cross public and private lands, and this meant the route of the trail would always be subject to change. He also explored the feasibility of constructing huts that could offer better lodging options in the field for hikers than the bare, empty plots that were designated as campgrounds within nature reserves. Even if Dvir found a way to raise the necessary funds, though, the zoning, environmental, and bureaucratic issues associated with constructing lodging in national parks and nature reserves were too challenging. Israel's long-distance trail, as well as its culture of long-distance hiking, would have to take forms that were more suited to the unique conditions of hiking in the Middle East.

In a unique application of the old aphorism that "the trail is wiser than the one who walks it," Dvir decided to go ahead with the project despite the uncertainties and trust that the problems would be solved along the way. Going ahead, however, first meant planning a route, and that presented challenges that extended far beyond zoning restrictions and bureaucratic processes. Creating a trail across the country that was designed to offer Israelis a special experience with the Land of Israel involved resurrecting impassioned debates that had begun during the early days of Zionism.

Lines upon the Land: Defining Israel

In 1912, during the era of the halutzim, the Labor Zionist leader Ya'akov Zerubavel argued that Jewish youth in Eretz Israel should be discouraged from making the annual religious pilgrimage to the northern village of Meron on the festival of Lag ba-Omer. Meron housed the tomb of Rabbi Shimon bar Yochai, the purported author of the Zohar, and thousands of religious Jews converged there every year to commemorate the anniversary of the mystic's death. Zerubavel asserted that Zionist youth should be encouraged instead to make pilgrimage to Modi'in, the site in the center of the country where the Maccabees had begun their revolt against the Seleucid king Antiochus and where the Hasmonean kings had eventually been buried. In a time when Jewish pioneers in Palestine were being killed by Arabs, he argued, Zionist youth needed to emulate heroic figures who were willing to fight for their country and not identify with passive scholars who wrote religious texts during the period of exile. For Zerubavel, this was not simply a pedagogical matter; it was fraught with existential significance. "Meron and Modi'in . . . which of the two is stronger?" he wrote. "Which of them will win? Which of them will define the process of our future history?"[19]

As discussed in previous chapters, hiking in the Yishuv had been regarded not only as an important pedagogical tool that taught young men and women about the Land, but also as a tool for shaping individual and group identity and for reconstituting the Jewish nation in the historic Jewish homeland. Civil-religious pilgrimage destinations, as well as the paths that Zionist youth walked in order to access those sites, were based in part on pragmatic considerations but were also largely defined by ideology. As different groups organized treks to sites they deemed important, they navigated not only the physical terrain of Palestine but also its symbolic landscape, which they viewed through the lenses of their respective ideologies. Those who went to Masada, for example, made choices about how they would access the site: if possible, they would walk there along unpaved paths rather than travel most of the way by boat because walking offered more direct contact with the Land and gave youth a more formative and dramatic experience to recount after they returned home. Once the Snake Path became an available option for ascending the mountain, it became preferable to the less-difficult Roman ramp because it enabled hikers to walk in the footsteps of the ancient defenders of the fortress.[20]

Discussions and debates over the Jewish relationship with the Land of Israel were different in the 1980s than they were in the 1930s, but they were still passionate, and they still shaped opinions regarding where Jewish youth should walk and what they should seek to attain in doing so. With the rise of a right-wing government in 1977, the settlement movement had moved into high gear and, through the acts of building and construction, had begun making its own articulation of what constituted the boundaries of the Land and which territories rightfully belonged to the Jewish people. National-religious youth had begun using yedi'at ha-aretz as a tool for rooting themselves deeply in the West Bank and for legitimizing their presence there.[21] For them, walking—whether in the form of nature hikes in the Judean and Samarian hills or in the form of marches through contested sites like Hebron—represented an important means of knowing and claiming territory.[22] Such efforts were supported by many of yedi'at ha-aretz experts from Dvir's generation who became supporters of the "Land of Israel" or "Greater Israel" movement after 1967. Azaria Alon was one such figure; in a 1974 interview, he said, "There are important sections of the country which are not inhabited by Jews and they are in danger. Hiking is thus a tool for displaying Jewish presence in those areas."[23]

Meanwhile, during the course of the peace negotiations between Israel and Egypt at the end of the 1970s, and in response to the increasing influence of Gush Emunim on Israeli policymakers, the Peace Now organization had begun arguing that Israel needed to consider withdrawing from occupied territories for the sake of long-term security. During the Israeli invasion of Lebanon in 1982, and its subsequent occupation of the southern portion of the country, Peace Now was able to successfully mobilize a large segment of the Israeli public. Following the massacre of Palestinians in the Sabra and Shatila refugee camps, the group organized a demonstration in Tel Aviv that drew 350,000 participants and set in motion a chain of events that eventually led to the resignation of Defense Minister Ariel Sharon. Tensions between the Israeli right and the Israeli left, which ultimately hinged on the issue of which areas were the rightful domain of the Jewish people, continued to rise. In 1983, a right-wing Jewish extremist killed the Peace Now activist Emil Grunzweig with a hand grenade during a demonstration in Jerusalem. In 1984, when Dvir and Tamir were envisioning their long-distance trail, Meir Kahane became a member of Israel's parliament under the banner of his far-right Kach party, which openly advocated the ethnic cleansing of Arabs.[24]

Unlike many of his contemporaries in the world of yedi'at ha-aretz education during the 1980s, Dvir never actively participated in these debates. As a private individual, he had his own political views regarding the future of the Land of Israel, but the exact nature of those views was often a mystery to the people who worked with him. Prior to statehood, as a youth, he had been deeply involved in the binationalist Ha-Shomer ha-Tzair youth movement, which opposed the partition of Palestine on the grounds that Jews and Arabs should rule the country in cooperation with one another. However, it is difficult to discern the degree to which Dvir adhered to every plank of the organization's political platform as a teenager or the degree to which his early positions continued to influence him later in life because as a public figure, he never discussed his political positions. In his writings and interviews, Dvir separated walking from claims of ownership over territory and constantly sought ways to open new spaces for exploration, asserting, "My position, which doesn't necessarily represent my political stance, was that we would mark nice paths through any place in which it was possible to walk."[25]

His eldest daughter, Carmel, who followed in her father's footsteps by becoming a scholar of the Land of Israel in her own right, describes Dvir as motivated not by politics but by creativity and curiosity.[26] Wherever he was, his desire to explore extended outward. Moti Ben-Shitrit, an SPNI guide who worked with Dvir for years on the ITC, said that Dvir was tenacious in his quest to know the whole Land, and if he found himself on an unknown trail, he would walk it until he was forced to stop because he was sure there would be a surprise at the end.[27] If there were spaces in Eretz Israel that were inaccessible, whether for bureaucratic or security-related reasons, Dvir wanted to go and explore them. If there were areas next door to Israel that were inaccessible for political reasons, he longed for peace so that he could go and explore them as well. In an interview that took place after Israel's 1994 peace agreement with Jordan, Dvir said, "Years ago, I used to promise, to anyone who would listen, that the day would come when I would guide in the Old City of Jerusalem. After the Six-Day War, this came true. My children heard from me endlessly that I'd yet be in Petra, and that I'd get there even if they had to push me in a wheelchair, but we managed without it. Today I am optimistic that maybe I will visit Damascus."[28]

Dvir's primary sphere of interest was the Land of Israel, but he harbored no ill will against those who traveled outside; he himself hiked in other countries and led overseas tours every year. Within the Land, his main concern was making sure that as much of the country as possible was open and accessible to hikers. When Israel withdrew from the Sinai Peninsula, Dvir's lament in his book *Nekudat Chen* was not that the Jewish state had relinquished territory that had rightfully belonged to it, or that Jewish communities there would be uprooted, but rather that the redeployment of the IDF in the Negev would curtail hiker movement and result in more paved roads.[29] Even when environmentalists sought to close lands to hikers on the grounds that trails would harm sensitive ecosystems, Dvir generally sided with hikers. When the Horeshat Tal nature reserve at the foot of the Golan Heights was turned into a national park, preservationists regarded the development as a disaster. Dvir's complaint, in contrast, was that only half of the reserve was open to hikers.[30]

In his capacity as the custodian of Israel's hiking trail system, Dvir's general inclination was to say "yes" every time he was asked whether a trail should be marked through a given area. Similarly, as a guide and an educator, he generally encouraged people to travel wherever they could in the Land if it was possible for them to do so, and the West Bank was no exception. The "beauty marks" referred to in Dvir's television show *Nekudat Chen* appeared all over the body of pre-1967 Israel as well as the West Bank and the Golan Heights and were gathered together as a single collection in the book, defining most of the land between the Jordan and the Mediterranean in the exact way Dvir preferred to envision it: as a unified whole. As a writer, as a guide, and as a trail marker, Dvir explored that space extensively and encouraged others to do the same. "I don't mix politics with my work," he once said, "but it is natural for a man to want to walk through his country."[31]

Dvir walked through "his" country but did not use overtly political rhetoric when writing about it. On the contrary, he frequently used his knowledge of the Arabic language and his familiarity with Christian and Muslim lore to enrich his readers' knowledge of Israel's history and its past and present habitation by different ethnic and religious groups. Dvir's writing appealed to Jewish Israelis, but he saw it also as relevant to Palestinians; the book *Nekudat Chen* was translated into Arabic. Similarly, Dvir marked trails on both sides of the Green Line, except in places where it seemed likely that his work would be co-opted by political movements. During a time when the SPNI was establishing an institutional presence in the West Bank and the simun shvilim project depended on field schools all over the country as hubs for waymarking activities, Dvir avoided marking trails around the new field school at the settlement of Ofra. Waymarking took place quickly all over the country except in two conspicuous places: the northern West Bank and the area around Hebron in the southern West Bank. The maps that covered those areas were the last to be published in the countrywide simun shvilim series.

While Dvir's exploration of the country and desire to share it with others may have seemed boundless, then, he did operate at times under self-imposed limits. Limits were necessary when planning the route of Shvil

Israel because in order for the trail to work as a walking route, it needed to seem like it was going somewhere and not zigzagging haphazardly in an effort to reach every site in the country worth visiting. In the end, though, the limits Dvir set for the Israel National Trail seem to have been informed by more than just the pragmatic necessities of ensuring that the trail would be user-friendly. In opposition to the expectations of a wide segment of the Israeli public, the route of the country's de facto national trail, once completed, avoided all of the regions of Eretz Israel held most dear by the settlement movement. Whether Dvir made these decisions according to his understanding of what hikers wanted, his own political positions, or a desire to detach the country's "national trail" from territorial claims on the occupied territories, the route he chose for Shvil Israel became the subject of debate across a wide sector of Israeli society.

Officially, the route of Shvil Israel was defined by a set of specifications that Dvir drew up and submitted to the ITC prior to discussions of the regions and sites that would be featured along the trail. Hillel Birger had created a similar list of guidelines prior to the creation of trail networks in the Judean Desert. Just as Birger's rules for simun shvilim established many of the characteristics that were later taken for granted in Israel's countrywide trail system, the nine "Principles of Shvil Israel" approved by the ITC constituted the genetic code of the Israel National Trail and defined many of its contours well before it was sketched on maps or marked on the ground.[32]

Most of these principles guided the trail in a particular direction: away from the Green Line, away from Palestinian areas, away from Jerusalem, and away from any politically contentious areas in general. Given the profusion of various types of Jewish settlements across the country, and the large tracts of JNF land that filled many of the spaces between them, it might have been possible to create a Shvil Israel that emphasized the Jewish character of Israel. The first principle, however, which emphasized diversity in the ethnic communities and religious sites visited by the trail, ensured that such a route would never take shape. The trail that Dvir envisioned would expose hikers to an Israel that was composed not only of diverse ecosystems and geographic regions but also diverse ethnic and religious groups.

Similarly, the fourth guideline, which emphasized security, ensured that the trail would not be routed through the West Bank; guided hikes across the Green Line often required leaders to carry weapons or groups to be accompanied by hired security guards. Therefore, that whole area would be off-limits for Shvil Israel. The fifth principle, which discusses weather and climate, is interesting because on the one hand it immediately excludes the Judean Desert as a space visited by the trail on the grounds of hot summer weather, yet it acknowledges that hot weather in the Negev is unavoidable. Whatever the logic behind this guideline, one of its practical effects was to block loopholes that might have allowed the trail to travel through the West Bank along more secure routes. If anyone were intent on running the trail through the Judean Desert, it might have been possible to establish a route along the eastern side of the West Bank through the Jordan River Valley or to go through Jerusalem and use a route that paralleled the highway to Jericho and the Dead Sea. With the Judean Desert off the table, such plans would not even have to be addressed.

The sixth guideline, while likely motivated by the desire to offer hikers sustained encounters with nature as they walked the Land, restricted the trail from entering cities and, therefore, had the effect of removing Jerusalem from the itinerary of Shvil Israel as well. The seventh and ninth guidelines both had to do with the marking system and subsequently had little to do with the trail's route. The eighth principle, however, establishes that the trail's northern terminus will be at Dan. Again, the historic status of that site as constituting one of the boundaries of Eretz Israel offered a strong reason for beginning the trail there. However, beginning the trail at Dan also effectively eliminated any discussion about Shvil Israel entering the Golan Heights. Including the Golan in the trail's route would have been considerably less problematic than including the West Bank and would have allowed hikers to begin their Shvil Israel experiences atop the snowy Hermon or at the springs of Banias. Like Jerusalem and the West Bank, though, it was not open for discussion.

Finally, by officially naming the trail Shvil Israel, the eighth principle raised the stakes of the entire endeavor by suggesting that the trail was not just a trail but a representation of Israel. Without defining the exact meaning of "Israel," which could signify a land, a people, or a state, it left open the possibility that the trail, through the places it visited and the communities it included, embodied all three. In a culture for which hiking and trails had long been connected with existential themes, as illustrated by Zerubavel's 1912 article, and during a time of intense struggles to define the boundaries of the Jewish people and the Land of Israel, the creation of an "Israel Trail" could easily be understood as an attempt to mark and map not just a walking route but the nation itself. That perception, which Dvir did little to dispel, embroiled the trail for a time in ideologically based debates but, on the other hand, forcefully brought the trail to the attention of the Israeli public.

Planning the Route

In the Hebrew Bible, the boundaries of Eretz Israel are repeatedly defined as running from Dan in the north to Be'er Sheva in the south. When Tamir suggested a trail that crossed the length and breadth of the Land, he used the formulation "from Dan to Be'er Sheva" as one possibility for where the route might begin and end. He also offered a more modern articulation of the Land's extreme northern and southern boundaries in the formulation "from Metulla to Eilat." When Dvir approached the idea more than a decade later, he combined the two by placing the trail's northern terminus at Dan and its southern terminus at Eilat. In doing so, he capitalized on the Hebrew phrase that was familiar to Israelis—"mi-Dan ve-ad Be'er Sheva"—but changed it to "mi-Dan ve-ad Eilat." "From Dan to Eilat" became the watchword for Shvil Israel while it was in the planning stages; in the beginning, it was the only sure thing about the trail.

The process of planning the route began in the north. In 1986, Dvir assembled a group of yedi'at ha-aretz experts who were particularly familiar with the Upper Galilee region, and had them meet with personnel from the SPNI's northern field schools and representatives of the Nature Reserves Authority.[33] Together, working from the set of nine principles Dvir had previously established regarding the regions and sites that should characterize Shvil Israel, the group envisioned possibilities and tried to square them with realities on the ground.[34] They met with a plethora of dilemmas that might seem arcane to any outsider: Could the trail pass through Metulla?[35] At the end of the Ramot Naftali ridge, should the trail run toward the Mediterranean Sea or the Sea of Galilee?[36] Other questions were more obvious and could hardly be addressed in the initial stages; for example, how to deal with the Tel Aviv-Jaffa conurbation in the center of the country, which constituted a wall of development that ran inland for miles.

One possibility that tempted trail planners was to run the trail—or at least an optional spur of it—straight south from Nazareth, across the Jezreel Valley, past the Israeli town of Afula, up the ridge of Mount Gilboa, and south into the mountains of the West Bank. The old mountain route that had been paved by the Romans could form the basis of a beautiful, modern hiking trail that would follow ridgelines all the way across the central highlands from Jenin in the north to Hebron in the south, by way of Jerusalem and Bethlehem. "We thought we could mark the Israel Trail as a main trail and as an extension," Dvir later wrote. "The main route would remind people of the historic Via Maris, and the secondary route would remind them of the Kings' Way from the approaches to Mount Hebron to the Jezreel Valley."[37] Elsewhere, Dvir elaborates on the character of the discussions surrounding the West Bank portion of the trail: "The possibility was raised that 'when peace comes,' we could prepare two extensions of the trail: one, along the sea, would ascend into the Judean Mountains via the corridor to Jerusalem and would descend again to the plain and the Negev; and the second would eventually continue along the 'way of the patriarchs,' or the 'mountain way.'"[38]

For Dvir, whose main focus was simply to walk wherever it was possible to walk and to know as much of the Land as possible along the way, the West Bank route was an intoxicating prospect but not one that could be fulfilled in the tense climate that prevailed between Israelis and Palestinians in 1986 and 1987. Dvir also understood the political problems associated with creating such a route and knew that different individuals and groups across the Israeli political spectrum would have different opinions on whether Shvil Israel should ever enter the West Bank. For the time being, he shelved the idea, but he never closed off the possibility.

While the question of the trail's route across central Israel was left unanswered for the time being, its tentative route across the Negev took shape. Establishing a route across the southern desert was relatively simple, but not for reasons Dvir liked. The increased presence of the IDF had turned the desert into a patchwork of open areas, closed military bases, and firing zones that were only open for hikers on holidays and weekends. Most of these areas were classified and therefore were not marked on civilian maps, including the new simun shvilim maps for the Arava Desert that were currently in production. On maps, then, and even on the ground, where the boundaries of firing zones were often unmarked or sparsely marked, the Negev appeared to be mostly open but actually represented the most difficult space within Israeli territory for marking a continuous hiking trail, much less a trail that fulfilled all of the conditions Dvir had set forth for the creation of Shvil Israel.

Any trail through the Negev already essentially violated Dvir's principle number five, which dictated that Shvil Israel should be set up in areas where the climate allowed people to hike during all seasons. Because of the desert's sheer size and the long distances between human settlements, including ruins, the route also ran the risk of violating the first principle, which stated that the trail should aim for diversity in its encounters with natural, historical, and cultural sites. If Dvir had been free to mark his own ideal route across the Negev, though, he could have attenuated the monotony of the desert landscape by interspersing canyon hikes, scenic overlooks, and natural curiosities like sand dunes and rock formations along the trail. Moreover, he could have guided the trail toward any number of restored archaeological sites and national parks, as well as modern settlements that could serve as desert oases. Too many military obstacles existed, however, to allow for the creation of such a route, unless significant portions of the trail could only be hiked on holidays, and Dvir was not willing to make this concession. The possibilities, then, were limited.

Dvir chose the ruins of Mamshit, which lay near Dimona in the northern Negev, as the beginning of the southern section of Shvil Israel. From there, the trail could run south to skirt the cliffs along the northern rim of the geological formation known as the Large Crater, and then continue southwest to the town of Mitzpe Ramon via the small settlements of Sde Boker and Ein Ovdat. Then the trail could descend into the huge Ramon Crater and push south toward the Eilat Mountains by way of the wide Ovda Valley and the mountain of Shacharut, which overlooked the Arava Valley. Once Shvil Israel had entered the Eilat Mountains, it would be free to zigzag a little within the trail network Dvir had marked two decades earlier and would reach the Red Sea not exactly at Eilat but a point southwest of the city near the Egyptian border crossing at Taba. On paper, the route looked good, but the section between Mitzpe Ramon and Shacharut was essentially a straight line that followed roads and military reservation boundaries for more than a hundred kilometers. That section of Shvil Israel did not look like a trail anyone would want to hike, and Dvir spent the next several years searching for better solutions.

Opening the Route to Public Debate

In the meantime, Dvir and the ITC went public with the plan for Shvil Israel in the hopes of opening the discussion to the wider public. In March 1987, the Ma'ariv newspaper printed an article describing the vision for the trail and outlining some of the challenges associated with creating a cross-country hiking route. The article calls the trail Shvil Israel, estimates its eventual length at about nine hundred kilometers, and enumerates the landmarks along the planned northern section. In addition, it includes a map that gives a rudimentary outline of how the trail might look, including the unplanned central section between Caesarea and Mamshit. (See fig. 5.1.) In the article, Dvir is honest about the difficulties inherent in finalizing the trail's route, such as securing rights-of-way through the agricultural areas around kibbutzim. He also makes straightforward statements in the article about the trail's emphasis on diversity: "Our intention is to cross all of the parts of the landscape that exist in the Land. We also want to utilize the fact that Eretz Israel is the center of many different religions, and therefore the trail passes the sacred sites of different religions."[39]

At the same time, though, it is clear that not everyone's definition of "Israel" would be satisfied by the route of Shvil Israel; the article includes a small map of Israel with a black line drawn boldly across it, staying strictly within Israel's pre-1967 boundaries and giving the West Bank a wide berth. Indeed, the line on the map appears less like a representation of Israel than as a long shadow of the Green Line, cast across Israel proper. The article concludes by asking whether the trail would cross into the West Bank, and offers Dvir's answer without quoting him directly: "Dvir explains that the solution was simple: In Samaria there are no sites that are more important than those that are found along the coastal plain. That said, the mountains of Judea are home to some of the most important sites, like Bethlehem and Hebron, and they were forced to give them up."[40] In other words, Dvir's answer was no.

Controversy immediately followed Dvir's statements in the article. None of the discussions Dvir had with the experts and field personnel he consulted were held completely privately; wider circles of Israelis had heard about what was taking place and had developed their own expectations as to how the trail would look. According to Dvir, when supporters of the Israeli right wing saw the article and the accompanying map, they immediately opposed the project on the grounds that the trail planners were "giving up on Judea and Samaria." Meanwhile, details of the previously held discussions regarding the possible eventual creation of a trail across the West Bank became known to supporters of the Israeli left, who subsequently accused Dvir and the ITC of trying to mark the occupied territories. "We got a lot of calls from members of the Knesset, from both the right and the left," Dvir later wrote.[41] Elsewhere, he wrote, "For some members of the Knesset, the matter was explained in writing and verbally, and the winds quieted after a short time."[42]

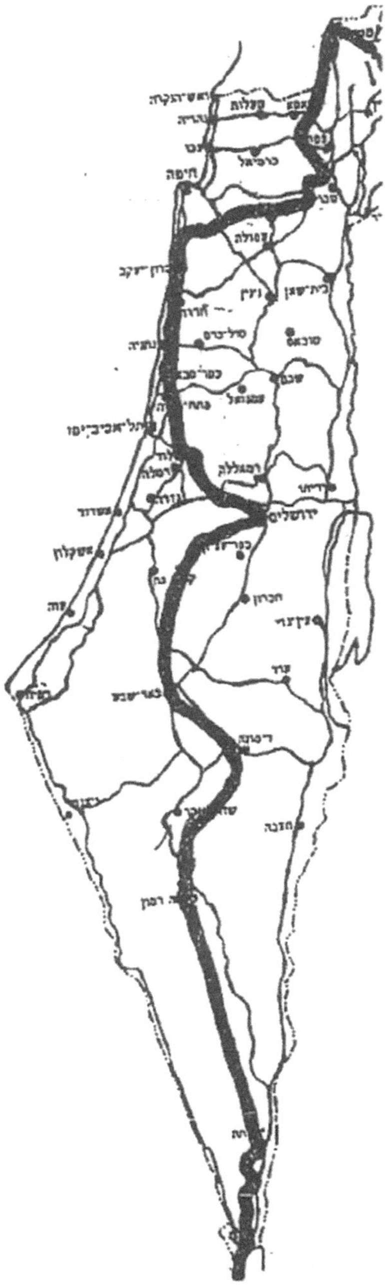

Figure 5.1. Early Shvil Israel map, sketched by Ori Dvir. *Published in the Ma'ariv newspaper, 1987.*

In late 1987, only a matter of months after the Ma'ariv article was published, the debate subsided, not through any argument of Dvir's, nor through any change in plans, but instead as a result of violence associated with the First Palestinian Intifada.[43] The issue of marking Shvil Israel across the West Bank came up from time to time, but Dvir continued to justify the exclusion of the occupied territories on security grounds: "Even when we were in the preliminary steps of marking, the right came against us. It didn't help to explain that you can't mark without an armed escort, and worse, you can't hike the trails without an actual military escort."[44] For the most part, though, after the beginning of the Palestinian uprising in 1987, Dvir was free to concentrate on marking Shvil Israel within the country's pre-1967 boundaries. The issue did not rise again in earnest until after the cessation of hostilities in the early 1990s, the beginning of the Israeli-Palestinian peace process, and the signing of the Oslo Accords.

Marking the Trail

The first part of Shvil Israel was technically marked in 1986. When Tamir first heard in 1984 that the trail project would probably take at least fifteen years to complete, he responded by telling Dvir to work more quickly because he had hoped to hike the trail in celebration of his eightieth birthday. Dvir never forgot that request. Just before the day arrived in 1986, Dvir marked a short experimental portion of the trail near Nahal Tavor in the Lower Galilee and invited a journalist to join him and Tamir on the first hike of Shvil Israel.[45] Later, after Tamir died in 1988, the route of the trail had to be changed, and the experimental section was not included in the final route. Nevertheless, Tamir was satisfied, and Dvir never failed to give him credit for his role in initiating the Israel National Trail project and for urging the ITC to move quickly in making it a reality.

Marking the route appears to have begun in earnest in the Upper Galilee in 1989, after Dvir had finished obtaining the types of permission always required when beginning a simun shvilim project. One section of the trail was marked in Nahal Amud, the deep ravine that runs just west of Safed all the way to the Sea of Galilee, and another was marked around the summit of Mount Meron to the north.[46] Around the same time, another section was marked along the Jordan River just south of the Sea of Galilee, between the Yardenit baptismal site and the historical marker at Umm Juni, where Kibbutz Degania was founded in 1909.[47] All of the sections were marked with experimental metal signs that bore the new emblem of the Israel National Trail: an orange arrow pointing to the left interlocked with a blue arrow pointing to the right, inscribed with the name of the trail in Hebrew, English, and Arabic. The emblem marked the first use of the Arabic name for the trail: Darb al-Balad, which was not a direct translation of Shvil Israel, but rather a name that meant "trail of the land" or "trail of the country"—a depoliticized name that made no reference to the State of Israel.

If Dvir intended this as a precaution against erasure or removal of the signs, it was ineffective; already in early 1990, a matter of months after the signs were posted, many of them had been either removed or defaced. In the latter case, the signs were vandalized with special focus on the word "Israel." Afterward, Dvir wryly remarked, "Does someone have something against Israel?"[48] In any case, the emblem was designed to set Shvil Israel apart from other marked trails in Israel, not only because it was the country's de facto "national trail" as the Appalachian Trail was in the United States, but also because in many cases, it lay atop the existing network of marked trails and needed its own identifying mark. The destruction of signage eventually led Dvir and the ITC to begin marking the trail with paint, as other trails were marked, but with blazes modeled after the original signs: interlocking orange and blue arrows upon a rectangular white field.

More experimentally marked sections were quickly added. In the spring of 1990, Dvir announced that hikers could visit three new marked sections in the Negev: one that started at Mamshit and ran along part of the rim of the Large Crater, one in Ovdat Canyon near Sde Boker that ran to the spring of Ein Ovdat and upper Nahal Tzin, and another that began at Mitzpe Ramon and descended into the Ramon Crater along an ancient path that had been newly marked by IDF volunteers.[49] Still, Dvir harbored no unrealistic expectations about the timeline for completing Shvil Israel. The plans for the northern and southern sections were almost complete, and had changed little from the sketch Dvir had offered in 1987. Only a tiny percentage of those sections had actually been marked, though, and the central section was still undefined; the only sure thing, Dvir wrote, was that it would pass Jerusalem. He estimated that the trail would be completed sometime within the next twelve years.[50]

In the north, though, the trail continued to be marked at a rapid pace, with new sections added throughout the remainder of that year and throughout 1991. Also in 1991, it was obvious that the method of marking the trail with the intricate blazes modeled after the original white signs was too time-consuming and difficult. Experienced trailblazers like Uzi Chaplin could carry out the work quickly, but for brand-new volunteers and field school employees, the interlocking orange and blue arrows atop a rectangular white field was like a work of art that had to be painted every few hundred meters on rock surfaces.[51] Dvir began experimenting with blazes. One short-lived incarnation that preceded the final form was a two-striped blaze consisting of offset, vertically oriented orange and blue bars. As with the markings for the rest of Israel's trail network, the colors Dvir designated were specifically numbered hues; in this case, Blue 49 and Orange 63.[52] In the end, Shvil Israel was marked with the blazes that appear today along its length: vertically oriented, offset tricolor blazes in orange, blue, and white. (See figure 5.2.)

Around the same time, with work progressing quickly in the north, Dvir began to focus attention on the unsurveyed central section. If a good solution for the trail's route was difficult to find in 1986 and 1987, before the start of the intifada, it was doubly so once the uprising was in full swing. The West Bank was regarded as a high security risk for hikers, and this not only meant that Shvil Israel would have to run west of the Green Line but also that it would probably have to stay a good distance away from it. This negated many of the best options for traversing the narrow coastal plain, which was mostly flat except for the low hills that lay along its eastern side. For this reason, Dvir and the ITC had long assumed that Shvil Israel would have to be marked along the seashore, which was preferable to routing the trail upon roads through open fields but would require hikers to walk through developed areas near the coast. Moreover, between Haifa and Jaffa, the beaches along the coastline were not wide and sandy as they were farther south but generally lay at the foot of rocky cliffs. If the trail had to be routed along the narrow strip of beach, hikers would be forced in some places to walk in the water at high tide.

In 1992, as the First Intifada was nearing an end, Dvir assigned Shai Rozen, one of the guides at the Poleg Field School near Netanya, to scout out alternative routes for the trail's central section that could bring hikers inland instead of keeping them near the coast. The route Rozen proposed had to navigate a complicated physical and political landscape. It began at Caesarea and at first adhered to the original plan of following the shoreline because that enabled the trail to circumvent the city of Hadera. Once south of Hadera, however, the trail cut straight east, skirting the northern edge of

Figure 5.2. Israel National Trail blaze. *Photograph by author.*

the city of Netanya and, once clear, swung southward until it again paralleled the coast. By that point, though, the route was only about two kilometers west of the West Bank city of Tulkarm. From there, it zigzagged south and southwest, away from the Green Line, but eventually swung east again to pass through the narrow open area between the Israeli city of Kfar Saba and the West Bank town of Qalqilya. Farther south, it then shot the narrow gap between Petach Tikva—part of the Tel Aviv metropolitan area—and the town of Rosh ha-Ayin. As it continued to skirt the Green Line on its journey south, the surveyed route managed to stay within pre-1967 Israeli territory, and also to avoid developed areas almost the entire time, which was a considerable achievement. Near Latrun, Rozen's route returned to the original plan, and entered the forested corridor that led upward into the Jerusalem foothills.[53]

At the same time Rozen was surveying this alternative route for Shvil Israel, the Israeli government was drafting a plan for a new multilane highway that followed the same corridor. Highway Six was a controversial project aimed at relieving the congestion that characterized the main roads along the coastal plain and similarly sought an open corridor that circumvented the major cities of central Israel.[54] The SPNI opposed the plan to build the new highway, but today one can look at a map of Israel and see the blue line of Highway Six following almost the exact route Rozen had mapped out for Shvil Israel along the edge of the West Bank. Dvir and the ITC had no choice but to abandon the inland route and follow the shoreline from Caesarea almost all the way to Tel Aviv and then to cut east toward Rosh ha-Ayin, where the metropolitan area thinned out and the open land was wide enough to accommodate both the Trans-Israel Highway and the Israel National Trail. Such a route was less than ideal—at many points, hikers would have to walk with the waves of the Mediterranean lapping at their ankles—but it was a quick solution for the central section.[55]

By 1993, much of the northern section had been completed, and parts of it had even been mapped. Metulla's local government had opposed the marking of the trail near the town, so Dvir had to divert the trail. Instead, it ran around the north side of Kiryat Shmona to Kfar Giladi and Tel Hai and ascended the ridge that overlooked the Huleh Valley. Aside from that problem, the creation of the trail's northernmost section had been uneventful, and its route was set to appear on the next edition of the corresponding simun shvilim map.[56] Overall, things were moving more quickly than Dvir had foreseen; Shvil Israel was taking shape and was on track to be completed several years ahead of schedule.

Map 5.1. Route of the Israel National Trail (as of July 2021).

The Negev portion of the trail had developed quickly as well, in large part because the problems that characterized the trail's route south of the Ramon Crater were not solved. A large segment of the trail still ran in a straight line all the way from Mitzpe Ramon and across the Ovda Valley to the Shacharut ridge in the southern Negev. The first hints at a solution came in 1993, when a portion of the Negev previously reserved for military training was opened for civilian use. By then, the trail network in Israel had become much larger and more noticeable to the point that employees of the SPNI and the Nature Reserves Authority were uneasy with the number and frequency of painted markings that were visible in nearly every part of the country. Near the end of the completion of Shvil Israel, with only seven maps left to be published in the countrywide map series, the simun shvilim project met its first principled resistance.

Opposition to Waymarking: Debates about the Relationship between People and Land

The most serious opposition to waymarking came from guides who worked at SPNI field schools. In the course of the withdrawal from the Sinai Peninsula, the SPNI closed its field schools in the area and returned its personnel to Israel. Many of the guides and staff from the Tzukei David Field School, which had been built near Saint Catherine's Monastery in the rugged mountains of south-central Sinai, moved to the Har ha-Negev Field School, which was situated atop the high cliffs overlooking the huge Ramon Crater in the central Negev Desert. The sparsely populated belt of Israeli territory over which the school presided was more like the Sinai than any other part of Israel. It included the mountainous highlands surrounding the crater to the west—the "mountain of the Negev" for which the school was named—and the broken land that descended toward the Arava Valley to the east. There, and at the Hatzeva Field School located farther north in the Arava near the Small Crater and the Large Crater, SPNI guides maintained the wild culture of hiking that had presided in the Sinai and that hearkened back to the culture of hiking that existed in the early days of the Yishuv.[57]

Between 1984 and 1986, the anthropologist Orit Ben-David studied the way SPNI field school guides conducted hikes. Ben-David argues that the guides maintained a radical distinction between "society" and "nature."[58] This dichotomy bears a close resemblance to the two-sided view of Eretz Israel espoused by early Labor Zionist pioneers during the first decades of the twentieth century. As described in chapter 1 of this book, the halutzim of the Second and Third Aliyah saw the Land of Israel, on the one hand, as a space that needed to be tamed and made fruitful and, on the other hand, as a place whose wild beauty needed to be left alone. Zionist youth in the pioneer era actualized their relationship with Eretz Israel in two ways: first, by coming into contact with the Land through acts of building, construction, and development; and second, by coming into contact with the Land through the act of hiking along unpaved paths and leaving nature unmarked.

However, whereas the youth at the vanguard of the pioneer generation in the Yishuv had been ambivalent about the marks of development upon the Land, SPNI guides at the forefront of Israel's environmental movement in the 1980s were not; as young men and women who had grown up in an already developed country, they opposed any further building or construction that could harm nature. The personnel of the SPNI saw themselves as bearing the torch of the Romantic tradition and ensuring that open spaces were preserved from development.[59] The staff of the southern field schools took this to extreme levels and opposed the encroachment of human civilization on the desert in the form of settlements, roads, radio stations, and even in the form of the organized hikes they themselves were charged with leading. "The guides incorporate all other hikers, including members of the SPNI, in the category of society, considering them as destroyers of nature while regarding themselves as part and parcel of nature."[60]

From the shattered vessel of the image of the Sabra scout, SPNI guides had preserved modes of behavior and dress that had always set elite Zionist hikers apart from the rest of the Jewish population. Like the halutzim of the Ha-Shomer defense organization and the reconnaissance scouts of the Palmach, the field school guides spoke Arabic, sought to emulate the lifestyle of the Bedouin, and wore Arab-style head coverings. Meron Benvenisti describes such behavior and dress as vestments that he himself once wore as "a high priest in the cult of moledet" while leading hikes in the Judean Desert after Israeli statehood.[61] The pioneering explorers of the 1910s and 1920s, the youth movement and paramilitary hikers of the 1930s and 1940s, and the explorers of the nascent State of Israel during the 1950s and 1960s had all characterized themselves as belonging to the Land and loving the Land to the degree that they were willing to fight to maintain their place within it. The SPNI guides who had been forged in the Sinai during the 1970s and returned to Israel in the 1980s upheld that tradition but articulated their fight for Eretz Israel in terms of environmental preservation, not armed defense.

As long as such guides believed the goals of simun shvilim were in line with the principles of nature preservation, they served as useful allies in marking useful trails in remote areas. For the larger simun shvilim project, the cooperation of the Har ha-Negev Field School was essential because the two maps of the surrounding region—one covering the area west of Mitzpe Ramon and one covering the area to the east—would connect with three previously published maps and complete an arc of mapped territory that started near Jericho and ran south and west all the way to the Egyptian border. The school did cooperate, though, and in an article Dvir wrote in 1989 announcing the publication of the two simun shvilim maps, he explicitly mentioned the staff of the field school as the driving force behind that waymarking initiative.[62]

Even for people who did not like the idea of painted markings appearing across Israel's backcountry areas, simun shvilim was a necessary evil because of the 1979 law requiring hikers to stay on marked trails inside the boundaries of nature reserves. Even after Dvir marked and mapped an area, though, some unmarked paths always remained. Often, Dvir did this on purpose, in accordance with his desire to leave some secret places in the Land unmarked so that hikers could discover them on their own and in keeping with the precedent he had established with the creation of the Eilat Mountains network between 1963 and 1967.[63] Sometimes, though, parts of the Land remained unmarked quite by accident. This was the case with the Eastern Har ha-Negev map, upon which no trails were marked across a large area beginning near the east side of the Ramon Crater and extending all the way to the Arava Valley and the Jordanian border.[64] The area was designated a military firing zone, but in reality, the area was barely accessible by vehicle, and the IDF rarely trained there.

As a result of what amounted to an oversight by Israeli planners, the area came to be known as Eretz Bereshit, or the "Land of Genesis," because few marks of human civilization existed there. SPNI guides from the Har ha-Negev Field School and the Hatzeva Field School in the northern Arava ranged freely across the space, reveling as the pioneers had in the sense of primacy they felt when encountering the unspoiled Land. In fact, even when hiking a marked trail was an option, such as along vestiges of the overland trade route that in ancient times connected Petra with Gaza, guides intentionally and illegally led groups alongside the marked trail rather than use the trail itself.[65]

During the early 1990s, Eretz Bereshit lost its status as a firing zone and became classified as a nature reserve. Dvir returned shortly thereafter, not only to add new trails to the Eastern Har ha-Negev simun shvilim map but also to search for possible solutions for the problems along Shvil Israel's southern portion. In response, the guides from the desert field schools who regarded the Land of Genesis as their personal domain for hiking and yedi'at ha-aretz began to mount their opposition to the simun shvilim project, casting it as a form of development that threatened to impose the ravages of civilization upon the Land's last untouched areas.

In 1993, Noa Mal'at, one of the guides at the Hatzeva Field School wrote a remarkable letter entitled "Simun Shvilim Vandalizes," which was published in the SPNI journal *Teva va-Aretz*. In it, the author cites the SPNI's recent success in blocking the construction of a Voice of America radio station in the Arava Valley and expresses frustration at now having to oppose more development in the same region but this time at the hands of people within Israel's environmental movement.[66] She describes Eretz Bereshit and its value as an unspoiled corner of the Land in terms that resonate with the writings of the early Zionist halutzim.

> Why can't you, like your fathers, sit and look around at the desert, in the sunset, in the sunrise, on the hills and on the trails, and see only them, and not another marking? Maybe only after we have marked the area, and after we have put up explanatory signs, and after—so that people will be really comfortable—we have placed trash cans and bathrooms in overnight campgrounds, because of course people will need to be taken care of . . . and when the day arrives in which we want to enter a place where there are no signs left by the hand of man, we won't find it here anymore.
>
> Indeed, according to the law, it is forbidden to hike with groups in unmarked areas that are within the boundaries of a nature reserve. This area was only recently declared a nature reserve. So it is reasonable to vandalize it for the sake of admitting hikes there in accordance with the law?? It will certainly be strange if the virginity of the area is vandalized at the hands of the very hiking public who are looking for this uncommon virginity. . . .
>
> We hope that there will still be some people who want to walk in this area as it is. And even if they have a problem with navigation, that they will ask one of the people who has knowledge in the matter, so that they will come and see this place, because there might not be much time left.[67]

Dvir had little patience for such expressions of protest. From his point of view, the motivation behind the field school guides' opposition was not concern for nature or love for the Land, but rather a desire to control territory and limit the ability of outsiders to visit it. The guides' donning of the mantle of the Palmach may have impressed members of the public who visited the field schools and relied on the guides' knowledge to help them safely make their way across the rugged desert, but it did not impress Dvir, who had helped forge the very culture of hiking the guides now claimed to lead and who had long since moved on from wearing the keffiyeh and making a show of his native status within the Land. To him, the guides' opposition to simun shvilim only proved their insecurity, irresponsibility, and ignorance because in the process of hiking away from marked trails, they created new lines of damage upon the sensitive desert environment, and in the process of eliminating the only legal routes by which people could visit nature reserves, they severed the Israeli relationship with a beautiful part of the Land. His response to Mal'at's letter reflected this attitude and defended the waymarking project:

> This system also makes it possible to "sit and look around at the desert, at the sunset, at the sunrise," and to do other good things of this sort, as Noa writes—but not only for the chosen few, and not only under experienced guidance. . . .
>
> The concluding statement in Noa's letter leaves a bitter taste, because like Noa, many certainly wish "that there will be a few more people who want to walk in this area," but why, Noa, why, if they have trouble navigating, do they have to ask one of the people who are skilled in such things? Why do the many simply have to be dependent on those knowledgeable in the matter? What's more is that for most people, such a request involves having to pay the person who they ask for help. . . .
>
> The most important reason for having marked trails is for the sake of preserving nature. Instead of creating countless new paths or wandering aimlessly, the trail directs and channels hikers. The problem of "parallel trails" is characteristic of individual hikers, but more often of guides who not only try not to walk on designated trails, but at times walk their hikers almost parallel to the established trail, only to give themselves the "feeling of primacy" or to heighten the leader's identity as "someone who knows how to find his way without a trail."[68]

Dvir's response did not change attitudes in the Har ha-Negev and Hatzeva Field Schools, but in the end, trails were marked through Eretz Bereshit simply because there was no other legal way for SPNI guides to operate tours there. SPNI guides could protest simun shvilim on the ground by avoiding marked trails and even by illegally erasing markings, but as long as Dvir and the ITC made recurring visits to the area and elicited the support of the field schools' parent organization, the guides could not effect much real change. More serious opposition came from Menachem Marcus, a former SPNI employee and yedi'at ha-aretz expert who had worked in the Sinai and the Negev field schools, had since then written a detailed series of volumes on Israel's history and geography, and had also traveled extensively overseas.[69]

In the early 1990s, as an employee of the Nature Reserves Authority, Marcus criticized not only the simun shvilim project but also the entire endeavor of placing signs upon the Land. In an article entitled "It's Also Possible without the Cult of Signs," Marcus contrasts the hiking trails of Europe with those of Israel and concludes that in the Land, the parties responsible for placing signs and marking trails are out of control.

> Most of the alpine trails are marked and their markings really arouse respect: a small yellow triangle, and on it, the number of the trail, posted on the face of a rock alongside the trail—modest, clear, easy for navigation, and almost unseen in the field. That is to say, in the moment you're on the trail, you'll clearly identify the marking without difficulty, but no one thinks that the marking needs to shout out to you, or that every hundred meters, some rock or another needs to be painted. . . .
>
> And when there is a directional sign, it's small and modest, and you look and you ask yourself, for what purpose is this megalomaniacal signing that has suddenly popped up in the Land, on the sides of highways and roads? Who needs this strange cult that gives us, for example, at the entrance to Nahal Katlav in the mountains of Jerusalem, one sign from the Trail Marking Committee; one from the Nature Reserves Authority, big and orange; and next to it a wooden sign, huge and expensive, belonging to the Jewish National Fund, and every one of them says the same thing, writ large: To Nahal Katlav.[70]

Dvir wrote a long reply to Marcus that appeared in a subsequent issue of *Teva va-Aretz* and in which he took a position similar to the one he had taken in response to Mal'at's letter.[71] He pointed out the degree to which marked trails freed hikers—especially less-experienced hikers—from having to constantly worry about navigation. He argued that most Israelis appreciated simun shvilim and quoted a letter the ITC had received from the writer Haim Be'er expressing thanks for the waymarking project. He wrote that the ITC used a great deal of restraint when adding new trails to the map and reiterated that in areas like nature reserves, they offered the only means by which most people could access large parts of the country. Finally, he accused Marcus, the yedi'at ha-aretz expert, author, and veteran hiker, of putting the concerns of professionals and elites above the needs of everyday people.

> It's not clear to me that it's preferable, for example, to have a little wooden sign, as Menachem wrote, rather than a painted marking upon a stone, which is smaller, less noticeable, and less bothersome to nature. It's also not clear to me what "signing according to need" is, in the opinion of Menachem. "According to need"—for whom? For the hiker. For a "normal" hiker, or for the professionals like Menachem and others? The true test is not whether markings appear every 100 meters on this stone or another, but whether they succeed

> in guiding, according to the needs of whole segments of the population. The appropriate combination between marking trails, and leaving some trails in unmarked areas, is the right solution.[72]

Despite Marcus's protests that simun shvilim was part of a megalomaniacal project of placing signs and markings on the ground, the marked and mapped trail network was a fait accompli. By 1994, most of the country was covered by hiking trails and their corresponding topographical maps; the few areas for which maps had not yet been printed were being marked and surveyed in the field. Marcus, however, remained part of a small but vocal contingent that continues to advocate for unmarked trails to this day; fourteen years after his original complaint, Marcus said to the *Ha'aretz* newspaper, "Marking trails take [*sic*] away one of the main thrills—the navigation challenge. This challenge is one of the things that excite [*sic*] me, besides the view. Let me be a bit alarmed, let me make some mistakes. After all, it's an important part of the experience."[73]

At their core, these discussions hearken to tensions inherent in the Jewish relationship with land as defined by the early Labor Zionists. The "pioneer generation" had idolized and mythologized a direct and unmediated relationship between Jews and the Land of Israel. Generations of Israelis had been taught to partake of that relationship if they could, and the guides of the SPNI carried on that tradition. Dvir himself enjoyed partaking in that relationship, but ultimately was a pragmatist. One of the other goals of Labor Zionism had been to create a Jewish state that bore all the hallmarks of "normal" states, in which citizens engaged in an array of trades and occupations, from technological development to agriculture. The masses of Israelis who lived everyday lives would never don the mantle of the ascetic "Sabra scout" of the 1930s, nor should they; that phase of nation-building had passed. Rather than encourage a mythologized Israeli identity that was only attainable by a privileged few, Dvir chose to expose large numbers of Israelis to the country's mythologized landscapes.

Conclusion: Inaugurating the Israel National Trail and Completing the Map Series

Shvil Israel was inaugurated during Passover 1995, during the period that followed the Oslo Accords and preceded the assassination of Prime Minister Yitzhak Rabin. A peace agreement with Jordan had been signed the year before, and many in Israel had high hopes that a similar agreement would eventually come to pass with the Palestinians. In that atmosphere, the route of the eight-hundred-fifty-kilometer Israel National Trail appeared to be a stroke of genius; by keeping the trail outside the occupied territories, Dvir had created a long-distance footpath that now seemed appropriate for the time. Ironically, though, the ceremony was held at the Armored Corps Museum in Latrun, which was the only place in the entire country where the trail crossed the Green Line. The speakers included President Ezer Weizmann, who officially inaugurated the trail; Yossi Sarid, the minister of the environment under the Rabin government; Azaria Alon, the former chairman of the SPNI who had been involved in simun shvilim from the very beginning; and of course, Ori Dvir.[74]

After the formal opening of the trail, Dvir stepped down as the head of the ITC, although he officially retained the title of chairman for years afterward, just as the printed map series continued to bear his name as the chief editor. He stayed heavily involved in the simun shvilim project, writing his monthly magazine columns and giving updates on the state of the countrywide map series. Once in a while, he would visit the crews who were still marking and maintaining Israel's trails and revisit the old feeling of kneeling in the dirt, scratching a rock with a wire brush, and gently brushing a colored mark onto a stone.[75] Regarding his life's work as the custodian of Israel's trails, he said, "For me, this is not a mission, but myself. It's my essence."[76]

Over the next fifteen years, Dvir was able to watch Shvil Israel blossom into a thriving long-distance trail, complete with its own unique thru-hiking culture. While in some ways it was similar to that which existed along the Appalachian Trail, with "trail angels" who provided services to hikers in need and special businesses and hostels that catered specifically to backpackers, it was a completely Israeli experience in other ways. Families and elementary school classes hiked the trail in sections, completing the trail piece by piece over the span of several years. Religious hikers used it in partial fulfillment of the commandment to make pilgrimage to Jerusalem. Young men walked it in association with their bar mitzvah coming-of-age ceremony. Recent high school graduates walked it in preparation for their military service. Newly discharged soldiers hiked it as a way of preparing for the next stage of their lives. Every year, more and more people hiked Shvil Israel, and it became an Israeli cultural institution.[77]

Dany Gaspar, a renowned guide who had worked for years at the SPNI field school in Be'er Sheva, was tapped by Dvir to oversee the simun shvilim project as the countrywide trail network neared completion. Gaspar was ideal for the job in many ways; he had helped plan and mark the route of Shvil Israel and had led the first group hike along its whole length in 1994, before the completion of the trail was even announced. Under Gaspar's watch, some of the supposed shortcomings of the Israel National Trail were addressed. Gaspar found a route through Eretz Bereshit that could enable the trail to access the Arava Valley rather than follow straight lines along highways through the central Negev. This and other improvements rendered the trail more and more attractive to hikers and increased the number of Israelis who took up the challenge of hiking the whole country from end to end.[78] For those who insisted on being able to incorporate hikes outside the body of pre-1967 Israel into their cross-country treks, Shvil ha-Golan, or the "Golan Trail," gave hikers the option of crossing the length of the Golan Heights from north to south.[79] Similarly, Shvil Yerushalayim, or the "Jerusalem Trail," departed as a side trail from Shvil Israel near Ein Kerem and formed a loop all the way around the city, pushing as far east as Mount Scopus before returning to rejoin the main route.[80]

Other issues, however, remained unaddressed. Dvir had always dreamed of a path that ran through the West Bank, and in some ways, that dream was as far off as ever. Under the agreement between Israel and the Palestinian Authority, the West Bank would be divided into a series of zones of three different types, known as Areas A, B, and C. Out of respect for that decision, Dvir announced that trail markings in Areas A and B would not be renewed; in Area C, which still lay under Israeli jurisdiction, trails would remain. As it happened, most of the open rural areas of the West Bank were covered by Area C, so it was still possible for Israelis to hike extensively on marked trails throughout the Judean Desert, up the Jordan River valley, and even around settlements like Ofra. National-religious settlers, too, longed for their own trail through the West Bank that would, in their view, correct the flawed route of Shvil Israel and enable them to further tie Judea and Samaria to the parts of the body of the Land that lay beyond the Green Line. Dvir had a different type of trail in mind, and in 1998, he began testing the waters on the Palestinian side to see how it would be received.

> At an Israeli-Palestinian conference that was organized in Bethlehem, the waymarking project and the Israel National Trail were presented, noting the fact that many trails marked by the [Israel Trails] Committee were unused on our side, as they were now passing through the area of the Palestinian Authority. It was proposed to the Palestinians that they continue the Israel National

> Trail from the Lower Galilee and from the Carmel to the region of Judea and Samaria, and thus make the "Way of the Patriarchs" or the "Mountain Ridge Way" a reality. The warm responses were not long in coming. Shortly after the conference, another meeting was organized in Tel Aviv with the people who would initiate the continuation of marking and updating the trails on the Palestinian side. They also had a name for the continuation of the Israel National Trail—the "Peace Trail." Nothing remained at that point but to raise support for the continuation of the project.[81]

Once again, the mere mention of such a trail in a public forum opened Dvir up to attack as he was accused of harboring ambitions of running an Israeli trail through the West Bank against the wishes of the Palestinians, and once again, the outbreak of violence rendered the idea an impossibility.[82] Yet even in 2000, as tensions between the Israelis and Palestinians again threatened to boil over, Dvir held out the hope that peace would eventually come and that Israelis could one day hike a long-distance trail across the highlands of Judea and Samaria. The impulse to mark that trail, Dvir believed, would emerge from outside the simun shvilim project: "The redemption of the route through Judea and Samaria will come, we will see, actually from the Palestinian direction."[83]

In September 2000, shortly after Dvir wrote those words, the Second Palestinian Intifada, or the al-Aqsa Intifada, began. A year later, in the midst of suicide bombings across Israel and widespread violence across the West Bank, the final sheet in the countrywide simun shvilim map series—Number 5/6, entitled "Jordan Valley and East Samaria"—was released to the public. Despite the fact that the violence made it impossible for Israelis to hike in the very area covered by the new map, Israel's yedi'at ha-aretz community, as well as prominent public officials, found cause for celebration. The magazine *Eretz ve-Teva* published a special edition on trails in Israel, with a section that featured a series of congratulatory letters and reminiscences written by famous hikers and guides. Prime Minister Ariel Sharon, Minister of Tourism Rehavam Ze'evi, and Speaker of the Knesset Avraham Burg were just a few of the prominent politicians who shared their memories of exploring backcountry routes and congratulated Dvir and the ITC on the completion of what amounted to a national project.[84]

While that issue of the magazine was still on shelves in October 2001, Ze'evi was killed outside his room at the Hyatt Hotel in Jerusalem by a group of men representing the Popular Front for the Liberation of Palestine. The attack was a sobering reminder that the struggle in which Ze'evi had engaged for control of the country during his years as a Palmach scout was still continuing. It also came at a turning point in the development of Israel's marked and mapped trail network. After the violence of the Second Intifada died down, Israelis and Palestinians began approaching trails differently in the field. Dvir, in his constant pursuit of new possibilities for hikers, had created a space upon which hiking could be undertaken by anyone and which could be used by anyone as a space upon which to project political statements. What had begun as a space for exploration now became a space for protest, particularly in Area C of the West Bank, where both Israelis and Palestinians claimed the right to walk unpaved paths.

The concluding chapter of this book deals with some of the postscripts written upon the palimpsest of the land between the Jordan River and the Mediterranean Sea—lines recently inscribed by individuals and groups who have recognized the potential of hiking and waymarking on the countryside to effect larger changes across societies. Waymarking initiatives—both official and clandestine—are today taking place on both sides of the Green Line in support of various economic, political, and religious goals. The future of Israel's marked and mapped trail networks will be defined in large part by how the ITC and the SPNI respond to outside efforts to create hiking routes and whether they decide to continue emphasizing the mark and the map in a world increasingly navigated by smartphones and satellites.

6

Postscripts, 2001–2021

Trails as Articulations of Multiple Identities

For nearly four decades, Ori Dvir stood at the helm of the simun shvilim project. Enormous societal and territorial changes had taken place during that time, and the trail network had evolved in response to those changes. At the same time, Dvir had been a stabilizing force in the world of Israeli hiking. Amid controversies over waymarking and nature preservation, he had engaged in a sort of cultural preservation by creating a countrywide space upon which Jewish Israelis could engage in practices first developed by early Zionists. As the uncontested curator of that space, Dvir was able to shape the experience of hiking, which is to say that he shaped the experience Jewish Israelis had with the land they knew as the Land of Israel, which is to say that he played an enormous role in defining what it meant to be Israeli. Now, as Dvir phased himself out of the simun shvilim project, other people recognized the power trails had in shaping Jewish-Israeli identity and the popular vision of the Jewish state's territorial dimensions.

Dvir himself had set the stage for some of the changes that soon occurred. Shvil Israel had opened up a new universe of possibilities for trail planners. With the completion of the countrywide trail network, simun shvilim had reached its logical end, but by stitching dozens of smaller trails together, Dvir had created a themed super-trail that crossed the country. Now, Dvir's successors could begin envisioning new super-trails that could be laid upon the existing network.

With the end of the Second Palestinian Intifada in 2005, the new head of the ITC, Dany Gaspar, was able to plan new trails. Gaspar was a well-known figure in Israel's hiking community. He had walked the country as much as anyone and was instantly recognizable with his tall frame, his trademark cap, and his long goatee. Like Dvir, he was a skilled writer who could effectively promote the work of the ITC through regular columns in popular yedi'at ha-aretz publications. Gaspar moved quickly to create two new trails: the Jerusalem Trail in 2006 and the Golan Trail in 2007. The 125-kilometer Shvil ha-Golan, or the "Golan Trail," was marked with green-blue-white blazes, and the 42-kilometer Shvil Yerushalayim, or the "Jerusalem Trail," was marked with blue-gold-blue blazes.

Even if such initiatives were never described by the ITC as corrections to the route of Shvil Israel as dictated by Ori Dvir, they were understood as such by hikers and even by outside parties involved in the new trails' creation. When the plan to create the Jerusalem Trail was announced in 2005, the city's mayor, Uri Lupoliansky, said it was "unbelievable that the Israel National Trail, a trail that spans almost the length of the country, and serves thousands of visitors every year, does not come through Jerusalem. Jerusalem deserves its own trail."[1]

These add-ons to the Israel National Trail appeared at a time when new technologies were also beginning to open possibilities for hikers. Hikers in Israel had always been able to "hike their own hikes," to paraphrase the watchword of the Appalachian Trail in the United States, and they often did. The culture of thru-hiking Shvil Israel was thoroughly anarchic, with hikers adding and subtracting sections as they pleased, hitchhiking around parts they found boring, and taking breaks for days or weeks at a time as they saw fit. But in the new era of GPS and Web-based mapping technologies, hikers were able to plan their own themed trails, record their routes, and share maps electronically. It was even possible to hike entirely off-trail and record those journeys as well; other hikers could download the tracks onto their own GPS receivers and recreate the treks on their own, with no need for painted blazes or printed maps. The democratization of trails, as a result of Dvir's absence and the rise of new technologies, gave rise to grassroots efforts to create new and unique trails in Israel proper. These projects resulted in the first serious efforts to open Israeli trails for foreign tourists.

Meanwhile, changes were also taking place on the ground in the West Bank. After the Second Intifada ended, the old agreements Israel and the Palestinian Authority (PA) had made in the 1990s remained in place. The PA controlled the small, mostly urban islands of territory of the West Bank, which the Oslo Accords had collectively defined as Area A, and it shared control with Israel in the surrounding semi-urban sections of land known as Area B. In keeping with its longstanding policy, the ITC limited its waymarking activities in Areas A and B, but continued working in Area C. Because that territory was under Israeli security control and hosted numerous Israeli nature reserves, the SPNI and the ITC saw it as falling within their mandate for environmental protection and waymarking.

However, for the first time, other parties began making serious attempts to mark trails in the West Bank as well: Jewish settlers who wanted to "correct" the Israel National Trail and create new political trails; anti-occupation activists and Palestinian tourism developers who wanted to create Palestinian trails; and even international organizations with trail development plans for the whole Middle East. Under Ori Dvir, any such initiatives had been branded "pirate trails," and any blazes discovered in the field by waymarking teams were erased. Dvir had been ruthless in establishing the dominance of simun shvilim on the grounds that marked trails were only safe and navigable if they matched the routes depicted on maps. Now, an efflorescence of independent waymarking projects, aided by new technologies and created in parts of the West Bank where Israeli waymarking teams rarely worked, challenged the hegemony of the ITC and threatened to turn the West Bank into a battleground where trails became weaponized in the service of competing national ideologies.

The Jesus Trail: New Directions for Waymarking in Israel

Millions of tourists visit Israel every year, and many arrive as religious pilgrims who are interested in walking in the footsteps of their spiritual ancestors. Many Christian tourists want to do this in the literal sense, wherever possible; in Jerusalem, for example, walking the Via Dolorosa, which commemorates the journey of Jesus to his crucifixion, is an essential part of the pilgrim experience. Protestant Christian visitors to Israel, in particular, are interested in seeing sites as they might have looked during Jesus's time. The Garden Tomb complex, just north of the Old City walls, is but one example: its unadorned and sunlit first-century Jewish tomb is surrounded by olive trees, native flowers, and ancient winepresses, which stand in sharp contrast to the marble-encased and gold-encrusted tomb inside the nearby Church of the Holy Sepulchre. During the high tourism season, visits to the Garden Tomb must be booked in advance. The view of the Holy Land first articulated by nineteenth-century Christian explorers like Edward Robinson and

Charles Warren—to see things as they might have looked in the Bible—is still in high demand.

One might expect Israel's thriving pilgrimage tourism industry to have responded to that demand by opening some trails for foreign visitors. All over the country, trails access remote sites that lie outside the itineraries of most big-bus tour packages, but which are well-known to people who study the Bible. The Valley of Elah, for example, is described in the Bible as the place where David fought his famous battle with the giant Goliath. It is a well-known site, near Beit Shemesh in the hills below the Jerusalem mountains, at the junction of Highways 38 and 375. The area is scenic and frequented by local hikers; trails marked in blue, red, black, and green, as well as the Israel National Trail, zigzag and intersect around the immediate vicinity. Some tour groups do stop next to the highway to take a quick look, but few of the tourists onboard the buses have any idea that walking around the area is even possible. Most foreign visitors to the Valley of Elah are never given the chance to take a short trail down to the dry watercourse and perhaps pick up a smooth stone; instead, they see the site from the road and vanish in a puff of diesel exhaust.

As noted at the beginning of this book, Israel's trail network originally took shape as a Jewish and Hebrew-language space, and for most of its history, no serious efforts took place to open it up to non-Israelis. The pioneer generation was blind to the possibility that anyone might desire Palestine, or the Holy Land, in any way resembling their own desire for the Land of Israel. The Israelis who envisioned and marked the trail network, and who inherited the pioneer outlook, never assumed that outsiders would have any interest in "walking the Land." Ori Dvir, with his translated books, might have been an exception; one of his principles while planning Shvil Israel was that the trail should be accessible for foreign hikers. In 1995, the Survey of Israel printed a special English-language edition of the Eilat Mountains simun shvilim map.[2] That map, however, was not publicized and was never reprinted. But even upon the completion of the Israel National Trail, Dvir and the ITC never capitalized on international backpackers' interest in such a route, or translated more trail maps, or worked with the Israeli Ministry of Tourism to promote trails for foreign visitors.

When a trail designed for tourists finally did take shape in the late 2000s, the ITC, SPNI, and the Ministry of Tourism had nothing to do with it. The Jesus Trail began as a grassroots initiative at the hands of Israeli and American tourism entrepreneurs. As a new source of supply for several tourism demands that had gone largely unanswered in Israel—frameworks for independent travel, meditative pilgrimage experiences, and community-based tourism projects, to name a few—the Jesus Trail attracted international press coverage and became popular around the world. After it became successful on its own, and an established fact, the SPNI supported the project and incorporated it into the countrywide trail network as a specially marked medium-distance trail. In the end, the Jesus Trail became the model for a new series of regional trails and put Israeli hiking on the international map in a way Shvil Israel never did.

In 2007, Maoz Inon, an Israeli entrepreneur who operated a guesthouse in Nazareth's Old City, and David Landis, an American who coordinated educational travel programs in Israel and the West Bank, began working together to map a route across the Galilee that connected important sites in the life of Jesus as described in the Gospels. Both had hiked Shvil Israel and other popular long-distance trails around the world, and they understood how pilgrimage routes like the Camino de Santiago in Spain had been transformed into modern tourism projects for independent travelers. Both were also interested in how trails could offer tourists meaningful personal experiences and also economically benefit less-visited rural areas that lay outside mainstream tourism frameworks. They began planning a trail that would offer access to beautiful and lesser-known Christian sites located in Arab villages across the Galilee.[3]

The city of Nazareth and the archaeological site of Capernaum near the Sea of Galilee were logical endpoints because they were important to Christian travelers and already popular tourist destinations. Between them lay a number of Christian holy sites, historical and cultural sites, and mountain peaks that overlooked whole sections of the Galilee. Connecting such sites, however, presented several challenges. The first had to do with the Arab settlements in the region that received little financial support from the Israeli government: lack of funding for public services had resulted in huge trash dumps on the outskirts of towns and villages. Another was that Nazareth and Capernaum were about sixty kilometers apart, which meant that hikers would need overnight accommodations. The type of lodging hikers and backpackers would need—inexpensive rooms in the small towns and villages across the Galilee—could be found in a few Jewish kibbutzim and moshavim but not in the Arab villages along the way. Creating the trail, then, involved not only finding a viable contiguous walking route, but partnering with Arab communities to develop infrastructure for independent travelers.

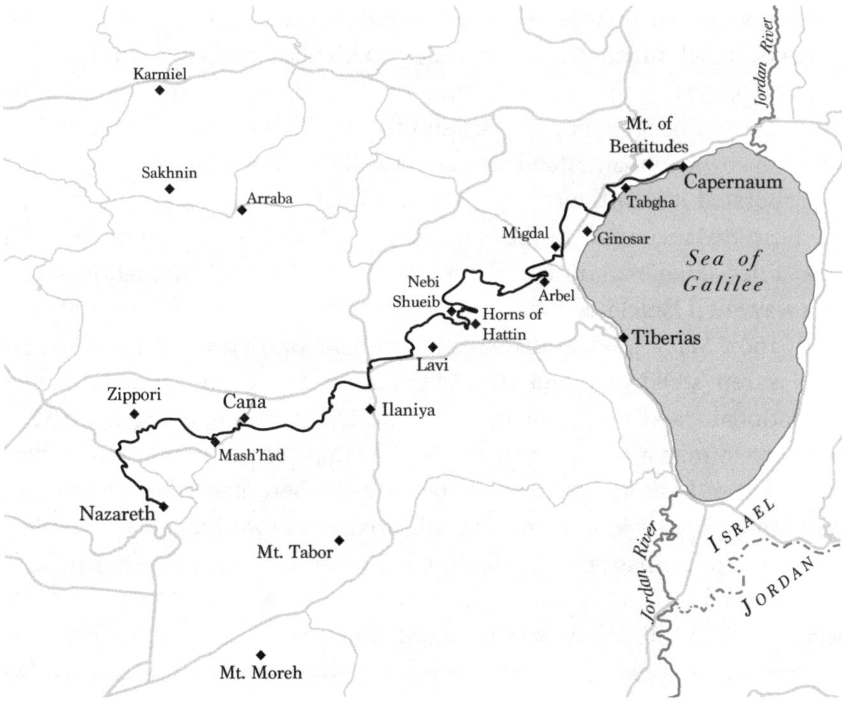

Map 6.1. Route of the Jesus Trail.

The Jesus Trail's sixty-five-kilometer route was finalized in 2008. It began in Nazareth, near the Basilica of the Annunciation, and then traveled north to Tzippori, which was the region's economic and cultural center during Jesus's time and whose well-preserved ruins lay within an Israeli national park. The trail then ran east to Kafr Kana, or the village of Cana, described in the Gospels as the site of Jesus's first miracle. From there, the trail crossed open countryside and JNF forests to Lavi, a kibbutz near the Horns of Hattin. The trail traversed the peaks where Saladin defeated the Crusader forces in the twelfth century and then visited the Druze shrine of Nebi Shu'eib. Then it continued east through the ruins of the depopulated Arab village of Hittin before cresting Mount Arbel and descending its vertical cliffs with the aid of ladder rungs driven into the limestone. From the Ginosar Valley, the trail followed the northwestern shore of the Sea of Galilee to visit a number of Christian holy sites and finally ended at Capernaum, the site described in the Gospels as the hometown of the Apostle Peter.[4]

Some of the Jesus Trail's route followed unmarked paths, and some of it followed existing ITC trails. The unmarked portions, of course, needed to be marked so that tourists could find their way. All of the route needed to be mapped in languages other than Hebrew. Landis created electronic resources using GPS and Google Earth, built a website, and made all of the data accessible for free. Inon offered GPS navigation systems to guests at his hostel and worked with residents of Arab villages along the trail to create informal lodging and meal options in local homes.[5] Similar frameworks had already taken shape along Shvil Israel, where "trail angels" offered all sorts of free or inexpensive lodging, transport, and resupply services for long-distance hikers. Meanwhile, Landis and Inon recruited volunteer crews to clean up the areas around the trail.[6]

The Jesus Trail was inaugurated in the spring of 2008 and quickly began to attract international attention.[7] For the first time, foreign tourists began traveling to Israel in significant numbers solely for the purpose of hiking. As the ITC became aware of the trail planners' desire to spur economic development and environmental preservation in the frameworks of "responsible tourism" and "leave no trace," its new chairman, Moti Ben-Shitrit, began exploring the possibility of incorporating the Jesus Trail into the marked and mapped network.[8] In 2009, ITC waymarking personnel began marking the route ahead of Pope Benedict XVI's visit to the country later that year.[9] The ITC had no plan for producing English-language maps for the Jesus Trail but treated it as a pilot for similar future projects, giving it a special white-orange-white blaze that denoted long themed and regional trails.[10]

In April 2010, Landis and his partner Anna Dintaman published the first Jesus Trail guidebook, which answered the need for printed maps. By then, thousands of foreign visitors were hiking the trail each year. By 2012, when the New York Times published a long profile on the Jesus Trail, the route was developed in the way Inon and Landis had envisioned from the start: its entire route was marked; a large amount of information was available in English in the form of printed guides and online materials; and guesthouses and restaurants had sprung up in the Arab villages along the trail's route.[11] The trail's contribution to an international awareness of Israeli hiking, however, reached a high point later in 2012, when Backpacker sent a writer to hike the trail and published the magazine's longest-ever profile of a trail outside the United States.[12]

The Jesus Trail appeared during an efflorescence of waymarking initiatives that developed outside the framework of the simun shvilim project during the late 2000s. Because it had been created with a high degree of forethought, and because its creators actively sought the participation of the ITC in marking and mapping its route, the Jesus Trail was successfully integrated into the countrywide network and even served as a model for the network's future development. In 2011, the ITC inaugurated another orange-blazed regional trail: a one-hundred-fifty-kilometer route called Shvil Emek ha-Ma'ayanot, or the "Valley of the Springs Trail," along the base of Mount Gilboa on the eastern end of the Jezreel Valley. Dvir, who was still writing monthly trail news articles, categorized the new trail alongside the Israel National Trail, the Golan Trail, and the Jesus Trail, and hinted that other themed, long-distance trails were in the planning stages.[13]

Not everyone supported the Jesus Trail in the way Dvir, the ITC, and the SPNI did. In 2011, the Israeli Ministry of Tourism inaugurated its own hiking trail across the Galilee called the Gospel Trail. While the Ministry of Tourism made no official mention of the Jesus Trail, it was clear that the government project, which cost three million shekels, was designed to compete with the grassroots initiative. The Gospel Trail began in Nazareth and ended in Capernaum, exactly as the Jesus Trail did. Rather than visit Arab communities in the Galilee, however, it stayed almost completely in JNF forests and offered no practical lodging options for hikers. Since Christian holy places were mostly located in Arab towns and villages, the Gospel Trail only featured such sites at the very end, where it paralleled the Jesus Trail's route along the shore of the Sea of Galilee. The JNF sought no assistance from the ITC or SPNI and departed from established waymarking practices by placing 150 steel-reinforced stone cairns along the trail. The Ministry of Tourism published maps that showed the route of the Gospel Trail along with every single ITC trail except one. The route of the Jesus Trail was deleted.[14]

Today, almost all of the stone cairns originally erected along the length of the Gospel Trail have been vandalized or destroyed, and the entire effort has been largely forgotten. The Gospel Trail failed because at its core, it was more a political project than a hiking trail. Given the trail's avoidance of Arab communities, the Gospel Trail was understood by most observers at the time as an attempt to undermine the Jesus Trail and its effort to boost Arab communities' tourism economies. Inon concluded as much on the day the Gospel Trail was opened, stating that in the future, the Ministry of Tourism needed to work on behalf of, and not against, the residents of the

Galilee.[15] In the end, local hikers took little notice of the Gospel Trail, and the Jesus Trail continued to grow.

"Pirate Trails" and Short-Lived "National Trails" in the West Bank

Throughout most of the 1990s and the 2000s, the simun shvilim project had left only a marginal imprint on the West Bank, with the exception of the northern Judean Desert and the Jordan River Valley. Because of safety concerns that had arisen during the Intifadas, and the overall question of the territory's political future, the ITC did not invest the same amount of time and resources in the central areas of the West Bank as it had in other parts of the country. By the late 2000s, when the security situation had stabilized and Israeli withdrawal from the West Bank seemed unlikely in the near future, ITC waymarking personnel found that Jewish settlers had begun blazing their own trails. In 2009, one of the staff members from the SPNI's Ofra Field School, which was located in a large Jewish settlement in the mountains north of Ramallah, wrote in a regional newspaper that "pirate trails"—unofficially marked trails that projected Israeli presence in the West Bank through the use of counterfeit three-striped blazes—had gone out of control, and now threatened hiker safety by undermining the reliability of the established waymarking system:

> A familiar and well-known phenomenon in our area, the placing of trail markings in the watercourses of the Binyamin region, has recently become unbearable. Such marking is done unprofessionally and without any long-term consideration. In the coming days, we are going to mark established trails, and also add some new ones. Trails that are marked by local people constitute nothing but damage. The importance of waymarking by the Israel Trails Committee exists on several levels. First, the marking is performed by professional staff who are experts in their field and know how to do their job. Second, this type of marking is placed on the simun shvilim maps that are sold all over the country, and which even appear on the internet, and have exposure on the national level, not just on the local level, which is not the case with "pirate marking." Third, professional marking is undertaken in an attempt to harm nature as little as possible.[16]

Throughout the history of simun shvilim, individuals and groups had made their own ad hoc additions to the country's trail network, and they exhibited varying degrees of skill and professionalism. Ori Dvir wrote that during the early days of the waymarking project, there were few rules regarding who was allowed to mark trails, so people would occasionally

Figure 6.1. "Pirate" trail blaze painted by Israeli settlers, Wadi al-Makoch, West Bank, 2012. *Photograph by author.*

paint giant arrows on rocks simply to give directions for a one-time hike.[17] Sometimes more systematic marks appeared that were modeled after the three-striped blazes characteristic of the simun shvilim project. (See fig. 6.1.) Dvir gives the example of a trail in the Galilee marked with blazes that looked normal, except for the fact that the outer stripes were black instead of white.[18] Such occurrences were rare, though, and do not seem to have slowed down larger waymarking efforts in any way. In the West Bank at the beginning of the twenty-first century, though, informally marked trails had indeed become a problem for all the reasons cited by the author of the article.

By then, the ITC was prepared to address "pirate trails" in a systematic way. Under Ben-Shitrit's leadership, the committee had moved away from recruiting large numbers of volunteers to mark trails and instead hired a full-time team of four or five people who traveled the country year-round to mark and renew trails, moving north and south according to the seasons.[19] While this burdened the ITC's small budget, it was viewed as a worthy investment because it recentralized the management of the countrywide trail network, made the process of trail maintenance and renewal more thorough and efficient, and guaranteed that marking methods across the country would occur according to a single standard. Eliminating "pirate trails," then, was just one part of the overall standardization process. When the waymarking crew found trails in the field that did not appear on maps, they used hammers to break the blazes from the rocks on which they had been painted.

One of the most prominent "pirate trails" painted by Israeli settlers in the West Bank was a route known as Shvil Israel ha-Alternativi, or the "Alternative Israel National Trail," which sought to realize on the ground the old vision of a long-distance hiking route across Judea and Samaria. The organizers' plan was to start at Kfar Tavor—a point on Shvil Israel that lay straight north of the Samarian highlands—and create a new trail that ran straight south, crossed the entire West Bank, and rejoined the main Israel National Trail near Arad in the northern Negev. The first section was marked with green-white-blue blazes, almost identical to those of the Golan Trail, and inaugurated during Passover 2009. The trail's organizer, who hailed from the large settlement of Itamar, described the trail as an attempt to incorporate Judea and Samaria into Israel.[20] The right-wing *Arutz Sheva* news outlet described the trail project as a means of transforming Eretz Israel back into its original condition as the Jewish homeland: "The trail passes foundational sites in the history of the people of Israel, and in the process of waymarking, Hebrew names will be restored to sites that received Arabic names."[21] The project was short-lived after that and never completed.

Another ideologically motivated waymarking project that occurred in the West Bank, outside the framework of simun shvilim, was the Palestine National Trail. Initiated in 2011 by the Israeli-Palestinian organization Combatants for Peace, the trail began in the southern West Bank and was designed to be a Palestinian competitor to Shvil Israel. It aimed to follow essentially the same route as the southern portion of the trail planned by the West Bank settlers. Starting just across the Green Line from the Israeli town of Meitar, activists painted blazes in the form of small Palestinian flags on boulders along a fifteen-kilometer route that ended near Hebron. The influence of simun shvilim on the project was clear: the flags' stripes were oriented vertically, and the markings were almost exactly the size of those that appeared along Israeli trails.[22] Like the Alternative Israel National

Trail, however, the Palestine National Trail faded into obscurity after the first section was marked.

A more serious plan for marked walking routes in the West Bank was partially revealed in February 2010, when Prime Minister Benjamin Netanyahu spoke at the Herzliya Conference—an annual forum in which academics, military leaders, and government officials met to discuss pressing issues facing Israel. The prime minister's keynote address, which had become something of a tradition at the conference, had served in the past as a setting in which to deliver landmark policy speeches. As mentioned in the introduction to this book, Netanyahu's address in 2010 surprised his audience. During a time when issues like the Iranian nuclear threat dominated the public discourse, Netanyahu stood behind the podium at the Interdisciplinary Center (IDC) Herzliya and delivered a speech arguing that Israel's long-term security depended on the ability of its youth to know and love the Land of Israel. He then unveiled a broad plan to renovate historical sites across the country and to establish two new long-distance trails that could supplement Shvil Israel by accessing places the de facto national trail did not visit, and perhaps more importantly, by crossing "Judea and Samaria."[23]

Throughout the history of the waymarking project, the Israeli government was aware of simun shvilim and had tacitly supported it but never tried to dictate its course. Most of its involvement in waymarking had occurred at the hands of the IDF, which constituted the most significant Israeli presence on the country's frontiers during the years immediately following independence. While the army's support for simun shvilim had been crucial in the formation of the Ein Gedi and Eilat Mountains trail networks, the Israeli military had always followed the lead of the civilian trail markers in charge of the overall project. The only time the IDF specifically requested that trails be marked in a given area was in the Golan Heights in 1973, but even then, Dvir made all of the major decisions while the army supported the effort with equipment and manpower. One could argue that the simun shvilim project was successful precisely because the government was not involved; rather than mark travel routes according to administrative fiat, Dvir generally allowed the character of Israeli trails to be shaped by the needs and demands of Israeli hikers. The trails he marked also reflected his own curiosity and creativity; they were scenic, interesting, and enjoyable to walk.

Even during the 1980s, when discussions regarding the planning of Shvil Israel took on a decidedly political character and elected officials began weighing in on whether the route should enter the West Bank, the Israeli government stayed out of the debate. After all, despite the degree to which Israelis viewed the trail network as a national project, simun shvilim had never officially received government funding. The support it received from the military had always come informally and never in the form of finances. Similarly, SPNI support for the project was essentially limited to allowing the ITC to use its existing resources, including personnel at its field schools and office space at its headquarters in Tel Aviv. The ITC was only funded by the SPNI in the sense that simun shvilim maps were sold at SPNI bookstores in Tel Aviv, Jerusalem, and Haifa, and the proceeds from the maps were channeled back into marking and maintaining trails.[24] Otherwise, as mentioned, Dvir never drew a salary for his waymarking work as the architect of Israel's trail network and was famous for using his own car—an underpowered Peugeot 305—to travel to remote sites in the field.[25] Despite its close relationships with the IDF, the SPNI, and the Nature Reserves Authority, the ITC was essentially autonomous.

In his speech, Netanyahu does not call for alterations to the route of Shvil Israel, for the simun shvilim project to take a different direction, or for the government to begin funding waymarking. Instead, he calls for the government to make its own foray into the realm of trail planning on the grounds that connections between Jewish youth and Eretz Israel comprise the ultimate security issue and that such connections are not being sustained through currently existing frameworks. Netanyahu describes the relationship between youth and the Land of Israel in existential terms: "Our existence depends not only on a weapons system, our military strength, the strength of our economy, our innovation, our exports, or on all these forces that are indeed essential. It depends, first and foremost, on the knowledge and national sentiment we as parents bestow on our children, and as a state to its education system."[26]

Farther on in the speech, Netanyahu makes a more explicit connection between hiking trails and the future of the country. Young men and women who have traveled extensively across Israel, he argues, are more motivated to serve in the military. He cites Shvil Israel as a prime example of the sort of experience that connects youth with the Land of Israel and mentions the trail's success in bringing large numbers of Israelis of all ages into contact with the beautiful landscapes of the country. He then states, however, that Shvil Israel alone is not enough and that Israelis do not have adequate access to the profusion of important national sites scattered across the country:

> According to the plan I will present to the government, we will, within five years, inaugurate two additional trails alongside the Israel National Trail. One is the historic Land of Israel Trail, which will connect dozens of ancient archaeological sites. Within our tiny piece of land, there are 30,000 ancient sites, 800 of which have clear national importance. Sadly, only 50 of those sites are open to the public, and even they are not in great shape. That is going to change on a huge scale. The second trail will be the "Israel Experience" trail. This trail will include the treasures of our country, and will serve as a living Land of Israel museum. It will connect between dozens of stops celebrating the history of the Jewish Yishuv.[27]

The following month, when Netanyahu released maps of the trails he envisioned, it became clear that in his view, Shvil Israel's shortcoming was that it did not enter the West Bank, Jerusalem, or the Golan Heights. The new trails were not two simple routes but instead a sort of ladder-shaped system that knitted all Israeli-controlled territory together, calling to mind the pioneer idea of the "body of the Land of Israel." Parts of the system's branching structure more or less followed sections of Shvil Israel, but other parts cut east into the Golan Heights, pushed into the southern West Bank, and cut through the Jordan River Valley. East-west trails connected the main north-south lines, and one even ran to the very edge of the Gaza Strip.

Overall, the system was confusing, and the response from hikers was underwhelming. After the Office of the Prime Minister released the map of the trails, the government made no serious moves to begin developing them. Most subsequent discussions focused on the constellation of heritage sites across pre-1967 Israel and the West Bank that were slated to be renovated within the plan. Perhaps if hikers had voiced overwhelming support, something more substantive would have taken place. However, even for hikers who sympathized with Netanyahu's overall goals for reasserting old Zionist ideas of national identity and connectedness to land, lines on a map were not enough. Trails in Israel remained closely bound to national politics, but hikers were not simply foot soldiers for political causes. Dvir had known that even if a line on a map appealed politically to Israeli hikers, they would not walk that line unless it enabled them to know and experience the beauty of the Land of Israel, as they had been taught to understand it.

Palestinian Hiking: The Nativity Trail

The three initiatives above—the Alternative Israel National Trail, the Palestine National Trail, and Netanyahu's heritage and historical trails—all involve long, north-south trails across the West Bank. Had they been completed, they would have been marked mostly in the Israeli-controlled Area C as defined by the Oslo Accords, which covers more than 70 percent of the West Bank, and includes nearly all of the territory's rural spaces. On maps of the Oslo-based administrative divisions in the West Bank, Areas A and B appear as an archipelago of small Palestinian islands within a sea of Israeli-controlled territory. While Israelis are forbidden by Israeli law from entering Area A, they can move freely within Area C and can hike through most of the West Bank without difficulty. It should not be surprising, then, that all three initiatives, including the Palestine National Trail, were largely undertaken by Israelis.[28]

Palestinians, on the other hand, face numerous barriers to movement within Area C and therefore have difficulty traveling long distances across the West Bank on roads and highways. For all practical purposes, the network of Israeli roads that crisscrosses the West Bank, and which is only for use by Israeli citizens, constitutes a system of barriers that can only be crossed at certain points. On the roads that Palestinians are able to use, IDF checkpoints make travel difficult, and the number of checkpoints rises and falls according to changes in the overall security situation. Israeli settlements, military bases, firing zones, and nature reserves add to the number of obstacles that limit Palestinian movement through the West Bank. In many places, the most reliable travel routes are unpaved roads. Footpaths represent viable transportation routes in some areas, but many of the trails marked through the simun shvilim project, or through the efforts of Jewish settlers to create "pirate trails," are traveled by armed Israelis, so Palestinians generally avoid them.[29] Travel on foot generally occurs over shorter distances along unmarked paths.

However, these relatively recent limitations on movement belie venerated Palestinian traditions of long-distance walking. In his book *Palestinian Walks*, Raja Shehadeh describes the practice of sarha, in which young men take a break from everyday life in order to regain perspective and familiarize themselves with their country. In *A Rift in Time: Travels with My Ottoman Uncle*, Shehadeh follows his uncle's early twentieth-century journey across Palestine and other parts of the borderless Ottoman Empire. Both works show how Palestinians once ranged far and wide across the country and the region and suggest that walking can serve as a tool for reclaiming lost heritage and building national identity. Shehadeh is not alone; over the past two decades, a number of Palestinian political activists, environmental activists,

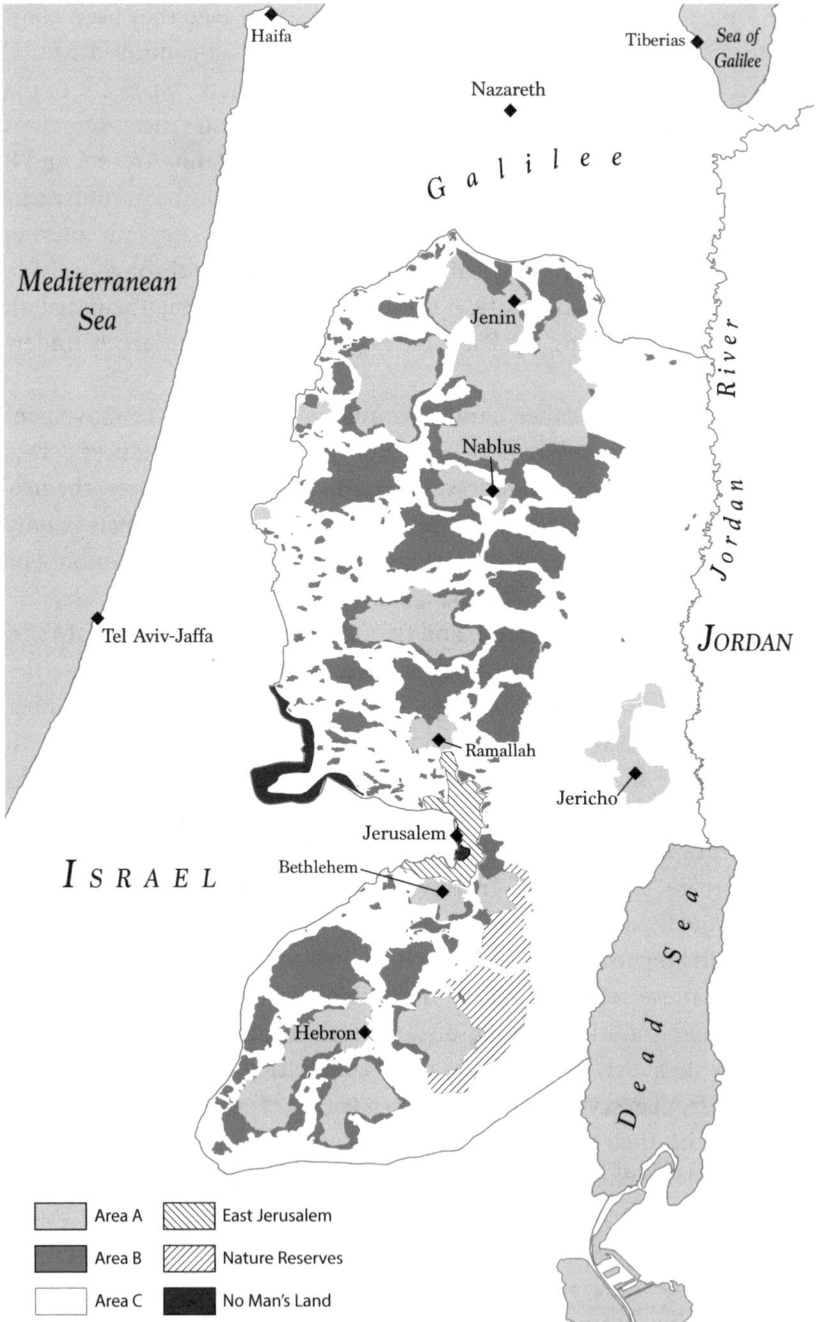

Map 6.2. West Bank Areas A, B, and C.

and tourism entrepreneurs have worked to create walking routes that connect Palestinians with their history and homeland. Palestinian walking has a character all its own; as Shehadeh describes, the practice of sarha is less goal-oriented than Western-style hiking. It follows that Palestinian trail infrastructure would be likely to develop along different lines than Israeli trail infrastructure.

On December 18, 1999, a group of eleven hikers made their way into Bethlehem and arrived in Manger Square just as PA President Yasser Arafat lit the Christmas tree to begin the city's holiday festivities. The group, composed of Americans, Europeans, and Palestinians, had begun ten days earlier in the city of Nazareth and had walked one hundred sixty kilometers across Israel and the West Bank. The hikers' journey had taken them through the Jezreel Valley, across the mountains of the northern West Bank, into the Jordan River Valley, and through the Judean Desert. Along the way, they had lodged and eaten their meals in Palestinian homes and Bedouin tents. The trail they had followed was composed in part of Israeli-marked trails but was largely unmarked; instead of walking according to signs or symbols painted upon stones, they took their cues from the local Palestinian guides who led them and explained not only different sites' natural and historical significance, but also their significance in relation to the Israeli occupation of the West Bank.[30]

Such was the inaugural thru-hike of the Nativity Trail, a long-distance walking route created with the goal of fostering new frameworks for Holy Land tourism and offering visitors to the country a view of the land of Palestine. The trail was organized within the framework of the Bethlehem 2000 project, an initiative organized in 1996 by the PA in an effort to capitalize economically and politically on the prominence of the Holy Land for Christian tourists on the cusp of the new millennium.

After the Oslo Accords, the PA regarded tourism as an important revenue source for building a viable and independent Palestinian state and saw a window of opportunity for investing in new tourism initiatives. Pope John Paul II had declared 2000 a year of jubilee for the Catholic Church, which meant that travel through the Holy Land would bear special significance for Christian pilgrims. Bethlehem, in particular, was expected to be an important destination for foreign visitors intent on celebrating the two-thousand-year anniversary of Jesus's birth in the city where he had been born. As part of that initiative, the Nativity Trail was set up to offer the ultimate experience for Christian pilgrims: a journey that connected the hometown of Mary

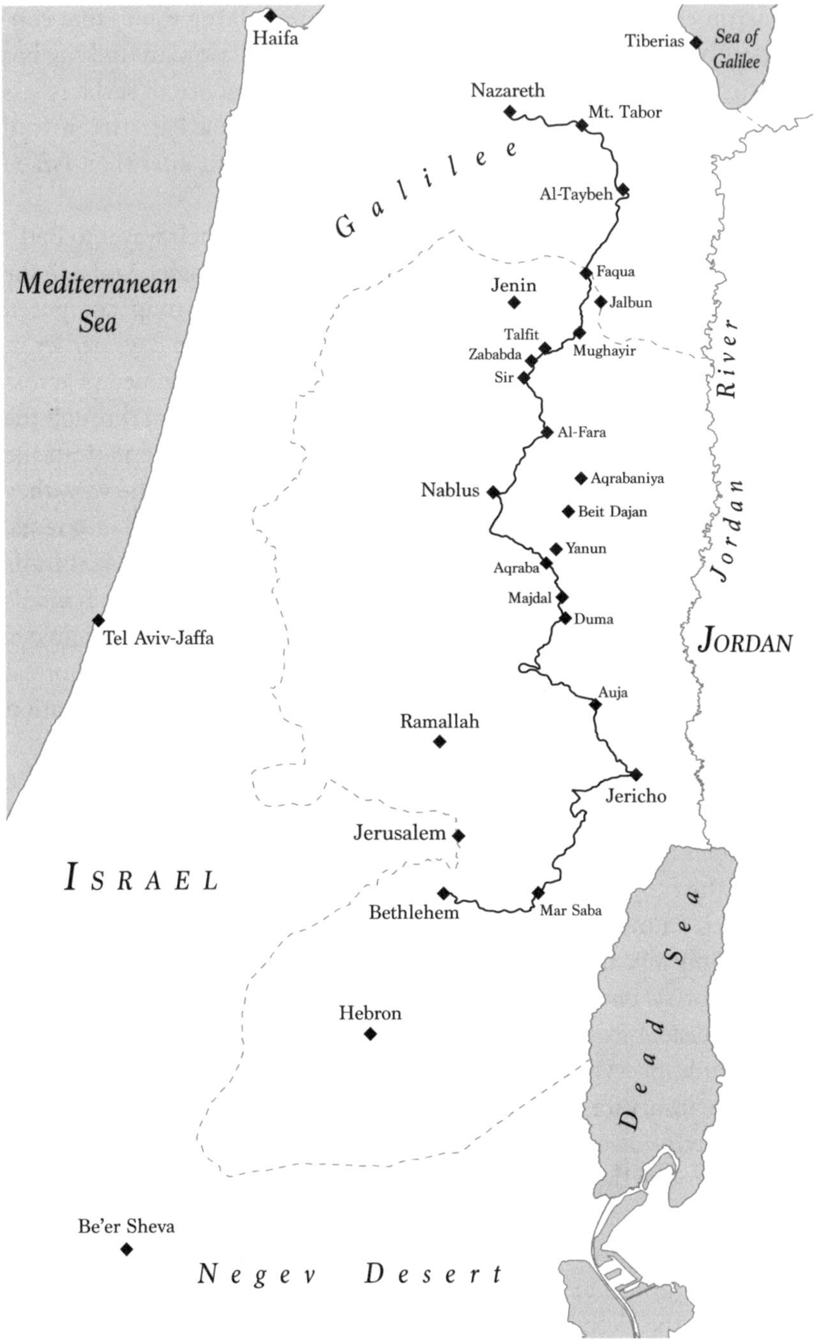

Map 6.3. Route of the Nativity Trail.

and Joseph to the birthplace of Jesus and followed in the footsteps of the Holy Family.

From its inception, the Nativity Trail was sensitive to regional instability. In the trail's early days, before the start of the Second Intifada, hikers were able to begin in Nazareth, walk south across the Jezreel Valley along marked Israeli trails, and enter the West Bank through the Highway 60 checkpoint north of Jenin. As the violence of the Second Intifada was intensifying, a guidebook that was also funded as part of the Bethlehem 2000 project went to print and was quickly condemned by Palestinian tour guides who argued that it put visitors to the area in danger.[31] In 2004, however, more tourists came to walk the trail. Within a tighter security framework, hikes had to take place entirely within the West Bank and typically began at the village of Faqu'a inside the Green Line northeast of Jenin.[32] From there, the route ran along the eastern edge of the mountains overlooking the Jordan River valley before descending into Jericho. Marked Israeli trails guided the way through the Judean Desert from the Nebi Musa shrine to the Mar Saba monastery and then the route ascended westward into Bethlehem.[33]

Rather than face the significant challenges of creating a marked Palestinian hiking trail through the parts of the West Bank under Israeli security control and try to build an infrastructure of campsites and private lodging options that would allow for independent travel, the Nativity Trail's organizers left the route unmarked and undeveloped. Visitors, therefore, relied on local guides while walking and spent their evenings staying with Palestinian families and eating home-cooked meals. In rural areas of the West Bank where residents were always on the lookout for Israeli settler encroachment, understood painted marks on the ground as signs of Israeli presence, and were uncomfortable with strangers camping out in the fields, the guide-and-homestay model was safe and sustainable.

The guide-and-homestay model was also an experiment in diversifying the Palestinian tourism economy, which at the time was centered mostly on East Jerusalem and Bethlehem. Most foreign tourists who visited those cities and their religious and cultural sites entered from Israel, used Israeli guides and bus companies, and flew in and out of the country through Tel Aviv. Often, they came only for day trips and did not spend nights in Palestinian hotels. Part of the logic of the Nativity Trail was to attract independent travelers who might not spend as much money as bus-tour participants, but who would stay for longer time periods and bring tourism income to rarely visited rural communities. Compared to traditional tourism initiatives, the supply chain of Nativity Trail tourism was much more Palestinian.

The Nativity Trail also played a national public-relations role for Palestinians by exposing tourists to the conflict and the occupation from a Palestinian point of view. According to promotional materials from the Siraj Center for Holy Land Studies, the Beit Sahour-based tourism organization that manages the project, homestays and guided tours "reveal the 'human face' of the people of Palestine that unfortunately is not often portrayed through Western media."[34] At the time of this writing, the Nativity Trail has not been enormously successful in terms of its overall number of visitors, but it has served as an important template for more ambitious and ongoing trail development projects.

Palestinian Waymarking: The Abraham Path/Masar Ibrahim

The longest unbroken corridor of movement for Palestinians in the West Bank is not a road or highway, but a three-hundred-thirty-kilometer trail called the Palestine Heritage Trail. It was initially called Masar Ibrahim al-Khalil, which translates literally from Arabic as the "Path of Abraham the Friend." It was originally born at Harvard University, where it took shape as part of a larger effort to create a walking route across the Middle East. In the summer of 2014, this author was hired by the Abraham Path Initiative (API) as a research consultant in the organization's Jerusalem field office and helped formulate a waymarking plan for the trail, which was implemented the following year. Some of the information below is firsthand, and all of it is part of a story that is still unfolding.

William Ury and Josh Weiss, the founders of the Global Negotiation Project at Harvard University, first envisioned the Abraham Path in 2004 as a long-distance walking route that would trace the cultural memory of the patriarch Abraham across the Middle East. The project initially took shape less as a hiking trail than as a long-term experiment in negotiation and peacemaking, set against the backdrop of long-running political and ethnic conflicts. Plans in the short term called for "the Path" to work toward connecting two important beginning and ending points of Abraham's journey as described in the book of Genesis: the present-day city of Urfa in southeast Turkey to the city of Be'er Sheva in Israel. Later, the idea expanded to envision extensions that would run to other places mentioned in Jewish, Christian, and Islamic versions of the Abraham story, including Egypt, Saudi Arabia, and Iraq.[35]

Over the next decade, the Abraham Path Initiative (API) became a non-profit organization, and an overall route began to take shape. Getting permission to scout and map routes, much less mark them, was difficult. In most of the Middle East, European-style hiking and backpacking were not popular practices. People who lived near planned routes often questioned the motives of foreign scouting teams who carried cameras and GPS units. Sections of walkable routes took shape in areas where the political climate allowed it and where local residents supported it. By the early 2010s, tentative routes had been mapped and hiked in southeast Turkey. In Jordan, large parts of the trail had become well-defined and could be hiked with the aid of guiding services. In Syria, a section of the trail had been inaugurated by President Bashar al-Assad and former US President Jimmy Carter.[36] In Israel, the project was met with enormous enthusiasm, but API had to tread lightly; for many of its partner organizations in Arab countries, any explicit mention of a trail connected to Israel was politically problematic. API shelved the Israeli section, knowing that it could be completed quickly when necessary.

Instead, one of the heaviest areas of initial investment was the West Bank, where the Israeli-Palestinian conflict represented an attractive target for the Global Negotiation Project, and where the Nativity Trail offered an initial template for independent travel and trail-based tourism.[37] API began working with a Palestinian tourism organization in Beit Sahour called the Siraj Center, which had played a lead role in establishing and promoting the Nativity Trail.[38] The West Bank section of the Abraham Path adopted the guide-and-homestay model that the Nativity Trail had used, and API began further articulating the idea of using hiking trails to foster economic development in rural Palestinian communities.[39] The project's Palestinian partners created a new organization, Masar Ibrahim al-Khalil (MIAK), to work full-time on the grassroots dimensions of trail development. The trail itself became known by the same name, or "Masar Ibrahim" for short. In 2014, API and MIAK received a $2,320,000 grant from the World Bank to deepen the tourism infrastructure along the planned route from Jenin to Hebron and make the Abraham Path in Palestine a full-fledged hiking trail.[40]

As of 2014, MIAK became the lead organization in developing the route, in keeping with API's overall approach of prioritizing local stakeholders and working toward local ownership of trails. API hired David Landis, mentioned previously as one of the developers of the Jesus Trail, to manage its field office in Jerusalem. Landis and the API Jerusalem staff helped manage the logistics of building a trail in Area C of the West Bank where Israel could easily stop Palestinian scouting and waymarking teams from freely operating. No formal relationship existed between Israeli organizations that operated in the West Bank (mainly the IDF and the SPNI) and the Palestinian organizations instrumental in building the Abraham Path (mainly the PA and MIAK), so the API Jerusalem office played a mediating role when necessary.

In the spring of 2015, waymarking began on sections of the Abraham Path/Masar Ibrahim. The API Jerusalem office drew up most of the waymarking standards, and MIAK drew up plans and timetables for implementing the standards in the field. Rather than mimic the Israeli system of vertically oriented three-striped blazes, the waymarking standards followed the European GR system used for blazing long routes across the continent. The horizontally oriented two-striped blazes—red and white in color—were similar enough to the Israeli system that anyone encountering them in the field would likely recognize them as signaling the presence of a hiking trail, but different enough that they would not appear to be part of the Israeli trail network or "pirate trails" masquerading as such. In this way, API and MIAK hoped to avoid erasure by the SPNI on the one hand and erasure by local Palestinians who feared the presence of Israeli settlers on the other.[41]

In the end, all three hundred thirty kilometers of the Abraham Path/Masar Ibrahim were marked, rendering the trail the longest continuous route of Palestinian movement in the West Bank, and the only such route traversing Areas A, B, and C. After 2015, trail infrastructure was maintained solely by MIAK, and based on field visits carried out most recently in 2018 and 2019, the condition of the waymarking varies widely along the route. The ongoing Israeli-Palestinian conflict, characterized most recently by frequent flareups between Israel and Hamas, has challenged the stability of the trail as a tourism project, with numbers of visitors fluctuating as tensions in the region rise and fall. After the 2020 Abraham Accords, which resulted in normalization of relations between Israel and several Arab countries, the trail became the Palestine Heritage Trail. Regardless of its name, the trail has become one rallying point in a growing culture of Palestinian hiking.

Shvil Israel Mizrach, or the "Eastern Israel National Trail"

In 2016, a group of hikers from the Kfar Etzion Field School revisited the question of whether an alternative route for the Israel National Trail could

Map 6.4. Abraham Path/Masar Ibrahim al-Khalil (renamed Palestinian Heritage Trail in 2021).

be built across the West Bank. Unlike the Alternative Israel National Trail idea attempted several years earlier, the Kfar Etzion hikers were from the mainstream Israeli hiking community. They had just completed a thru-hike of Shvil Israel and wondered whether it would be possible to undertake a similar cross-country trek that took them east of the central mountain range rather than along the coastal plain.[42] Rather than frame their project as an "alternative" to the regular trail, they sought to create a new route that would realize Ori Dvir's original idea of creating an eastern route for the Israel National Trail. Dvir's idea had aroused controversy from the outset and had been rendered moot by the beginning of the First Intifada. Now, however, more than a decade after the end of the Second Intifada, personnel from the field school began working seriously on the idea.[43]

The Kfar Etzion Field School is not officially part of the SPNI network of field schools that Yossi Feldman began at Ein Gedi. It is based in the Gush Etzion region of the West Bank, whose residents are classified internationally as Israeli settlers, but who view their own status differently because they live on land that was Jewish-owned before 1948 and conquered by Jordan during the war. In practice, the Kfar Etzion Field School works in solidarity with other settlement groups and participates in SPNI activities as well. Like all of the SPNI field schools, the Kfar Etzion school conducts environmental education programs and also organizes outdoor excursions that carry on the tradition of yedi'at ha-aretz and teach children to think of the country as the Jewish homeland.

When the director of the field school, Yaron Rosenthal, unveiled the plan in 2017, he did so in a way that sought to engage a wide segment of the Israeli public and not just political right-wingers who supported the settlement project. He appropriated the Israel National Trail brand and applied it to the Kfar Etzion trail project, referring to the new trail as the "Eastern Israel National Trail" and the original as the "Western Israel National Trail." Speaking in language that might have been used by Labor Zionist hikers before the establishment of the State of Israel, Rosenthal focused on land, not politics: "At the end of the day, our goal is for the people of Israel to know the Land of Israel. . . . We want them to love and take care of the Land of Israel."[44]

Israeli critics of the plan discounted Rosenthal's attempt to depoliticize the project. Some assailed it as the most recent attempt by Israeli settlers to extend their control over sections of the West Bank. Others pointed out that the logistics of creating, hiking, and maintaining a long-distance Israeli trail across the West Bank were impractical. Shai Yagel, who had served for several years as the simun shvilim coordinator under Moti Ben-Shitrit, argued that hiking groups would be required to carry guns along the trail and that this by itself threatened the viability of the whole project. In response to such criticisms, Rosenthal appealed to the legacy of pre-statehood Zionist hiking: "They say to me, how can you send people to hike in such a dangerous place? And I say, the groups of students who went to the Judean Desert and Masada in the 1940s and 1950s weren't endangering themselves?"[45]

Accessing the Judean Desert and Masada was just one of the perceived shortcomings of the Israel National Trail that the new trail sought to address. Echoing the slogan associated with the INT, "From Dan to Eilat," the Eastern Israel National Trail took the phrase, "From the Hermon to Arad," implying that the trail would include the Golan Trail as well. Overall, the trail was well-planned; the Kfar Etzion Field School posted a series of maps on its website that detailed every stage of the route as it split from the INT at Umm Juni, south of the Sea of Galilee, and wound its way to the city of Arad in southern Israel, where it rejoined the INT. Most of the planned route ran east of the spine of the central mountains, away from the most densely settled Palestinian areas and away from the route of the Abraham Path/Masar Ibrahim.[46]

The plan for the Eastern Israel National Trail appeared to gain sudden momentum in November 2017, when the Minister of Tourism, Yariv Levin from the Likud party, announced his ministry's support for a "Trans-Israel Trail." The goal of the project, approved by the Office of the Prime Minister, was to "establish a tourist trail along the length and breadth of Israel." Since the announcement did not mention the INT or any other existing trails, most people in Israel's hiking community assumed that the announcement amounted to approval of the Kfar Etzion plan. The budget for the new trail was a staggering ten million NIS.[47]

In the end, however, the language of the new project effectively blocked it from taking place in the West Bank. The trail was supposed to be a "tourist trail," and the inter-ministerial committee that explored the idea determined, in accordance with Yagel's criticism of the Kfar Etzion plan, that foreign hikers would be unlikely to travel through places where guns were mandatory equipment. Shortly thereafter, domestic political chaos prevented much else from taking place.[48] At the time of this writing, construction of a serious alternative to the Israel National Trail appears unlikely in the near future.

Endings: Where Israeli Trails May Go from Here

For most of the history of the simun shvilim project, the system of marking Israel's trails on the ground with colored blazes and printing them on maps as correspondingly colored lines never faced any serious competition. Before the advent of systematic waymarking in Israel, human guides and written guidebooks had been the mediators that enabled hikers to understand their surroundings and to move safely from one place to another. This system worked most of the time, but human guides were always limited by the amount of knowledge they had and by their own fragility; if a guide lost track of a known route or became incapacitated, the larger group's ability to travel safely vanished. Similarly, guidebooks were limited by the knowledge possessed by their writers and by the finite ability of verbal descriptions to accurately convey conditions in the field. Books were also heavy to carry, especially on desert treks that required hikers to haul large amounts of water in their packs. Some hikers went so far as to memorize the verbal descriptions of trails from guidebooks; other hikers sought other sources, like secondhand maps, to supplement written texts. In the Yishuv and the early days of Israeli statehood, planning a long hike was often a collaborative process in which hikers gathered and shared all the materials they could so as to render the country's little-known spaces slightly more known.

One way to understand the revolutionary nature of the simun shvilim project is to examine the way it collected, processed, and transmitted information. When Yossi Feldman set about creating a whole network of marked and mapped trails around Ein Gedi, he prepared for the endeavor in a manner similar to the way youth hikers prepared for long trips on foot across the Negev. He began with his own significant body of knowledge on desert trails, as well as the yedi'at ha-aretz texts and topographical maps of various sorts that were available to him at the Ein Gedi Field School, and then convened a wide group of experts who could help him fill the gaps in his knowledge. Hillel Birger, with his extensive exposure to trail networks in Europe, his personal library of books on topography and navigation, and his ability to read such texts in five different languages, was one such expert. Tzion Sheetrug, who had access to the Survey of Israel's considerable resources, and who also had a unique set of skills that enabled him to collect topographic data in the field, was another. Altogether, the group of people Feldman assembled possessed a total body of knowledge that could be immensely useful to hikers, but which was too large to fit in any guidebook.

Instead of trying to translate this knowledge into the Hebrew language and compile it all within a written text, Feldman translated it into the simpler language of simun shvilim and wrote it directly onto the ground. Because that language possessed only a few words, which took the form of differently colored and differently shaped blazes, it stripped away any information that was not directly related to navigation. The blazes communicated simple messages: the existence of a trail, the change of a trail's direction, and the intersection of one trail with another. Since the land itself was the surface upon which the blazes were written, no verbal descriptions of the Land were necessary. Statements like, "the trail turns left at the white rock," then, were replaced by the trail itself, the white rock itself, and the painted mark signaling the turn. The language of simun shvilim was elegant and intuitive, and once a hiker learned it, the land with its markings became its own map and guidebook.

Printed maps, of course, remained necessary. If the system worked properly, and the markings had not been obscured or erased, then hikers would be able to walk without maps, as long as they knew the destinations of their chosen trails when they set out. If there was a problem with the markings, or if a hiker encountered another trail and wanted to know where it led, or if a hiker had an accident and needed to find the shortest route back to civilization, then the printed map showing the whole of the surrounding area was essential. It served as an index to the larger one-to-one scale relief map upon whose surface the hiker walked. Between the colored markings that appeared on the ground and the colored markings that appeared on the map, the hiker had all the information necessary for safely walking across even the most difficult-to-traverse parts of the country. The additional data often contained in guidebooks—such as the subtle difference between two species of acacia trees or the historical provenance of a particular ruin—could be learned at home but could also be useful in the field. Eventually, simun shvilim maps began carrying such information on their reverse sides.

For most of the history of systematic waymarking in Israel, nothing else could compete with the simun shvilim system that Birger adapted from European systems and which Feldman applied on a large scale to the face of Eretz Israel. The durability and simplicity of the sign upon the stone hearkened to the most tried-and-true methods of written human communication, and at the same time, the high-resolution topographical map functioned as one of the most lightweight and effective modern tools for route finding and navigation. Dvir, as the chairman of the group of experts known in the beginning as the Public Committee for Waymarking in Israel, and eventually as the Israel Trails Committee, became the broker of the body of yedi'at ha-aretz that lay at the foundation of the project. During his decades as the editor of the simun shvilim map series, as the prime decision-maker regarding which trails would be marked and which would not, and as the chief scribe responsible for marking the Land, Dvir himself came to embody the trail network, and even the Land itself, in the minds of many Israelis.

During the period between the First Intifada and the Second Intifada, two technological developments appeared that initially had subtle effects on Israel's culture of hiking but eventually gave rise to major challenges for the simun shvilim project. First, the rise of the Internet in the 1990s made it possible for people to create and print their own maps. Second, increased civilian access to GPS technologies enabled hikers to pinpoint their exact locations in the field, record their routes as they walked, and plot them onto map layers downloaded from online databases. By the 2000s, these technologies were becoming dominant among hikers and supplanting hard-copy maps and guidebooks.

By the time the Second Intifada ended, and Israel's trail planners were ready to begin creating new long-distance trails, people operating outside the ITC were able to scout their own routes and mark them electronically. The speed with which these changes took place is illustrated by the fact that as late as the 1980s, topographic maps in Israel were still considered sensitive intelligence documents. The civilians who bought the first 1:50,000-scale simun shvilim maps from the SPNI were required to state their parents' names and place of residence and show their identity cards. Less than twenty-five years later, in 2005, civilians were able to download applications like Google Earth and access recent and detailed satellite images of virtually any place on the planet. By the 2010s, the above technologies had become integrated to the point that they were common on smartphones, making it possible for almost anyone to take a hike almost anywhere in Israel spontaneously and simply rely on tools already in their pockets for navigation. At the time of this writing, a number of privately created Israeli smartphone applications offer hikers a cheap and convenient alternative to printed simun shvilim maps. The most prevalent is called Amud Anan whose meaning, "Pillar of Cloud," refers to God's divine guidance of the Israelites across the desert in the book of Exodus. Even in the smartphone era, the pioneer tradition of viewing the land metahistorically lives on.

It is difficult, then, to imagine the future of the trail network, at least in its current incarnation. Israel's trails will not disappear overnight, nor will the simun shvilim project as a whole. As printed maps become less relevant for hikers, the trail network's traditional funding source will continue to shrink, to the point that maintaining the enormous trail system will become impractical for the small group of people who make up the ITC. Unless an organization like the SPNI, or even the Israeli government, formally takes on the task of raising funds and managing the trail system, the markings may fall into disrepair, and some trails may disappear entirely. On the other hand, private organizations, regional councils, and local municipalities may pick up some of the slack and develop and maintain the trails that matter to them most. In that case, Israel's trail system may become smaller and less centralized, guided by a free market of hikers whose footsteps and personal actions determine which trails survive and which do not.

One might expect that at this moment of decision, Israeli hikers may take a turn similar to the one European hikers took after the Second World War. Most of the European trails that began as national trails for individual countries' Scouting organizations and youth movements have become international routes where tourists are welcomed. Recently, as a result of the same technological developments that have undermined the dominance of simun shvilim, international interest in Shvil Israel has grown dramatically. Individual hikers who have written trail reports, created websites, recorded GPS tracks, and posted information on Web forums have spread the word about the Israel National Trail, and Israeli hiking in general, to non-Hebrew-speaking audiences. What once rendered Israel's hiking trail network an oddity—its European-style marked routes that brought hikers not only to pastoral mountain landscapes but also across deserts, along hostile borders, and through minefields—has begun to attract adventurers who want to experience the unique challenge of walking a thousand kilometers across part of the Middle East. In 2012, the magazine National Geographic Adventure included the Israel National Trail in its list of the world's twenty greatest long-distance treks, on par with routes like the Camino de Santiago in Spain and the Appalachian Trail in the United States.[49]

At that time, Israel's culture of hiking was not ready to capitalize on such publicity. Neither the ITC, nor other organizations connected to trail development, like the SPNI or JNF, made any serious moves to market trails to foreign tourists. The Jesus Trail had represented an initial opening, but again, it began as a private project and was only incorporated into the trail system once it became successful. Its intentional engagement with non-Israeli and non-Jewish hikers has not spread to the rest of the trail network. The Israeli government's only effort in that direction had been Netanyahu's abortive heritage trail project and the Ministry of Tourism's failed Gospel Trail project. Even today, tourists who want to access Israel's hiking trails must do so largely on their own, either by scouring the internet for open-source information or by reaching out to individual Israeli hikers who can help them find entry points.

For now, Israel's trail system remains a national trail system: a Hebrew-speaking space where most hikers still encounter the country as the Land of Israel and as the Jewish homeland. As mentioned, few West Bank Palestinians venture onto the trails around Israeli settlements, but this is also true for Palestinian citizens of Israel. There are exceptions, of course, but they tend to prove the rule. For example, in 2020, Israeli media outlets ran a story about two Muslim Arab brothers serving in the elite Golani Brigade of the IDF. The case was remarkable for its rarity; while Druze and Bedouin men often serve in the Israeli military, Muslim Arabs do not. While part of the story involved the brothers' turn from a life of crime to a life of service, the larger story was about their entry into mainstream Israeli society. The turning point was when one of the brothers, at the suggestion of his counselor at a center for at-risk teenagers, thru-hiked the INT from Dan to Eilat. The seven-week trek marked the beginning of the young man's passage into mainstream Israeli society and set the stage for him and his brother to join an IDF combat unit.[50]

This underscores one of the key arguments in Tamar Hermann's 2019 book *Walking the Israel National Trail*—that the INT is a place where individual Israelis retreat from the country's complexities, gain a sense of solidarity with mainstream Israeli society, and remember what they imagine as simpler times.[51] This is illustrated perhaps most clearly in the real-life drama surrounding the creation of David Grossman's best-selling novel *To the End of the Land*. In 2006, Grossman's twenty-year-old son Uri was killed in the final hours of the Second Lebanon War. The country was captivated by the irony of the tragedy: Grossman, a longtime peace activist, had criticized Israel's policies during the war. In his bereavement, Grossman set out alone to hike the Israel National Trail and then used it as a powerful narrative device. In the award-winning book, which became an immediate classic of

Israeli literature, the characters experience figurative death and rebirth as they hike through iconic Israeli landscapes. In art and in life, Israel's trails are places for being and becoming Israeli.

Being and becoming, building and being built: such existential ideas were at the forefront of early Zionist hikers' minds in Palestine. As long as they still surge to the forefront of conversations about hiking in Israel, it seems unlikely that Israel's trail network will take a Europe-style turn and that its nationalist character will somehow wash away in a flood of foreign hikers. In 2019, the ITC and SPNI announced that part of the Israel National Trail's route would move eastward to access Masada for the first time.[52] Dvir had never considered such a move, and it brought the emblem of contemporary Israeli hiking closer to its early Zionist roots.

One of the clearest recent moments when the language of the halutzim reappeared in contemporary Israeli society on a large scale took place immediately after the death of Ori Dvir in 2011. During the years since Dvir had officially stepped down as the head of simun shvilim, he had maintained a strong presence in the world of waymarking. He had kept his office at the SPNI headquarters in Tel Aviv and had continued to weigh in on the decisions of the ITC. He had remained the editor of the simun shvilim map series and had kept writing his monthly columns on trails and hiking in different yedi'at ha-aretz publications. As the route of Shvil Israel was updated, and as new long trails were added to the map of the country, Dvir passed new information along to the public as he always had. Even as he battled cancer and as his health deteriorated, he remained the public face of hiking and waymarking in Israel. By virtue of his steady stream of writings and broadcasts, which flowed continuously for more than four decades, Dvir had become an Israeli institution that people took for granted. When he died at the age of eighty on July 2, 2011, Israelis spoke as though part of the Land of Israel had died with him.

Dvir was eulogized in every major print, broadcast, and online news outlet in the country, in language that rang with old tropes like "love for the Land of Israel," "knowledge of the Land of Israel," and so on. Leaders in the SPNI wrote about his accomplishments within the environmental movement and his familiarity with every remote corner of the country. Younger Israelis, including Stav Shaffir, who knew Dvir well, expressed deep personal admiration for the lessons he had sought to teach people as he led them on hiking trips and waymarking efforts. Shortly before she became well-known as a member of the Knesset, Shaffir wrote, "I suppose what always enchanted me about him, aside from his uncompromising knowledge of each and every trail, was that he loved the Land without hating anything."[53]

Every article made mention of simun shvilim as the defining project of Dvir's life and of the mark Dvir left upon the Land as evidence of his great love for it.[54] Many linked Dvir's identity with that of the Land of Israel, describing his body and its body as if they had merged, and become one. For example, one article referred to Dvir as "Ha-Movil ha-Artzi," or "the National Carrier," a name that normally refers to the system of pipelines that carries water throughout the country but alluded to Dvir as if he himself were a part of the infrastructure that kept the country alive.[55] The description was apt in another way; the Hebrew word *movil* also can apply to one who leads or guides others, and *artzi* literally means "of the Land."

Prime Minister Benjamin Netanyahu went even further, saying, "Like many others, I too was raised on Ori Dvir's descriptions on the radio of the beautiful corners of Eretz Israel. Ori Dvir was the beauty mark of Israel. He embodied in his life and in his actions the love of the Land."[56] Netanyahu's use of the term "beauty mark" was intentional; it referred to Dvir's long-running yedi'at ha-aretz program. Of course, the name also anthropomorphized the Land of Israel as a living being with a female body: an idea that had been transmitted through the generations directly from the early Labor Zionist halutzim.

As noted earlier in this chapter, language from the Zionist past still characterizes many conversations about trails in Israel, but not all of them. The voices of the halutzim echo forward from a particular historical moment: a time when Jewish immigrants to Palestine saw their nation-building project as a liberation movement and when they moved forward confidently in the belief that the reunion of the Jewish people with their homeland would culminate in the rebirth of a nation and, to a certain extent, the remaking of the world. More than a century later, conscious of the forces unleashed along with the realization of the pioneer dream, such as the displacement and dispossession of Palestinians after 1948, the occupation of the West Bank and Gaza after 1967, and all of the violence associated with the Israeli-Palestinian conflict, one recent project has reclaimed trails as spaces for inverting and repudiating the chief mode of interaction with land still associated with the halutzim.

In their 2018 project entitled "The Israel Trail Procession," the artists Ayelet Carmi and Meirav Heiman photograph and film the movement of

Figure 6.2. The Israel Trail Procession, 2017. *Courtesy Ayelet Carmi and Meirave Heiman.*

a group of people along a Shvil Israel that bears little resemblance to any national trail. (See fig. 6.2.)[57] Indeed, the people are not identifiable as Israelis, or as members of any particular country, nation, or time period. Clad in shimmering clothing, bearing blank, tan-colored flags that flap in the wind behind them, they stare toward featureless horizons, focusing all of their effort on remaining in motion, never coming to a standstill. But they are not walking; in fact, none of them are touching the ground. All of them are perched on precarious objects and complicated contraptions: some have wood blocks or balls bound to their feet, and they tilt and sway and edge their way forward; others balance on high stilts, or ride bicycles with welded-on perches that hold other riders high in the air; still others stand on giant wheels, using their feet and body weight to generate rolling momentum. A child rides a wagon across a field of loose rock, pushed by another child wearing roller skates. This is not a movement of confident pioneers, but a tribe of uncertain people, detached from land, making their way precariously toward an unknown future. For Israelis, the trail network remains, then, a space for articulating existential concerns: not just hopes but also anxieties.

NOTES

Introduction

1. Shafran, *The Red Rock.*
2. Collins-Kreiner and Kliot, "Why Do People Hike?"
3. Hermann, *Walking the Israel National Trail.*
4. Avraham, "Fighting Ravek."
5. Other trails in Israel have been constructed under the auspices of other organizations, such as the Jewish National Fund (JNF), the Ministry of Tourism, and local civil administrative bodies. However, these represent a relatively small number of hiking trails in Israel and, in many cases, have been incorporated into the trail system maintained by the ITC. Their construction and development, therefore, lie outside the scope of this project.
6. Amit, "Who Are the People Who Help Us Stay on the Trail?"
7. Harel, "Israelite and Roman Roads in the Judean Desert," 18–26.
8. This is the author's own conservative estimate, based on observations regarding the frequency of painted markings along Israeli trails, and also based on ITC descriptions of how often blazes should appear along a given route. A less-conservative estimate for the total number of blazes would be closer to two hundred thousand.
9. As shown throughout the book, waymarking methods and the appearance of Israeli trails evolved over time. One explanation of Israeli waymarking standards that more or less reflects the present-day character of the trail network can be found in Dvir, "How Is a Marked Trail Marked?"
10. See Borges, "On Exactitude in Science," 181.
11. Marcus, "It's Also Possible without the Cult of Signs."
12. Dvir, "The Most Marked Country in the World."
13. See Lekan, *Imagining the Nation in Nature*, 2009.
14. In terms of countrywide trail density (total length of trails in relation to country area), the top six are Luxembourg, Switzerland, Bulgaria, Germany, Austria, and the Czech Republic. These are the author's calculations, based on trail network data from European

Ramblers' Association, "Walking in Europe," and country data from United States Central Intelligence Agency, *The World Factbook*.

15. In this respect, Germany's countrywide trail network is more accurately described as a series of trail networks because they are marked by different organizations, and blazes can vary by trail or by region. The Swiss trail network, on the other hand, is marked just as uniformly as the Israeli network, although in a style that relies less on blazes and more on text-based signs placed at trail junctions.

16. Ben-Shitrit, "For the Trail Markers."

17. Barker, "Traditional Landscape and Mass Tourism in the Alps," 396. Barker points out that the first Baedeker guide to Switzerland was created in 1844, reflecting tourist demand to visit alpine areas long before the establishment of marked hiking routes.

18. Netanyahu, "Herzliya Conference."

19. Miller, "Herzliya Diary 2010."

20. Kimmerling, *Zionism and Territory*, 20.

21. Vladimir Dubnow to Simon Dubnow, October 20, 1882.

22. See, for example, Ha'am, "Truth from Eretz Israel," and Epstein, "The Hidden Question."

23. Hemda Alon, *Hiye Nakhon!*, 43–50.

24. Degani, "They Were Prepared." 12.

25. Benvenisti, "On the Question of Hiking Tragedies."

26. Tahon, *We Circled the Dead Sea on Foot*.

27. Shapira, *Land and Power*, 270.

28. Birger and Hershkowitz, *Siyurim u-Masa'ot*.

29. Kfar Etzion Field School, "Shvil Israel Mizrach."

30. World Bank, "Implementation Completion and Results Report."

31. Ha-Machanot Ha-Olim, *Bi-vritech*.

32. Shemer, "Hopa Hey."

33. Benvenisti, *Conflicts and Contradictions*, 31.

34. Ibid., 20.

35. Gurevitch and Aran, "*Al ha-Makom*."

36. Babylonian Talmud, *Ketubot* 111a.

37. Rubin, *Portraying the Land*, 1–12.

38. Scholem, letter to Franz Rosenzweig, 1926.

39. Neumann, *Land and Desire in Early Zionism*, 27.

40. Ibid., 39.

41. Peres, *Battling for Peace*, 42.

42. Aflaq, "Nationalism Is Love before Everything Else," 242.

43. Benvenisti, *Conflicts and Contradictions*, 20.

44. Ibid., 34.

1. The Construction of a Jewish Hiking Culture in Palestine, 1904–1935

1. Ben-Zvi, *Essays and Reminiscences*, 93.

2. These numbers are approximate; census data exists for 1890 and 1914. See DellaPergola, "Demographic Trends in Israel and Palestine," 11.

3. Few academic studies that deal with hiking give a specific definition of the term. One study on different types of leisure activities defines "walking," "hiking," and "backpacking" as separate categories, distinguished primarily by the duration of time involved in each, but

acknowledges even then that the setting in which each occurs, the equipment used in each, and the benefits participants seek in each, should all be considered. See Coble, et al., "Hiking Alone," 6.

4. Towner, "The Grand Tour," 300.
5. Jarvis, *Romantic Walking and Pedestrian Travel*, 14.
6. Amato, *On Foot: A History of Walking*, 43.
7. Jeffrey C. Robinson, *The Walk*, 6–7.
8. Solnit, *Wanderlust*.
9. Harris, *German Liberalism*, 6.
10. Laqueur, *Young Germany*, 5.
11. Williams, *Turning to Nature in Germany*.
12. Baden-Powell, *Scouting for Boys*, 1.
13. Williams, *Turning to Nature in Germany*, 232–34.
14. Luncz, *Guide to Eretz Israel and Syria*. Luncz also republished medieval Hebrew-language works relating to the geography of the Land, including ha-Parchi, *Kaftor va-Ferach*.
15. Ben-Yehuda had immigrated in 1881, and began his work at the Alliance-supported "trade school" when it opened in Jerusalem in 1882; other schools in Jerusalem then followed suit. See Bentwich, *Education in Israel*, 10.
16. Dror, "*National Education*," 226–27.
17. Ibid., 227.
18. Nardi, *Education in Palestine*, 18.
19. Dror, "*National Education*," 229.
20. Bar-Gal and Bar-Gal, "To Tie the Cords," 44–67.
21. Wilkomitz, "A Lecture on the Schools."
22. See Ben-David, "*Tiyul* as an Act of Consecration of Space."
23. Neumann, *Land and Desire*, 7.
24. Gordon, "People and Labor," 374.
25. Gordon, "Our Tasks Ahead," 381.
26. Gordon, "Some Observations," 377.
27. Gordon, "Letter III," 132.
28. Yosef Weitz, quoted in Neumann, *Land and Desire*, 3.
29. Avraham Shlonsky, quoted in Neumann, *Land and Desire*, 37.
30. Zerubavel, quoted in Neumann, *Land and Desire*, 56.
31. von Uexküll, *Theoretical Biology*, 1926.
32. Neumann, *Land and Desire*, x.
33. Ibid., 40.
34. Ibid., 3.
35. Ibid., 39.
36. Vilnay, "You Shall Love Your Neighbor."
37. Yael Zerubavel, *Recovered Roots*, 28.
38. Alterman, "Song of the Homeland," 29.
39. Neumann, *Land and Desire*, 89.
40. Ibid., 60.
41. Tal, *Pollution in a Promised Land*, 25–26.
42. Liebman and Don-Yehiya, *Civil Religion in Israel*, 33.
43. See Gordon, "Logic for the Future," 371–72: "And when, O Man, you will return to Nature—on that day your eyes will open, you will gaze straight into the eyes of Nature, and in its mirror you will see your own image."

44. Religious processions are understood by some anthropologists and human geographers as a primal boundary-establishing activity; see, for example, Tuan, "Sacred Space: Explorations of an Idea," 84–99.

45. One of the fundamental laws of trail formation is that if a visible or known trail appears to lead toward a desired destination, that trail constitutes the least-cost route and is the most likely to be used by travelers; see, for example, Bates, "Track Making by Man and Domestic Animals," 28. In the Israeli context, the phrase "חכם השביל מן ההולך בו," or "the trail is wiser than he who walks it," sums up the process by which the accumulated wisdom of travelers over time manifests itself in the form of a safe and efficient walking route.

46. Neumann, *Land and Desire*, 57–58.

47. Braslavi, *Along Unpaved Paths to Knowledge of the Land.*

48. For a wider sample of pioneer encounters with the Land that occurred along paths and in the course of walking across the country, see Neumann *Land and Desire*, 2, 51, 55, 56, 58, 61–64, 69, 71, 98–99.

49. Neumann, *Land and Desire*, 99.

50. See Turner, *The Forest of Symbols*, 48: "A symbol, then, is a blaze or landmark, something that connects the known with the unknown."

51. Ben-Zvi, "With the Shomer," 80–82.

52. The Reali School was a *realschule* supported by the Hilfsverein fur Deutschen Juden, a German philanthropic organization established in 1901 that, among other things, funded Jewish education in Palestine. While the Hilfsverein was more favorably disposed to Hebraism in its schools than the French Alliance Israelite Universelle, it also worked to spread German influence in Palestine. It makes sense, then, that some of the first European-style hiking clubs in the country began at the Reali School and at the Teachers' Seminary in Jerusalem, which was also affiliated with the Hilfsverein. See Halpern and Reinharz, *Zionism and the Creation of a New Society*, 198–99.

53. Hemda Alon, "The Scouting Movement," 19–36.

54. Biale, *Gershom Scholem*, 11–12.

55. Nardi, *Education in Palestine*, 177–78.

56. Oz Almog, *The Sabra*, 173–74.

57. Vilnay's iconic red-bound *Guide to Eretz Israel* was a sort of Baedeker guide to Palestine that detailed automobile and walking tours throughout the country and included maps and verbal descriptions of trips and sites. Updated editions of the guide were printed for decades in Israel. See Vilnay, *Guide to Eretz Israel*, 1935.

58. Reichman, "Evolution of Land Transportation," 55–90; see map on page 64.

59. See Troen, *Imagining Zion*, 70–71. This area of settlement became even more dense during the early 1930s: "In the five years between 1932 and 1936, on average one settlement was created per month, for a total of sixty-six."

60. Weintraub, et al., *Moshava, Kibbutz, and Moshav*, 14.

61. According to Reichman, "Evolution of Land Transportation" (79–80), the colonial experience in India led the British to oppose road construction between Arab settlements on the grounds that it would not improve the lot of subsistence farmers and would therefore be a waste of money and time. Even by 1947, most Arab towns and villages in the central mountain range remained unconnected to Palestine's network of paved roads.

62. Azaryahu and Kellerman, "Symbolic Places of National History and Revival," 101–23.

63. Chitty, *The Desert a City*, 14.

64. Reichman, "Evolution of Land Transportation," 64.

65. Harel, "Israelite and Roman Roads," 18–26. Harel identifies sixteen ancient travel routes that ascend from the Dead Sea depression to the Judean Desert highlands, mostly by way of the great wadis, including the Israelite-constructed "Ascent of the Essenes" near Ein Gedi; see map on p. 19.

66. Josephus, 387–88.

67. Edward Robinson, *Biblical Researches in Palestine*, vol. II, 240–42.

68. Warren, "Remarks on a Visit to 'Ain Jidy," (1869), 147.

69. Shapira, *Land and Power*, 270.

70. Almog, *The Sabra*, 173–74.

71. Reuveni, "Trip Around the Dead Sea."

72. Shalem, "The Journal of Natan Shalem," 147–54.

73. Ben-Yehuda, *Masada Myth*, 96.

74. Quoted in Pinchas Cohen and David Benvenisti, *Guide to Eretz Israel*, 753.

75. Eisenstadt, *Israeli Society*, 239.

76. Government of Israel, "Farewell Ceremony for the Late Minister Rehavam Ze'evi."

77. Meron Benvenisti, *Son of the Cypresses*, 22.

78. A detailed account of the creation of industrial and housing facilities on the northern end of the Dead Sea can be found in Troen, *Imagining Zion*, 128–36.

79. Three of the young men from the 1931 hike also participated in the famous 1934 circumnavigation of the Dead Sea, which is described in detail later in this chapter.

80. Azaria Alon, *Trails in the Desert*, 90–91.

81. David Benvenisti, "Hiking Tragedies," 6.

82. Meron Benvenisti, *Son of the Cypresses*, 22.

83. David Benvenisti, "Hiking Tragedies," 6.

84. This hike is described in detail in Tahon, *We Circled the Dead Sea*.

85. The route Tahon and his companions used to descend the north side of Ras Feshkha appears to have been the same that Hillel Birger and the Palmach marked in 1947 as Palestine's first hiking trail. The path's history and characteristics are discussed at length in chapter 2.

86. Tahon, *We Circled the Dead Sea*, 110.

87. As will be described in further detail in chapter 2 and chapter 3, the desert north of Masada was the site of repeated confrontations between Bedouins and Jewish hikers during the 1940s and in the early years of the state.

88. Azaria Alon, *Trails in the Desert*, 90–91. Alon writes that after 1934, few hikers visited the Judean Desert.

89. "Five Hikers in Dead Sea Desert Saved from Death," 1.

90. "On the Unsupervised Hike in the Judean Desert," 8.

91. "Less Arrogance and More Caution!," 8.

2. The Palmach and the First Marked Hiking Trail in the Middle East, 1935–1948

1. Peres, *Battling for Peace*, 42.
2. Neumann, *Land and Desire*, 5.
3. Oz Almog, *The Sabra*, 3.
4. Ibid., 3.
5. Shapira, *Land and Power*, 319.

6. Birger, "Father of Topography," interview with Yitzhak Aran, 1–2.
7. Ibid., 1.
8. Ibid., 3.
9. Birger, "History of the Azimuth," 56–59.
10. Birger, "Father of Topography," 3.
11. Ibid., 3–4.
12. Ibid., 5.
13. *Fosh* is an acronym for the Hebrew term *plugot sadeh*, which means "field companies."
14. Birger, "History of the Azimuth," 57–58.
15. Ben-Ze'ev, *Remembering Palestine in 1948*, 47–48.
16. Birger, "History of the Azimuth," 57.
17. Birger, "Father of Topography," 5.
18. Birger and Hershkowitz, *Siyurim u-Masaot.*
19. *Hish* is an acronym for the Hebrew term *cheil ha-sadeh*, or "field corps." *Palmach* is an acronym that stands for *plugot machatz*, or "strike forces."
20. Birger, "History of the Azimuth," 56.
21. Sheetrug, "Hillel Birger: Father of Topography in the Land of Israel," 22.
22. Oz Almog, 175. Almog cites an August 1939 order restricting Jewish movement in large areas of the Negev Desert and the Judean Desert. See also Mordechai Naor, "Rambling in the Land," specifically the map on p. 254 showing three areas restricted to Jewish travel from December 24, 1942. These restrictions are mentioned in "Two New Military Commanders," *Palestine Post*, December 24, 1942, p. 3: "Three 'Controlled Areas' lying between the Jordan and the Jerusalem-Nablus Road, in the hills west of Nablus, and in Southern Palestine down to the Gulf of Aqaba area are by Gazette order now placed under the control of the Military Commanders who may restrict the entry into these Areas of persons not resident or employed therein."
23. Maharshek, quoted in Oz Almog, *The Sabra*, 173.
24. Gartal, "A Cow-Path Between Mountains," 291.
25. Oz Almog, *The Sabra*, 173.
26. Azaria Alon, *Trails in the Desert*, 51.
27. Ibid., 50.
28. Ibid.
29. Ibid., 52. Nahal Tze'elim is mentioned in chapter 1 as the place where Rafi Tahon and his group ambushed a group of Bedouins and stole their water eight years earlier while hiking around the Dead Sea.
30. Ze'evi, "Notebooks of the Reconnaissance Scouts," 246.
31. Azaria Alon, *Trails in the Desert*, 18–19.
32. Greenbaum and Yisraeli, "Grenades at Ein Gedi," 54–58.
33. Ben-Yehuda, *Masada Myth*, 95.
34. Yehiam Weitz, *Palmach: Sheaves and Sword*, 29. The large-scale masa'ot of the Palmach's Plugah Gimel visited Masada every year between 1942 and 1945, with one additional trek to Mount Hermon in August 1945. See *Scouting Routes and Journeys of Plugah Gimel, Southern Album*, Palmach Museum Photo Archive, 6–12.
35. Birger, "Father of Topography," 11.
36. Oz Almog, *The Sabra*, 171–73.
37. "Jewish Hikers Disarm Robbers," 3.
38. "Hikers Arrested on Eretz-Israeli Territory," 10.

39. "Adventure on Negev Highway," 3.

40. "Jewish Hiker Killed by Arabs."

41. Birger, "Marking Ramblers' Paths in the Judean Desert," 237–38.

42. Birger, letter to Ori Dvir, in Dvir, "Requiem for a Scout," 34.

43. However, in 1934, hikers stopped instead at Kalia; Beit ha-Arava was not established until 1939.

44. *Scouting Routes and Journeys of Plugah Gimel*, Palmach Photo Archive, Tel Aviv, 6–12.

45. Gartal, "A Cow-Path Between Mountains," 289–319.

46. Robinson, *Biblical Researches*, vol. II, 248: "From the south end of the Dead Sea, this great road follows the shore below as far as to 'Ain Jidy [Ein Gedi], and then ascends the pass. Along that part of the sea we heard of no road upon the high land above."

47. Masterman, "'Ain el-Feshkhah, El-Hajar el-Asbah, and Khurbet Kumran," 162.

48. Hyrcania was known to local Arabs as Khirbet el-Mird, and the valley below it was known as al-Buqeia; these are the names that appear on British maps during the late Mandate period, such as Survey of Palestine, *Sheet 10: Jerusalem*, 1:100,000, 1942. In contemporary scholarly literature, "Hyrcania" currently prevails.

49. Some researchers of the Judean Desert have written that Qumran was an important fortified site in ancient times precisely because of its proximity to the nearest major ascent that allowed a detour around Ras Feshkha. The road through the Hyrcania Valley would have been the chief route through the northern part of the desert and would therefore merit the fortifications found not only at Hyrcania but also at the other ruined sites along the valley's length. See Cross and Milik, "Explorations in the Judean Buqe'ah," 5–17; and Stager, "Farming in the Judean Desert," 145–58. These arguments illustrate the degree of difficulty ancient and modern travelers experienced in negotiating the Feshkha barrier. They are bolstered by Dorsey, who in *The Roads and Highways of Ancient Israel* shows no ancient routes along the western Dead Sea shore between Ain Feshkha and Ein Gedi.

50. Goren, *Dead Sea Level*, 148.

51. Wilson, "The Dead Sea," 365–68. It is worth noting here, in light of Wilson's rendering of the spring as "'Ain Feshka," that "Feshkha," as the place-name is spelled throughout this book, has many spellings and pronunciations. In Arabic the spring is described as "عين ,الفشخة" but English-language sources rarely describe it as "al-Feshkha" and transliterate the place-name in different ways. The matter becomes even more complicated in Hebrew, in which veteran hikers consistently describe the spring and the headland, respectively, as "Ein Feshkha" and "Rosh Feshkha," even though the official Hebrew names now shown on maps are "Einot Tsukim" and "Rosh Tsukim," or "Springs of the Cliffs" and "Head of the Cliffs," respectively. Problematic as all of these names may be, this book strives for consistency in using "Ain Feshkha" and "Ras Feshkha," which are the correct Arabic names for the places in question before Israeli geographers renamed them following the 1967 war. A final note on this place-name: Louis Felicien de Saulcy, in *Narrative of a Journey Round the Dead Sea*, vol. II, 81–85, strives to identify Ras Feshkha with the biblical Mount Pisgah based on apparent similarities between the Arabic and ancient Hebrew names.

52. Masterman, "Observation," 155–60.

53. Ibid., 156.

54. Masterman, "'Ain el-Feshkhah," 162. Edward Robinson also used this path during his 1838 journey through Palestine after having arrived atop Ras Feshkha via the highland route from Ein Gedi. He and his party used the path to descend the mountain, and Robinson described it as being in poor condition, "the rocks and stones not being at all cleared away."

As it happens, Robinson, too, almost lost a horse when it fell from a cliff; see *Biblical Researches*, vol. 2, 250–251.

55. Robinson, *Biblical Researches*, vol. 2, 247.
56. "Another Disaster in the Dead Sea Mountains," 1.
57. David Benvenisti, "Hiking Tragedies," 6.
58. Tristram, *The Land of Israel*, 257.
59. Ibid., 261.
60. Tahon, *We Circled the Dead Sea on Foot*, 107.
61. Harel, "Israelite and Roman Roads," 19.
62. Rozen, *Judean Desert*, 25.
63. Masterman, "Observation," 159.
64. For a summary of the fluctuation of Dead Sea water levels since 1800, see Gavrieli and Oren, "The Dead Sea as a Dying Lake," 287–306.
65. Masa'ot *of Company Gimel*, 18. No photographs exist of the journey around Ras Feshkha along the water line.
66. Azaria Alon, *Trails in the Desert*, 47.
67. This is the term Birger uses in a 1959 article advocating for waymarking in Israel along the lines of the experimental initiative at Ain Feshkha. See Birger, "Marking Rambler's Paths," 237–38; see also discussion of this article in chapter 4.
68. Survey of Palestine, *Ras Feshkha 19–12*.
69. Birger, "Marking Ramblers' Paths," 238.
70. Robinson, *Biblical Researches*.
71. Azaria Alon, *Trails in the Desert*, 47.
72. Birger, "There Is Nothing New Under the Sun," 35–37.

3. The First Israeli Hiking Trails, 1949–1963

1. Oz Almog, *The Sabra*, 3.
2. Feldman, "Streams in the Desert," 67.
3. See Gavish, "Foreign Maps," 174–84.
4. Between 1949 and 1956, the government was only able to establish about a dozen new settlements between Be'er Sheva and Eilat. See Weintraub, Lissak, and Azmon, 21–22.
5. Meron Benvenisti, *Sacred Landscape*, 12–14.
6. Ben-Gurion, *Israel: A Personal History*, 367–69.
7. Revivim had been established in 1943, along with Gvulot and Beit Eshel, in the hopes that the Negev would eventually be incorporated into Jewish territory. See Troen, *Imagining Zion*, 74.
8. Feldman, "Streams in the Desert," 67–68.
9. Tchernichovsky, *Shirim*, 466.
10. Feldman, "Out of the South the Blessing Shall Come Forth," 19–21.
11. Roman, "The Lure of the Trail."
12. Har-Zion, *Chapters of a Diary*.
13. Even after Har-Zion conducted his infamous cross-border raid to kill Bedouins in revenge for his sister's murder, Moshe Dayan described Har-Zion as "the finest of our commando soldiers"; see Dayan, *Story of My Life*, 191.
14. Roman, "The Lure of the Trail."

15. Feldman, "Streams in the Desert," 67.

16. For more on the mystique of the desert for Israelis as simultaneously a dangerous space and a mythical space, see Yael Zerubavel, *Desert in a Promised Land.*

17. Yaakov Morris, *Masters of the Desert*, 75.

18. "Israeli Force Descends Upon Ein Gedi," 1.

19. Feldman, "Streams in the Desert," 67.

20. The paths taken by this tiyul and many others followed routes that had served desert travelers since antiquity; just as Palmach hikers preferred to travel along well-established paths, Israeli hikers often used trails that had ancient provenance. The path between the Dead Sea and Rosh Zohar past the fortress of Meitzad Zohar, known to the Arabs as Rujm Zuweira, was identified during the 1950s by Yochanan Aharoni as *Derekh Edom*, or the "Edom Road," which was used by ancient armies to cross the Dead Sea depression. It was the only route that featured ascents gradual enough to allow the movement of stock and heavy equipment. For more on these and other ancient ascents from the Dead Sea into the Judean mountains, see Aharoni, "Forerunners of the *Limes*"; Harel, "Israelite and Roman Roads"; and Dorsey, *Roads and Highways*, 125–26.

21. Azaria Alon describes a similar incident in his memoirs, in which one of the senior members of the SPNI was fired upon and injured by Israeli soldiers at Ein Gedi; it is likely that the incidents are one and the same. Alon, however, writes that the haphazard gunfire was celebratory and that the soldiers were elated at the sight of visitors. See Azaria Alon, *Nature and Man.*

22. Feldman, "Streams in the Desert," 68.

23. "The fervent desire to be Jews of a new, better breed led to the self-conscious imitation of Arab dress, language, and folklore. . . . The adoption of Bedouin customs and attitudes was . . . a way of stating that the Sabra had shed the skin of the Diaspora and developed a native Land of Israel mentality." Oz Almog, *The Sabra*, 188.

24. Feldman, "Streams in the Desert," 68.

25. Dayan, *Story of My Life*, 159.

26. "Pedagogical Poem," 20.

27. Feldman, "Streams in the Desert," 67.

28. Ibid.

29. Glueck, *Rivers in the Desert*, x.

30. Feldman, "Streams in the Desert," 67.

31. See Anati, *Har Karkom: The Mountain of God.*

32. Feldman, "Streams in the Desert," 67.

33. "Pedagogical Poem," 20.

34. Evenari, Shanan, and Tadmor, *The Negev: The Challenge of a Desert*, 1.

35. Morris, 54; Evenari et al., 181; "Nabatean Farm Reconstructed at Shivta," 11.

36. Ad, "Reconstruction Work Finished," 8.

37. Feige, "Identity, Ritual, and Pilgrimage."

38. "Pedagogical Poem," 20.

39. Amiti, "Going Up to Ein Gedi," 1.

40. Ben-Yehuda, *The Masada Myth*, xx.

41. Rivlit, "Economic Cooperative Established," 3.

42. Birger, "Nothing New Under the Sun," 36.

43. Oz Almog, *The Sabra*, 175–76. Almog points out that the 1950 mass trek was followed by the "March of the Two Thousand" in 1951 and that the Gadna continued to organize mass

treks annually after that. These hikes were notable, though, precisely because the desert was otherwise so infrequently visited. For smaller groups, the desert was difficult to access and dangerous to cross.

44. Avitzur, "Traffic Signs in the Desert," 3.

45. Yehuda Almog, "Popular Initiative in the Dead Sea Desert," 2. Projects included repairing the unpaved road along the shore to Ein Gedi, paving the road from the shore road to Rosh Zohar, developing the Zohar hot springs, restoring the ruins at Masada and planting a forest there (!), renovating the shore area near Ein Gedi, and improving the Dead Sea shore in general. Almog mentions nothing in the letter about hiking or trails.

46. Birger, "On the Margins," 2.

47. Birger, "Rules of Waymarking," December 15, 1957.

48. These categorizations (iconic, indexical, and symbolic) are the most famous from Peirce's complicated hierarchy of signs and are also described as mimetic, denotative, and symbolic. For more on Peirce's system and on these three categories, see Singer, "Pronouns, Persons and the Semiotic Self," 235.

49. "Hostel Being Built," 2.

50. Talmi, "Negev Scouts Rescue Lost Hikers," 7.

51. Birger, "Neglect That Is Likely to Cause Disasters," 2.

52. Search and rescue efforts often required not only foot patrols and police and army jeeps, but also airplanes; in a 1959 accident, a Piper Cub was dispatched in an attempt to locate lost hikers from above. See "Student and Teacher Disappear," 1.

53. Yehuda Almog, "To the Hikers on the Trails of the Negev," 2; see also Yehuda Almog, "To the Hikers on Dead Sea Trails," 2.

54. "Path-Marking Initiative," 4.

55. Sayar, "Crazy People" 6. This 1961 article recounts previous efforts at simun shvilim and gives more details on the 1959 initiative at Rosh Zohar.

56. "Path-Marking Initiative," 2.

57. Ibid., 2.

58. Ibid., 4.

59. "Bus Line to Ein Gedi," 4. According to the article, the lone bus to Ein Gedi left every Friday from Tel Aviv in the early hours of the morning, spent the entire day making its way to Be'er Sheva and Sdom and then took the rough unpaved road to Ein Gedi. The bus spent Shabbat at Ein Bokek and returned to Ein Gedi on Sunday morning to pick travelers up for the return voyage.

60. "Don't Say in Sdom," 6.

61. Feldman, "Streams in the Desert," 68–69. Feldman did not tell Almog how he arrived so quickly.

62. See Yael Zerubavel, *Desert in the Promised Land*, 105–8.

63. Feldman, "Streams in the Desert," 69.

64. Tal, *Pollution in a Promised Land*, 122.

65. Feldman, "Streams in the Desert," 69.

66. Ad, "Group of Armed Arabs," 1; see also "Israeli-Jordanian Border Relations," 195, which quotes Jordanian radio reports that shots were fired in response to an earlier Israeli cross-border attack. To this day a monument stands atop Mt. Yishai in memory of Barzilai. In general, hikers who died in border areas, or even on hikes across borders, have been memorialized almost as martyrs, as if the contact of their blood with the ground sanctified that portion of the Land as Jewish and Israeli. Sarah Rabinovitch's death on the Feshkha

cliffs and the deaths of Arik Megger and others en route to Petra are just a few of many examples.

67. Dayan, *Story of My Life*, 152, 160.

68. In 1951, Ta'amira Bedouin found four caves in Wadi Muraba'at southwest of Qumran that contained artifacts. In 1952, Roland de Vaux and Gerald Lankester Harding excavated the caves and found scroll fragments connected to Bar-Kochba. See Cansdale, *Qumran and the Essenes*, 8.

69. In 1952 and 1953, Khalil Iskander Shahin, the famous Bethlehem antiquities dealer, brought a series of Bar Kochba-era finds to the Rockefeller Museum in East Jerusalem and claimed that they had come from Wadi Seiyal, or Nahal Tze'elim, which runs north of Masada and comes close to the Green Line but lies wholly within Israeli territory. The claim ensured that the discoveries were not in violation of the Jordanian antiquities laws aimed at preventing unauthorized treasure hunting. Subsequent finds by Yadin and Aharoni made it clear that the fragments sold by Shahin had originally come from Nahal Hever, which crosses the Green Line and has caves on both sides. For more on this, see Eshel, "Excavations in the Judean Desert," 381–402.

70. Yadin, *Bar-Kochba*, 15; Yael Zerubavel, *Recovered Roots*, 57.

71. Yadin, *Bar-Kochba*, 46.

72. Feldman, "Out of the South," 21; Mazar, et al., *En-Gedi: The First and Second Seasons*, 13.

73. Tal, *Pollution in a Promised Land*, 122.

74. Ibid., 123. In 1997, about one-third of the SPNI's budget came from the state.

75. Feldman, "Out of the South," 21.

76. The exact date of this initiative is unclear; it is likely, however, that it took place during Sukkot 1960. None of the people involved give accurate dates in later interviews and articles. A June 1961 news article mentions that the first stage of the project began the previous winter, and a December 1961 article describes the first stage as having taken place "about a year ago." See Ad, "First Attempts at Waymarking" and Sayar, "Crazy People," 6, which describes this first stage in some detail.

77. Sayar, "Crazy People," 6.

78. Feldman, "The First Map," 34.

79. Ibid., 6.

80. Dvir, "Wide World of Travel."

81. Ad, "First Attempts."

82. Feldman, "Streams in the Desert," 69; Sayar, "Crazy People," 6.

83. Ad, "First Attempts."

84. Feldman, quoted in Ad, "First Attempts."

85. Ad, "First Attempts."

86. Ibid.

87. The problems with numbering blazes would only have become apparent after some experiments in marking longer trails and may have been noticed by Birger in the course of the 1959 Masada youth hostel project. Numbering the blazes would render the marking system inflexible over time; adding even one new blaze would require adjusting the numbers of all the remaining blazes along a given trail. Erasing painted markings on rocks can only be done effectively in the field by breaking them away with a hammer. It would also make it impossible for two crews to move from opposite ends while marking a single trail. This is obvious if one observes current Israeli waymarking methods, but would have been difficult to foresee when the networks were first being created.

88. Ad, "First Attempts."
89. Sayar, 6.
90. "6000 Ascend to Masada," 4.
91. News articles written at the time describe the total length of the trail network as more than five hundred kilometers (see Ad, "First Attempts"), but measurements made on the later-published map (made by this author using a Scalex Map Wheel measurement tool) put the network's total length at three hundred twenty kilometers.
92. It is worth noting that the Survey of Palestine also produced a series of 1:20,000-scale maps of the country; however, despite their apparently high resolution, the fifteen sheets that cover most of the Judean Desert (the southern Dead Sea area is not covered by the series) are either based entirely on aerial surveys or are actually enlarged from the 1:100,000-scale maps. See, for example, Survey of Palestine, *Ras Feshkha 19–12*, 1942.
93. Survey of Palestine, *Sheet 10: Jerusalem*, 1:100,000, 2nd ed., 1944.
94. Survey of Palestine, *Sheet 13: Dead Sea*, 1:100,000 scale, 2nd ed., 1945.
95. Survey of Palestine, *Sheet 16: Jebel Usdum*, 1:100,000 scale, 2nd ed., 1945.
96. Ze'evi, "Notebooks of the Reconnaissance Scouts," 39.
97. Feldman, "The First Map," 34.
98. Sheetrug, "Hillel Birger: Father of Topography in Eretz Israel," 22.
99. Sheetrug, interview with Shantzer.
100. Sheetrug describes this process in the interview with Shantzer. While GPS has made field triangulation almost obsolete, it works along the same principles; rather than use a compass to find the intersection of landmark bearings, a GPS receiver uses signals to find the intersection of satellite bearings.
101. Talmi, "They Flow to the Bottom of the World," 8.
102. "Ein Gedi Prepares to Bring in 35,000," 13.
103. The only known source that records the exact date is a news article written earlier in the week mentioning that a meeting for participants in the simun shvilim initiative would take place at Ein Gedi the following Shabbat. In his interview with Shantzer, Tzion Sheetrug describes the location of the event and mentions the guests who attended.
104. Sheetrug, interview with Shantzer.
105. Dvir, "*Simun Shvilim* Maps," 49. A copy of one of the original maps, in the possession of this author and shown in figure 3.2, bears a handwritten inscription stating that it belonged to "Reuven B." from Kibbutz Mishmar ha-Emek in northern Israel.

4. The Foundations of the Countrywide Trail Network, 1963–1979

1. See Neumann, *Land and Desire*, 4: "I maintain that the encounter with the Land of Israel, as it was experienced until the 1960s and 1970s—that is, until the decline of the pioneer ethos and the transition from socialism to capitalism, or from Zionism to post-Zionism—was largely the work of the *halutzim*." Similarly, Oz Almog traces the influence of the Sabra generation to the mid-1960s.
2. Dvir-Edri, "Abba: Nekudat Chen," 14.
3. Roman, "Davar Metzada," 62–65. See also Guttman, *With Masada*.
4. Roman, "The Price of Fame," 19.
5. Dvir-Edri, "Abba: Nekudat Chen," 14–15.
6. Dvir, "Wide World of Travel."

7. Dvir-Edri, "Abba: Nekudat Chen," 15.

8. Azaria Alon, letter to Dvir, quoted in Dvir, "The Simun Shvilim Project and Shvil Israel," 187.

9. "*Yedi'at ha-Aretz* Contest for Students Concludes," 3.

10. "Second Country-Wide Contest," 6.

11. Dvir was trained in topography and navigation by Birger himself in the 1950s; see Dvir, "Requiem for a Scout," 34. Dvir's travels also brought him into contact with regional governmental officials like Yehuda Almog of the Tamar Regional Council, as mentioned in the previous chapter; see "Don't Say in Sdom," 6.

12. Dvir-Edri, "Abba: Nekudat Chen," 15.

13. Dvir, *Curriculum Vitae.*

14. Biger, *Boundaries of Modern Palestine*, 14–40.

15. Deuteronomy 2:8; II Chronicles 8:17.

16. Biger, *Boundaries of Modern Palestine*, 100.

17. "Eilat Highway Will Be Inaugurated," 4.

18. See Feige, "Identity, Ritual, and Pilgrimage." Feige discusses the pilgrimage dynamics of the IES meetings at length.

19. Biger, *Boundaries of Modern Palestine*, 35.

20. Nahal Gishron, a large wadi with high rock walls and a sand-and-gravel floor, is one such corridor. It serves as a natural line of movement through rugged mountains and parallels the border for some distance on the Israeli side before curving west and crossing into Egypt. Until the recent construction of the border fence it led numerous hikers into the Sinai Peninsula.

21. "Eilat Will Absorb 50–60,000 Residents," 3.

22. "Many Hikers in Eilat," 2.

23. According to Dvir, Egged's express purpose in supporting simun shvilim was "to promote hikes and trips to Eilat." See Dvir, "This Cannot Be," 32.

24. Dayan, *Story of My Life*, 159.

25. Erez, "*Simun Shvilim* Initiative," 18.

26. Dvir, "This Cannot Be," 32.

27. Erez, "*Simun Shvilim* Initiative," 18.

28. Edelstein, "Waymarking in the Eilat Region," 180. It is worth noting that while yellow represented a departure from the methods that had been used around Ein Gedi, it was one of the colors mentioned in Birger's 1957 document outlining his waymarking system. It is also possible that yellow was considered more visible than black when marking certain trails atop dark granite rock in the Eilat Mountains. See Birger, "Rules of Trail Marking."

29. Dvir, "This Cannot Be," 32.

30. Edelstein, "Waymarking," 180.

31. Dvir, "Wide World of Travel."

32. Ben-Gurion, *Israel: A Personal History*, 675.

33. For more on Smilansky's background and education, see Nitza Ben-Ari, "Hero or Anti-Hero?," 86.

34. Smilansky, "A Land Without Wildflowers," 24.

35. Ben-Gurion, *Israel: A Personal History*, 676.

36. Tal, introduction to Smilansky, "A Land Without Wildflowers," 19.

37. Tal, *Pollution in a Promised Land*, 120.

38. Erez, "Southern Negev," 22.

39. Similar logic was in play regarding roads when Makhtesh Ramon became a nature reserve; though activists opposed the construction of a highway through the crater, the Nature Reserves Authority allowed it, arguing that otherwise, Israelis would likely cross the crater anyway and create their own vehicle tracks. See Tal, *Pollution in a Promised Land*, 184.

40. Ad, "First Attempts."

41. Dvir-Edri, "Abba: Nekudat Chen," 15.

42. Edelstein gives the figure of five hundred kilometers in "Waymarking," 180; Erez gives the figure of thirty-five trails in "Southern Negev," 22.

43. Survey of Israel, *Waymarking Map of the Eilat Region*.

44. For more on the four new trails, see Feldman, "The First Map," 34. For more on the brand-new trail, later known as *Shvil Bnei ha-Moshavot*, see Eitan Golan, "The *Bnei ha-Moshavim* Ascent," 30. The Palmach path mentioned here is the famous trail that was first described by the Bedouin who witnessed its creation as *Naqab al-Yehud*, and it is generally known today by the Hebrew name *Ma'ale ha-Palmach*.

45. Survey of Israel, *Map of Waymarking in the Judean Desert*.

46. Azaria Alon, *Trails in the Desert*, 47. While Dvir mentions this waymarking effort later in his writings on simun shvilim, he does not mention taking part in it or being involved in the planning. Feldman was likely the key initiator in marking the northern Judean Desert.

47. As mentioned in chapter 2, the road through the Hyrcania Valley had been the main travel route through this portion of the Judean Desert since antiquity because of the steep cliffs at Ras Feshkha that prevented most wagons or livestock from moving along the shoreline. Now that the detour around Ras Feshkha via Hyrcania could be safely traveled, Birger's original route was again a minor byway.

48. Attempts by this author in December 2011 to find traces of Birger's original markings, or any other signs of the 1947 waymarking effort, were inconclusive.

49. Allon, "The West Bank and Gaza," 386–89.

50. Dvir, "Notes on Desert Trails," 34.

51. Ben-Yehuda, *Masada Myth*, 91.

52. Noy and Cohen, "Introduction," 4.

53. Dvir, "The Simun Shvilim Project and Shvil Israel," 185.

54. United Nations, "Resolution 242."

55. Sachar, *A History of Israel*, 681.

56. "Syrian Minefields Discovered," 8.

57. "Woman and Youth," 28.

58. Erez, "They Went for a Hike," 8.

59. Erez, "200–500,000 Mines," 8.

60. See "Large Fire in Golan," 2.

61. "Quiet Along Lebanese and Syrian Borders," 3.

62. Dvir, "Notes on Desert Trails," 34. Chaplin had been involved in the Eilat Mountains project and helped mark trails for more than two decades.

63. Dvir-Edri, "Abba: Nekudat Chen," 10.

64. Dvir, "The Simun Shvilim Project and Shvil Israel," 185.

65. "*Simun Shvilim* in the Golan," 204.

66. SPNI Golan/Hermon Field School, *Golan and Hermon*, 1:100,000 (1971).

67. Dvir, *Where Will We Hike This Week?*

68. Dvir, "The Simun Shvilim Project and Shvil Israel," 185.

69. Ibid., 185.

70. "SPNI News," 140–41.

71. The priority for destinations accessed by the trails appears to have been "interesting landscape sites," but famous historical trails were marked as well, including *Ha-Shvil ha-Mandatori*, or the "Mandatory Trail," which had been used by the Palmach to illegally move Jewish *Aliyah Bet* immigrants who had broken out of the Atlit detention camp. See "SPNI News," 141.

72. Dvir, "Notes on Desert Trails," 34.

73. Ibid., 34. Dvir remained Chairman of the Public Committee for Trail Marking and worked for free; Chaplin took the paid position of Coordinator of Waymarking. To this day, the Chairman fulfills the role of publicizing trails and raising funds for their continued upkeep, and the Coordinator organizes marking and maintenance efforts on the ground.

74. Survey of Israel, *Map of Hikes in the Eilat Region.*

75. Shaked, "Where Are the Trails Going," 38.

76. Edward Abbey, letter to Avraham Shaked.

77. Shaked, "Where Are the Trails Going," 38.

78. Government of Israel, "Amendments to Nature Reserves."

5. Completing the Network and Creating a National Trail, 1980–2001

1. Dvir, "Wide World of Travel."

2. See Smilansky, "A Land Without Wildflowers," 23; see also Moti Ben-Shitrit, quoted in Lev, "Ori Dvir: His Life's Project": "Everyone now knows what a marked trail is. It caught on in exactly the same way as the prohibition against picking wildflowers did."

3. For purposes of clarity, the committee formerly known as the "Technical Committee" and the "Public Committee for Waymarking in Israel" are described hereafter as the "Israel Trails Committee," abbreviated "ITC," even though that name did not become official until the early 1990s. During the 1980s, it changed its name several times; in the *Ma'ariv* article quoted below, the committee is described by its short-lived title, "Committee in the Land for Waymarking" (הוועדה הארצית לסימון שבילים), which probably reflects the change in outlook following the withdrawal from the Sinai. See Achimeir, "All Trails Lead to the Judean Desert," 51.

4. Ori Dvir, "How Is a Marked Trail Marked?" 68–71.

5. Students in the tour-guiding program, as part of their degree requirements, had to spend a certain amount of time volunteering either with archaeological expeditions, or with the simun shvilim project. See Dvir-Edri, "Abba: Nekudat Chen," 12.

6. Dvir, "To Scratch a Rock and Get a Spritz," 35.

7. Achimeir, "All Trails Lead to the Judean Desert," *Ma'ariv*, October 27, 1982, 51; for map indices shown above, see Horovitz, "Survey of Israel Map Series from 1948 to the Present."

8. Ori Dvir, "*Simun Shvilim* Maps," 49.

9. Ori Dvir, "From Dan to Eilat," 10.

10. See, for example, "Television Listings," *Davar*, March 1, 1981, 12.

11. Ori Dvir, *Nekudat Chen.*

12. By the time the new Judean Desert maps were published, Dvir was famous in Israel as a television personality and regarded as a mediator between Israelis and the Land of Israel who brought the country's landscapes into hundreds of thousands of homes weekly. See Achimeir, "All Trails," 51.

13. Tamir, "Eighty-Year-Old Grandmother," *Davar le-Yeladim*, March 5, 1973, quoted in Ori Dvir, "From Dan to Eilat," 10.

14. Ibid., 10.

15. Tal, *Pollution in a Promised Land*, 125.

16. Ori Dvir, "The Longest Trail of Them All."

17. Ibid.

18. Berger, *Advanced Backpacking*, 174.

19. Ya'akov Zerubavel, "Yizkor," 29–34.

20. The importance of maintaining symbolic purity along youth hikes is illustrated by Shmaryahu Guttman's account of discovering the Snake Path in 1933. In it, Guttman quotes Captain Charles Warren of the Palestine Exploration Fund, who discovered, walked, and even mapped the Snake Path in 1867, but alters Wilson's account in order to render the nineteenth-century discovery incomplete. In doing so, he portrays the Snake Path as a relic of Masada's past that was lost with the fall of the fortress and the dispersion of the Jews and rediscovered with the return of the Jews and the reoccupation of Masada without any important encounters in between by others. See Warren, "Remarks on a Visit," 147; and Guttman, *With Masada*, 16.

21. Feige, *Settling in the Hearts*, 109–10.

22. Katriel, "Touring the Land," 6–13.

23. Azaria Alon, interview with Israel Broadcasting Service, January 9, 1974, quoted in Kimmerling, *Zionism and Territory*, 208.

24. Sprinzak, *Brother Against Brother*, 205–7. The *Kach* party was later banned from participation in Israeli politics.

25. Dvir, "Longest Trail of Them All."

26. Dvir-Edri, "Abba: Nekudat Chen," 19.

27. Ben-Shitrit, quoted in Lev, "Ori Dvir: His Life's Project."

28. Dvir, quoted in Bar-On, "The National Carrier."

29. Dvir, *Off the Beaten Track in Israel*, 156.

30. Ibid., 36.

31. Dvir, quoted in Bar-On, "The National Carrier."

32. See Dvir, "From Dan to Eilat," 12. This 1990 article is the first time these principles appear in print, but the principles were finalized previously in discussions within the ITC perhaps as early as 1984, when Dvir and Tamir approached the group regarding the creation of the trail.

33. Shachaf, "Way-Markings—From Dan to Eilat," 21.

34. Few records of the meetings of the ITC exist; most appear to have been kept in Dvir's personal files, which were inaccessible at the time this research was being conducted. However, the minutes of an ITC meeting that took place on August 1, 1989, show that fifteen people attended. Some represented organizations, while others attended in their individual capacities as waymarking experts and yedi'at ha-aretz authorities. Notable names include Yossi Feldman, the organizer of the Ein Gedi trail network; Dany Gaspar, who later succeeded Dvir as the head of simun shvilim in the ITC; Tzion Sheetrug, who had remained involved with simun shvilim since his participation in the Ein Gedi initiative and who would become the head of the Survey of Israel in 1993; Uzi Paz of the Nature Reserves Authority; and Ze'ev Meshel, Dvir's childhood friend and a well-known scholar of the history and geography of the Land of Israel. See Public Committee for Trail Marking, "Conclusion of Meeting," 1989.

35. Dvir, "From Dan to Eilat," 11.

36. Shachaf, "Way-Markings—From Dan to Eilat," 21.

37. Dvir, "The Longest Trail of Them All."
38. Dvir, "The Simun Shvilim Project and Shvil Israel," 188.
39. Shachaf, "Way-Markings—From Dan to Eilat," 21.
40. Ibid.
41. Dvir, "The Longest Trail of Them All."
42. Dvir, "The Simun Shvilim Project and Shvil Israel," 188.
43. Dvir, "The Longest Trail of Them All."
44. Ibid.
45. Dvir, "The Simun Shvilim Project and Shvil Israel," 187. The journalist was Israel Radio correspondent Tirtza Erezi.
46. Dvir, "From the Notebook," (1989), 46.
47. Dvir, "From the Notebook," (1990), 17–18.
48. Dvir, "From Dan to Eilat," 11.
49. Ibid., 12.
50. Ibid., 11–12.
51. Chaplin, "There is a Stripe," 37.
52. Dvir, personal correspondence with Rozen and Dekel. Contrary to popular belief, the colors orange and blue were not chosen to symbolize earth and sky or south and north; Dvir simply liked their aesthetic appeal and thought they stood out well in the field.
53. Rozen, *Proposal for Shvil Israel, Center-West*, 1:250,000 (1992).
54. Tal, *Pollution in a Promised Land*, 150.
55. In a 2009 interview, Moti Ben-Shitrit, as head of the ITC, said that Shvil Israel was set to follow the inland route until the announcement of the construction plans for Highway Six and that this was later confirmed by the establishment of the security fence around the West Bank. See Aryeh Dean Cohen, "Voices of the Trail," 16.
56. Dvir, "From the Notebook," (1992), 26–27.
57. One may recall that Hatzeva was originally the site of a spring where a remote IDF camp was located immediately after the establishment of the State of Israel, and where Yossi Feldman received medical attention after the friendly fire attack at Ein Gedi in 1950, as described in chapter 3.
58. Ben-David, "*Tiyul*," 135.
59. Tal, *Pollution in a Promised Land*, 25.
60. Ben-David, "*Tiyul*," 136.
61. Meron Benvenisti, *Conflicts and Contradictions*, 31.
62. Dvir, "From the Notebook," (1989), 46.
63. Edelstein, "Waymarking in the Eilat Region," 180.
64. Survey of Israel and Israel Trails Committee, *Eastern Har ha-Negev Simun Shvilim Map*, 1:50,000 (1987).
65. Dvir claims to have witnessed this on at least one occasion. See Dvir, "How Is a Marked Trail Marked?" 69–70.
66. For more on the SPNI opposition to the Voice of America project, see Tal, *Pollution in a Promised Land*, 139–145.
67. Mal'at, "Simun Shvilim Vandalizes," 38–39.
68. Dvir, "Is It True That Simun Shvilim Vandalizes?," 38–39 [Hebrew].
69. Marcus's large body of work includes, for example, *The Judean Desert: Landscape Survey and Hiking Routes*, and *Disappeared in Bhutan: A Searchers' Journey in the Himalayan Mountains*.

70. Marcus, "It's Also Possible without the Cult of Signs," 42–45.
71. Dvir, "Without the Cult of Signs," 5–6.
72. Ibid., 6.
73. Gilad, "Showing the Way."
74. Israel Trails Committee, "Invitation to Inauguration of the Israel Trail," 1995.
75. Dvir, "To Scratch a Rock and Get a Spritz," 33.
76. Bar-On, "The National Carrier."
77. Dvir, "The Most Marked Country in the World," 97–98.
78. See, for example, Dvir, "Change to the Route of Shvil Israel," 16.
79. Dvir, "The Golan Trail," 14.
80. Fried, "Jerusalem Trail," 12. According to Fried, the express goal of the trail is to enable hikers from Shvil Israel to access Jerusalem, which was not previously possible because the trail passed the city via the mountains to the west.
81. Dvir, "The Simun Shvilim Project and Shvil Israel," 188.
82. Bar-On, "The National Carrier."
83. Dvir, "The Simun Shvilim Project and Shvil Israel," 188.
84. Dvir, "This Cannot Be," 27–40.

6. Postscripts, 2001–2021

1. Weil, "Jerusalem Calling."
2. Israel Trails Committee and Survey of Israel, *Elat Mountains*, 1:50,000.
3. Ibid., 30.
4. Dintaman and Landis, *Hiking the Jesus Trail*, 58–126.
5. Schneider, "A Spiritual Journey and Then Some," F1.
6. Landis, "'Clean Up the World Day.'"
7. Copans, "Following in the Footsteps of Jesus," 32.
8. See Dintaman and Landis, *Hiking the Jesus Trail*, 30: "The Jesus Trail was designed with responsible tourism in mind. Walking is a non-threatening, low-environmental-impact means of travel that stimulates interaction with local people. The trail encourages locals to take an active role in caring for the environment as stakeholders in a project that provides business for the community."
9. Lefkovits, "Walking the 'Jesus Trail,'" 5.
10. Dvir, "On Marked Long-Distance Trails in the Land," 13. Neither Dvir nor anyone else explains the rationale behind using orange blazes to denote regional trails, but the most likely explanation is that waymarking crews already carried orange paint for the purpose of renewing blazes along Shvil Israel. The homemade kits the trail markers carried had only six compartments for paint bottles, and with the four colors that were used for regular trails, plus the white paint that was used in every blaze, plus the orange that was used for the Israel National Trail, no room remained for another color. This is also a possible explanation for the green-blue-white blazes of the Golan Trail; those, too, employed colors that were already in use.
11. Wetzler, "Hiking Through Biblical Backcountry," 9.
12. Lewon, "The Jesus Trail," 70–80.
13. Dvir, "On Marked Long-Distance Trails," 13.
14. Gilad, "Gospel Trail."

15. Ibid.
16. Simon, "Green News Flashes."
17. Dvir, "The Simun Shvilim Project and Shvil Israel," 185.
18. Ibid.
19. Amit, "Who Are the People Who Help Us Stay on the Trail?"
20. Assaf Kidron, quoted in Ezra, "Alternative Route."
21. Ezra, "Alternative Route."
22. Poliak, "Palestinian National Trail," 18.
23. Netanyahu, "Herzliya Conference."
24. This arrangement is described on the reverse side of simun shvilim maps, thereby letting hikers know that purchasing the maps facilitates the continued existence of the trail network.
25. Dvir's assistant at the SPNI, Idit Herzog, writes that Dvir often tried to use his underpowered Peugeot 305 sedan as an off-road vehicle and that people who traveled with him often had to help him dig it out after it became stuck in mud or soft sand. See Herzog, "Stories from the Committee," 32–33.
26. Netanyahu, "Herzliya Conference."
27. Ibid.
28. Poliak, "Palestinian National Trail," 18.
29. For one description of such an encounter, see Feige, *Settling in the Hearts*, 124.
30. Laub, "Following in Mary's Footsteps," M23.
31. See "News and Tips," 4. According to the article, the back jacket of the unfortunately timed guidebook read "Set off with this book and an open mind, and you cannot go far wrong," and it was publicized during the time when IDF forces had besieged the Church of the Nativity in Bethlehem—the trail's southern terminus—in pursuit of Palestinian militants during Operation Defensive Shield. See also Taylor and Howard, *Walks in Palestine*.
32. Copans, "Pilgrims' Progress," W13.
33. Laub, "Following in Mary's Footsteps," M23.
34. "About Us," *Walk Palestine*, https://www.walkpalestine.com/en/aboutus.
35. Leary, Sebenius, and Weiss, "Negotiating the Path of Abraham," 10–049.
36. Ibid., 26.
37. Gilad, "In the Footsteps."
38. Ibid.
39. Masar Ibrahim al-Khalil, "Walking the Path."
40. World Bank, "Implementation, Completion, and Results Report."
41. Rabineau et al., "Masar Ibrahim/Abraham Path."
42. Reinstein, "The Eastern Israel National Trail."
43. Rinat, "The New Initiative."
44. Reinstein, "The Eastern Israel National Trail."
45. Ibid.
46. Kfar Etzion Field School, "Shvil Israel Mizrach."
47. Israeli Ministry of Tourism, "Government Approves Tourism."
48. Hermann, "The Israel National Trail," 1–17.
49. Schnitzspahn, "World's Best Hikes."
50. Times of Israel Staff, "Arab Muslim Twins."
51. Hermann, *Walking the Israel National Trail.*
52. Moshe Gilad, "A New Route for the Israel Trail."

53. Shaffir, "Last Trail on the Way." Shortly after writing this article, Shaffir became a leader in Israel's social protest movement and subsequently became a Member of the Knesset.
54. "Ori Dvir, 1931–2011."
55. Bar-On, "National Carrier."
56. Netanyahu, quoted in "Netanyahu: Ori Dvir Was the Beauty Mark of Israel."
57. Carmi and Heiman, "The Israel Trail: Procession."

BIBLIOGRAPHY

Abbey, Edward. Letter to Avraham Shaked, Oracle, AZ, USA, August 9, 1979. Private collection of Avraham Shaked, Tsur Hadassah, Israel.

Achimeir, Yosef. "All Trails Lead to the Judean Desert." *Ma'ariv*, October 27, 1982, 51 [Hebrew].

Ad, Meshulam. "First Attempts at Waymarking." *Davar*, June 10, 1961.

———. "Group of Armed Arabs Seen on Way to Border after Murder North of Ein Gedi." *Davar*, February 26, 1960, 1 [Hebrew].

———. "Reconstruction Work Finished at Nabatean City of Shivta." *Davar*, September 6, 1959, 8 [Hebrew].

"Adventure on Negev Highway." *Palestine Post*, April 14, 1947, 3.

Aflaq, Michel. "Nationalism Is Love before Everything Else." In *Arab Nationalism*, edited by Sylvia Haim, 242–49. Los Angeles: University of California, 1962.

Aharoni, Yochanan. "Forerunners of the *Limes*: Iron Age Fortresses in the Negev." *Israel Exploration Journal* 17 (1967): 1–17 [Hebrew].

Allon, Yigal. "The West Bank and Gaza within the Framework of a Middle East Peace Settlement." In *Israel in the Middle East*, edited by Itamar Rabinovitch and Jehuda Reinharz, 386–89. 2nd ed. Waltham, MA: Brandeis University Press, 2008.

Almog, Oz. *The Sabra: The Creation of the New Jew*. Los Angeles: University of California Press, 2000.

Almog, Yehuda. "Popular Initiative in the Dead Sea Desert." *Davar*, July 14, 1957, 2 [Hebrew].

———. "To the Hikers on Dead Sea Trails." *Herut*, February 14, 1959, 2 [Hebrew].

———. "To the Hikers on the Trails of the Negev." *Davar*, February 1, 1959, 2 [Hebrew].

Alon, Azaria. *Nature and Man*. Tel Aviv: Am Oved, 2012 [Hebrew].

———. *Trails in the Desert: From the Plains of Jericho to the Gulf of Solomon*. Tel Aviv: Ha-Kibbutz ha-Meuchad, 1969 [Hebrew].

Alon, Hemda. *Hiye Nakhon!* Tel Aviv: 'Am ha-Sefer, 1976 [Hebrew].

———. "The Scouting Movement from Its Beginning Until 1960." In *Youth Movements: 1920–1960*, edited by Mordecai Naor, 19–36. Jerusalem: Yad Ben-Zvi, 1989 [Hebrew].

Alterman, Natan. "Song of the Homeland." In *The Zionist Ideas: Visions for the Jewish Homeland—Then, Now, Tomorrow*, edited by Gil Troy, 29–30. Philadelphia: Jewish Publication Society, 2018.

Amato, Joseph Anthony. *On Foot: A History of Walking*. New York: New York University, 2004.

Amit, Yael. "Who Are the People Who Help Us Stay on the Trail?" *IDF Radio Magazine Online*, March 29, 2013. http://glz.co.il/1363-14754-he/Galatz.aspx [Hebrew].

Amiti, Tz. "Going Up to Ein Gedi: Settling a Desert Oasis." *Al ha-Mishmar*, March 1, 1953, 1 [Hebrew].

Anati, Emanuel. *Har Karkom: The Mountain of God*. New York: Rizzoli, 1986.

"Another Disaster in the Dead Sea Mountains." *Davar*, April 8, 1934, 1 [Hebrew].

Avitzur, Shmuel. "Traffic Signs in the Desert." *Davar*, June 25, 1956, 3 [Hebrew].

Avraham, Yael. "Fighting Ravek: The Tour Guide Who Did Not Give in to Waymarking." *Makor Rishon*, January 29, 2017. https://www.makorrishon.co.il/nrg/online/1/ART2/858/199.html [Hebrew].

Azaryahu, Maoz, and Aharon Kellerman. "Symbolic Places of National History and Revival: A Study in Zionist Mythical Geography." *Transactions of the Institute of British Geographers* 24, no. 1 (1999): 101–23.

Baden-Powell, Robert. *Scouting for Boys: A Handbook for Good Citizenship*. London: Horace Cox, 1908.

Bar-Gal, Yoram, and Bruria Bar-Gal. "'To Tie the Cords between the People and Its Land': Geography Education in Israel." *Israel Studies* 13, no. 1 (2008): 44–67.

Barker, Mary L. "Traditional Landscape and Mass Tourism in the Alps." *Geographical Review* 72, no. 4 (October 1982): 395–415.

Bar-On, Ya'akov. "The National Carrier." *News1*, July 13, 2011. http://www.news1.co.il/Archive/0024-D-61756-00.html [Hebrew].

Bates, G. H. "Track Making by Man and Domestic Animals." *Journal of Animal Ecology* 19, no. 1 (May 1950): 21–28.

Ben-Ari, Nitza. "Hero or Anti-Hero? S. Yizhar's Ambivalent Zionism and the First Sabra Generation." In *Struggle and Survival in Palestine/Israel*, edited by Mark Andrew LeVine and Gershon Shafir, 85–103. Los Angeles: University of California Press, 2012.

Ben-David, Orit. "*Tiyul* (Hike) as an Act of Consecration of Space." In *Grasping Land: Space and Place in Contemporary Israeli Discourse and Experience*, edited by Eyal Ben-Ari and Yoram Bilu, 129–45. Albany, NY: SUNY, 1997.

Ben-Gurion, David. *Israel: A Personal History*. Tel Aviv: American Israel Publishing Company, 1971.

Ben-Shitrit, Moti. "For the Trail Markers." In *Bishvil Ori*, edited by Rina Idan, Carmel Edri-Dvir, Dan Avidan, and Timi Ben-Yosef, 55–62. Israel: Beit Berl and SPNI, 2009 [Hebrew].

Bentwich, Joseph S. *Education in Israel*. Philadelphia: Jewish Publication Society of America, 1965.

Benvenisti, David. "On the Question of Hiking Tragedies." *Davar*, April 18, 1934, 6 [Hebrew].

Benvenisti, Meron. *Conflicts and Contradictions*. New York: Villard, 1986.

———. *Sacred Landscape: The Buried History of the Holy Land Since 1948*. Los Angeles: University of California, 2000.

———. *Son of the Cypresses: Memories, Reflections, and Regrets from a Political Life*. Los Angeles: University of California Press, 2007.

Ben-Yehuda, Nachman. *The Masada Myth: Collective Memory and Mythmaking in Israel*. Madison: University of Wisconsin Press, 1995.

Ben-Ze'ev, Efrat. *Remembering Palestine in 1948: Beyond National Narratives*. Cambridge University Press, 2011.

Ben-Zvi, Yitzhak. *Essays and Reminiscences*. Jerusalem: Yad Yitzhak Ben-Zvi, 1966 [Hebrew].

———. "With the Shomer." In *The Second Aliyah: An Anthology*, 80–82. New York: Zionist Youth Council, 1955.

Berger, Karen. *Advanced Backpacking*. New York: W. W. Norton, 1998.

Biale, David. *Gershom Scholem: Kabbalah and Counter-History*. 2nd ed. Cambridge: Harvard University, 1982.

Biger, Gideon. *The Boundaries of Modern Palestine, 1840–1947*. London: Routledge, 2004.

Birger, Hillel. "Hillel Birger—Father of Topography in the Haganah and the IDF." Interview with Yitzhak Aran, 12 March 1985. File 196.00054, Haganah Archive, Tel Aviv [Hebrew].

———. "History of the Azimuth." *Hed ha-Haganah* 56 [Hebrew].

———. "Marking Ramblers' Paths in the Judean Desert." *Teva va-Aretz* 6 (1959): 237–38 [Hebrew].

———. "The Neglect That Is Likely to Cause Disasters." *Davar*, April 6, 1958, 2 [Hebrew].

———. "On the Margins of the Popular Initiative in the Dead Sea Area." *Davar*, August 18, 1957, 2 [Hebrew].

———. "Rules of Waymarking (Temporary Standardization)." December 15, 1957. Folder D32, Document 46, Yad Tabenkin Archive, Ramat Efal, Israel [Hebrew].

———. "There Is Nothing New under the Sun, and We Are Not the First." *Teva va-Aretz* (April 1993): 35–37 [Hebrew].

Birger, Hillel, and Eliyahu Hershkowitz. *Siyurim u-Masaot*. 1940. Haganah Archive, Tel Aviv. File 34.154 [Hebrew].

Borges, Jorge Luis. "On Exactitude in Science." In *The Aleph and Other Stories*, translated by Andrew Hurley, 181. New York: Penguin, 2000.

Braslavi, Yosef. *Along Unpaved Paths to Knowledge of the Land*. Tel Aviv: Am Oved, 1973 [Hebrew].

"Bus Line to Ein Gedi by Way of Ein Bokek and Masada." *Herut*, April 9, 1959, 4 [Hebrew].

Cansdale, Lena. *Qumran and the Essenes: A Re-Evaluation of the Evidence*. Tübingen: Mohr Siebeck, 1997.

Carmi, Ayelet, and Meirav Heiman. *The Israel Trail: Procession*. In "Last Chance to See," curated by Drorit Gur Arie and Isabel Bourgeois. Petach Tikva Museum of Art, 2018.

Chaplin, Uzi. "There Is a Stripe." In "Tales of the Trails," 37. *Eretz ve-Teva* 75 (September/October 2001): 27–40 [Hebrew].

Chitty, Derwas J. *The Desert a City: An Introduction to the Study of Egyptian and Palestinian Monasticism under the Christian Empire*. Yonkers, NY: St. Vladimir's Seminary Press, 1966.

Coble, Theresa G., Steve W. Selin, and Beth B. Erickson. "Hiking Alone: Understanding Fear, Negotiation Strategies and Leisure Experience." *Journal of Leisure Research* 35, no. 1 (2003): 1–22.

Cohen, Aryeh Dean. "Voices of the Trail," *Jerusalem Post*, October 2, 2009, 16.

Cohen, Pinchas, and David Benvenisti. *Guide to Eretz Israel for the Rambler, Teacher, and Tourist*. Jerusalem: Jerusalem Publishing, 1937 [Hebrew].

Collins-Kreiner, Noga, and Nurit Kliot. "Why Do People Hike? Hiking the Israel National Trail." *Journal of Economic and Social Geography* 108, no. 5 (October 2017): 669–87.

Copans, Laurie. "Following in the Footsteps of Jesus." *Sunday Telegraph* (Australia), June 22, 2008, 32.

———. "Pilgrims' Progress." *The Advertiser* (Adelaide, Australia), December 25, 2004, W13.

Cross, Frank Moore, and Joseph Tadeusz Milik. "Explorations in the Judean Buqe'ah." *Bulletin of the American Schools of Oriental Research* 142 (1956): 5–17.

Dayan, Moshe. *Story of My Life*. New York: William Morrow, 1976.

Degani, Arnon. "They Were Prepared: The Palestinian Arab Scout Movement, 1920–1948." *British Journal of Middle Eastern Studies* 41, no. 2 (2014): 200–18.

DellaPergola, Sergio. "Demographic Trends in Israel and Palestine: Prospects and Policy Implications." *American Jewish Yearbook* 103 (2003): 3–68.

de Saulcy, Louis Felicien. *Narrative of a Journey Round the Dead Sea and in the Bible Lands in 1850 and 1851*, vol. 2. Edited and translated by Count Edward de Warren. London: Richard Bentley, 1854.

Dintaman, Anna, and David Landis. *Hiking the Jesus Trail and Other Biblical Walks in the Galilee*. Harleysville, PA: Village to Village, 2010.

"Don't say in Sdom . . ." *Davar*, April 9, 1959, 6 [Hebrew].

Dorsey, David A. *The Roads and Highways of Ancient Israel*. Baltimore: Johns Hopkins, 1991.

Dror, Yuval. *"National Education" through Mutually Supportive Devices: A Case Study of Zionist Education*. Bern: Peter Lang, 2007.

Dubnow, Vladimir. Letter to Simon Dubnow (Petersburg), Jaffa, October 20, 1882. In *Documents on the History of Hibbat Zion and Settlement in Palestine*, edited by Alter Druyanow and Shulamit Laskov, rev. ed., vol. 1. Tel Aviv, 1982 [Hebrew].

Dvir, Ori. "Change to the Route of *Shvil Israel* in the Negev." *Teva ha-Dvarim* 102 (April 2004): 16 [Hebrew].

———. *Curriculum Vitae*. Collection of Carmel Dvir-Edri, 2011 [Hebrew].

———. "From Dan to Eilat." *Moreshet Derekh* 33 (1990): 10 [Hebrew].

———. "From the Notebook of Ori Dvir." *Moreshet Derekh* 31 (1989): 46 [Hebrew].

———. "From the Notebook of Ori Dvir." *Moreshet Derekh* 32 (1990): 17–18 [Hebrew].

———. "From the Notebook of Ori Dvir." *Moreshet Derekh* 48 (1992): 26–27 [Hebrew].

———. "'The Golan Trail'—Another New Hiking Trail, This Time in the Golan." *Teva ha-Dvarim* 141 (July 2007): 14 [Hebrew].

———. "How Is a Marked Trail Marked?" *Teva va-Aretz* 31, no. 7 (April 1989): 68–71 [Hebrew].

———. "Is It True That *Simun Shvilim* Vandalizes?" In "Debate from Two Sides of the Trail," 39. *Teva va-Aretz* 255 (April 1993): 38–39 [Hebrew].

———. "The Longest Trail of Them All." Originally published in *Panim: Quarterly for Society, Culture, and Education* 51 (2010); available online at *Israel Teachers' Union*. http://www.itu.org.il/?CategoryID=1680&ArticleID=16176 [Hebrew].

———. "The Most Marked Country in the World." *Masa' Acher* 121 (2001): 94–98 [Hebrew].

———. *Nekudat Chen*. Tel Aviv: Modan, 1983 [Hebrew].

———. "Notes on Desert Trails." *Teva va-Aretz* 20 (September–October 1978): 34 [Hebrew].

———. *Off the Beaten Track in Israel: A Guide to Beautiful Places*. Tel Aviv: Modan, 1987.

———. "On Marked Long-Distance Trails in the Land." *Teva ha-Dvarim* 184 (February 2011): 13 [Hebrew].

———. Personal correspondence with Shai Rozen and Shlomo Dekel. Collection of Shai Rozen, February 9, 1991 [Hebrew].

———. "Requiem for a Scout." *Teva va-Aretz* (October 1988): 34 [Hebrew].

———. "*Simun Shvilim* Maps." *Moreshet Derekh* 2 (1982): 49 [Hebrew].

———. "The Simun Shvilim Project and Shvil Israel." In *Landscapes of Eretz Israel: Sefer Azaria Alon*, edited by Gabriel Barkai and Ely Schiller, 182–88. Jerusalem: Ariel, 2000 [Hebrew].

———. "This Cannot Be," in "Tales of the Trails," 32. *Eretz ve-Teva* 75 (September/October 2001): 27–40 [Hebrew].

———. "To Scratch a Rock and Get a Spritz." *Teva va-Aretz* 32, no. 5 (July 1990): 35 [Hebrew].

———. *Where Will We Hike This Week?* Tel Aviv: Levin-Epstein, 1972 [Hebrew].

———. "The Wide World of Travel." Originally published in *Eretz*, December 2010. Available online at *Eretz*. http://www.eretz.com/NEW/articlepage.php?num=12 (May 1, 2013).

———. "Without the Cult of Signs." Letter to the editor, *Teva ha-Aretz* 257 (June 1993): 5–6 [Hebrew].

Dvir-Edri, Carmel. "Abba: Nekudat Chen." In *Bishvil Ori*, edited by Rina Idan, Carmel Dvir-Edri, Dan Avidan, and Timi Ben-Yosef, 14–19. Israel: Beit Berl and SPNI, 2009 [Hebrew].

Edelstein, Mordechai. "Waymarking in the Eilat Region." *Teva va-Aretz* 3, no. 9 (April 1967): 180 [Hebrew].

"Eilat Highway Will Be Inaugurated January 1." *Herut*, January 6, 1958, 4 [Hebrew].

"Eilat Will Absorb 50,000–60,000 Residents in Its Second Decade." *Davar*, August 3, 1958, 3 [Hebrew].

"Ein Gedi Prepares to Bring in 35,000 Hikers During Hanukkah." *Davar*, December 7, 1962, 13 [Hebrew].

Eisenstadt, Shmuel Noah. *Israeli Society*. New York: Basic Books, 1967.

Epstein, Yitzhak. "The Hidden Question." *Ha-Shiloach* 17 (July–December 1907): 193–206 [Hebrew].

Erez, Ya'akov. "*Simun Shvilim* Initiative Begins in the Eilat Mountains." *Ma'ariv*, August 26, 1963, 18 [Hebrew].

———. "Southern Negev Will Be Declared a Nature Reserve and Tourism Site." *Ma'ariv*, December 22, 1965, 22 [Hebrew].

———. "They Went for a Hike in the Jalbina Area—And Got Pulled Out of a Minefield." *Ma'ariv*, July 9, 1968, 8 [Hebrew].

———. "200–500,000 Mines Still Scattered in Golan Heights." *Ma'ariv*, July 16, 1968, 8 [Hebrew].

Eshel, Hanan. "Excavations in the Judean Desert and at Qumran under Israeli Jurisdiction." In *The Dead Sea Scrolls in Scholarly Perspective: A History of Research*, edited by Devorah Dimant, 381–402. Leiden: Brill, 2012.

European Ramblers' Association. "Walking in Europe." February 1, 2021. https://www.era-ewv-ferp.org/walking/walking-in-europe/.

Evenari, Michael, Leslie Shanan, and Naphtali Tadmor. *The Negev: The Challenge of a Desert*, 2nd ed. Cambridge, MA: Harvard, 1982.

Ezra, Chezki. "Alternative Route for the Israel Trail." *Arutz Sheva*, April 10, 2009. http://www.inn.co.il/News/News.aspx/187888 [Hebrew].

Feige, Michael. "Identity, Ritual, and Pilgrimage: The Meetings of the Israeli Exploration Society." In *Divergent Jewish Cultures: Israel and America*, edited by Deborah Dash Moore and S. Ilan Troen, 87–106. New Haven: Yale University Press, 2001.

———. *Settling in the Hearts: Jewish Fundamentalism in the Occupied Territories*. Detroit: Wayne State University Press, 2009.

Feldman, Yossi. "The First Map." In "Tales of the Trails," 34. *Eretz ve-Teva* 75 (September/October 2001): 27–40 [Hebrew].

———. "Out of the South the Blessing Shall Come Forth." *Teva va-Aretz* 26, no. 3 (March/April 1984): 19–21 [Hebrew].

———. "Streams in the Desert." *Eretz ve-Teva* 130 (November/December 2010): 66–69 [Hebrew].

"Five Hikers in Dead Sea Desert Saved from Death." *Davar*, June 26, 1935, 1 [Hebrew].

Fried, Menachem. "Jerusalem Trail." *Teva ha-Dvarim* 127 (April 2006): 12 [Hebrew].

Gartal, Gil. "A Cow-Path Between Mountains." In *Palmach: Sheaves and Sword*, edited by Yehiam Weitz, 289–318. Jerusalem: Ministry of Defense, 2000 [Hebrew].

Gavish, Dov. "Foreign Maps: Offshoots of the 1:100,000 Topographic Map of Israel." *Imago Mundi* 48 (1996): 174–84.

Gavrieli, Ittai, and Aharon Oren. "The Dead Sea as a Dying Lake." In *Dying and Dead Seas: Climatic Versus Anthropic Causes*, edited by Jacques C. J. Nihoul, Peter O. Zavialov, and Philip P. Micklin, 287–306. Norwell, MA: Kluwer Academic Publishers, 2003.

Gilad, Moshe. "In the Footsteps and Spirit of Abraham." *Ha'aretz Online*, November 16, 2011. http://www.haaretz.com/culture/arts-leisure/in-the-footsteps-and-spirit-of-abraham-1.395851.

———. "A New Route for the Israel Trail in the Judean Desert." *Ha'aretz Online*, September 11, 2019. https://www.haaretz.co.il/travel/travel-in-israel/1.7832076 [Hebrew].

———. "Parting of Ways: What You Don't See along the Gospel Trail." *Haaretz Online*, December 4, 2011. http://www.haaretz.co.il/gallery/trip/1.1582255 [Hebrew].

———. "Showing the Way." *Haaretz Online*, April 12, 2007. http://www.haaretz.com/travel-in-israel/showing-the-way-1.217946.

Glueck, Nelson. *Rivers in the Desert: A History of the Negev*. New York: Norton, 1968.

Golan, Eitan. "The *Bnei ha-Moshavim* Ascent." In "Tales of the Trails," 30. *Eretz ve-Teva* 75 (September/October 2001): 27–40 [Hebrew].

"Google Earth." *Wikipedia*. Last modified July 26, 2013. https://en.wikipedia.org/wiki/Google_Earth.

Gordon, A. D. "Letter III." In *A. D. Gordon: Selected Essays*, translated by Frances Burnce, 128–39. Boston: Independent Press, 1938.

———. "Logic for the Future." In *The Zionist Idea: A Historical Analysis and Reader*, edited by Arthur Hertzberg, 371–72. Philadelphia: Jewish Publication Society, 1997.

———. "Our Tasks Ahead." In *The Zionist Idea*, edited by Arthur Hertzberg, 379–83. Philadelphia: Jewish Publication Society, 1997.

———. "People and Labor." In *The Zionist Idea*, edited by Arthur Hertzberg, 372–75. Philadelphia: Jewish Publication Society, 1997.

———. "Some Observations." In *The Zionist Idea*, edited by Arthur Hertzberg, 375–79. Philadelphia: Jewish Publication Society, 1997.

Goren, Haim. *Dead Sea Level: Science, Exploration and Imperial Interests in the Near East*. London: I. B. Tauris, 2011.

Government of Israel. "Amendments to Nature Reserves and National Parks Law (Order and Conduct)—1979." *Tourism Law*. http://www.tourism-law.co.il/tevareg.htm (accessed May 3, 2022) [Hebrew].

———. "Official Government Farewell Ceremony for the Late Minister Rehavam Ze'evi," October 18, 2021. *Government of Israel*. http://www.knesset.gov.il/vip/zeevi/heb/ceremony.htm [Hebrew].

Greenbaum, Roska, and Oded Yisraeli. "Grenades at Ein Gedi." *Eretz ve-Teva* 98 (2005): 54–58 [Hebrew].

Gurevitch, Zali, and Gideon Aran. *Al ha-Makom* ["On the Place."] *Alpaim* 4 (1991): 9–44 [Hebrew].

Guttman, Shmaryahu. *With Masada: Accounts of Exploration and Research*. Tel Aviv: Am Oved, 1963 [Hebrew].

Ha'am, Ahad. "Truth from Eretz Israel." In *Collected Writings of Ahad Ha'am*, 23–30. Tel Aviv, 1947 [Hebrew].

Halpern, Ben, and Jehuda Reinharz. *Zionism and the Creation of a New Society*. Waltham, MA: Brandeis University Press, 2000.

Ha-Machanot Ha-Olim. *Bi-vritech*. Tel Aviv, 1938.

Ha-Parchi, Ishtori. *Kaftor va-Ferach*. Jerusalem: Luncz, 1897 [Hebrew].

Harel, Menashe. "Israelite and Roman Roads in the Judean Desert." *Israel Exploration Journal* 17 (1967): 18–26.

Harris, James F. *A Study in the Theory and Practice of German Liberalism: Eduard Lasker, 1829–1884*. Lanham, MD: University Press of America, 1984.

Har-Zion, Meir. *Chapters of a Diary*. Tel Aviv: Levin-Epstein, 1969 [Hebrew].

Hermann, Tamar. "The Israel National Trail as a Place of Refuge." *Strategic Assessment*, special publication (October 2020): 1–17.

———. *Walking the Israel National Trail*. Haifa: Pardes, 2019 [Hebrew].

Herzog, Idit. "Stories from the Committee." In "Tales of the Trails," 32–33. *Eretz ve-Teva* 75 (September/October 2001): 27–40 [Hebrew].

"Hikers Arrested on Eretz-Israeli Territory by Syrian Police." *Davar*, February 7, 1947, 10 [Hebrew].

Horovitz, Chilik. "Survey of Israel Map Series from 1948 to the Present." *Survey of Israel*. http://www.gis.mapi.gov.il/mapi/gis/moreset_1_new/moreset_1_new/ofer/mis_moreset/makor_mis/sid_map.htm (January 9, 2015). Available via *Internet Archive*, https://web.archive.org/web/20150109013724/http://www.gis.mapi.gov.il:80/mapi/gis/moreset_1_new/moreset_1_new/ofer/mis_moreset/makor_mis/sid_map.htm (accessed May 3, 2022) [Hebrew].

"Hostel Being Built at Feet of Masada." *Davar*, January 10, 1958, 2 [Hebrew].

"Israeli Force Descends upon Ein Gedi, on Dead Sea Shore." *Al ha-Mishmar*, March 15, 1949, 1 [Hebrew].

"Israeli-Jordanian Border Relations." *Middle East Record* 1 (1960), edited by Yitzhak Oron, 194–95.

Israeli Ministry of Tourism. "Government Approves Tourism Minister Yariv Levin's Proposal to Build a Trans-Israel Trail." *Ministry of Tourism*, November 26, 2017, https://www.gov.il/he/departments/news/tour_path_26112017 [Hebrew].

Israel Trails Committee. "Invitation to Inauguration of the Israel Trail." April 19, 1995. Collection of Dany Gaspar [Hebrew].

Israel Trails Committee and Survey of Israel. *Elat Mountains*, edited by Ori Devir [Dvir], 1:50,000, 1995.

Jarvis, Robin. *Romantic Walking and Pedestrian Travel*. New York: St. Martin's Press, 1997.

"Jewish Hiker Killed by Arabs." *Palestine Post*, May 9, 1947.

"Jewish Hikers Disarm Robbers." *Palestine Post*, January 10, 1947, 3.

Josephus, Flavius. *Josephus: The Essential Works: A Condensation of Jewish Antiquities and the Jewish War*. Grand Rapids, MI: Kregel Academic, 1994.

Katriel, Tamar. "Touring the Land: Trips and Hiking as Secular Pilgrimages in Israeli Culture." *Jewish Folklore and Ethnology Review* 17, no. 1–2 (1995): 6–13.

Kfar Etzion Field School. "Shvil Israel Mizrach: Proposed Plan: Goals and Objectives," 2016. D7%96%D7%A8%D7%97_%D7%9C%D7%9E%D7%A9%D7%A8%D7%93_%D7%94%D7%AA%D7%99%D7%99%D7%A8%D7%95%D7%AA_%D7%92%D7%A8%D7%A1%D7%94_5.pdf [Hebrew].

Kimmerling, Baruch. *Zionism and Territory: The Socio-territorial Dimensions of Zionist Politics*. Los Angeles: University of California, 1983.

Landis, David. "'Clean Up the World Day' on the Jesus Trail." *Jesus Trail Updates*, November 22, 2009. http://jesustrail.com/updates/clean-up-the-world-day-on-the-jesus-trail.

Laqueur, Walter. *Young Germany: A History of the German Youth Movement*. New Brunswick, NJ: Transaction Press, 1984.

"Large Fire in Golan Heights Minefields." *Davar*, October 12, 1971, 2 [Hebrew].

Laub, Karin. "Following in Mary's Footsteps." *The Advertiser* (Melbourne, Australia), December 25, 1999, M23.

Leary, Kimberlyn, James K. Sebenius, and Joshua Weiss. "Negotiating the Path of Abraham." Harvard Business School Working Paper 10-049, draft v. 3.9, December 21, 2009.

Lefkovits, Etgar. "Walking the 'Jesus Trail.'" *Jerusalem Post*, May 14, 2009, 5.

Lekan, Thomas M. *Imagining the Nation in Nature: Landscape Preservation and German Identity, 1885–1945*. Cambridge, MA: Harvard University Press, 2009.

"Less Arrogance and More Caution!" *Davar*, July 10, 1935, 8 [Hebrew].

Lev, Liat. "Ori Dvir: His Life's Project." *Walla*, July 3, 2011. http://news.walla.co.il/?w=/2501/1837284 [Hebrew].

Lewon, Dennis. "The Jesus Trail." *Backpacker*, March 2012, 70–80.

Liebman, Charles S., and Eliezer Don-Yehiya. *Civil Religion in Israel: Traditional Judaism and Political Culture in the Jewish State*. Los Angeles: University of California, 1983.

Luncz, Abraham Moses. *Guide to Eretz Israel and Syria*. Jerusalem: Luncz, 1890 [Hebrew].

Mal'at, Noa. "*Simun Shvilim* Vandalizes." In "Debate from Two Sides of the Trail," 38. *Teva va-Aretz* 255 (April 1993): 38–39 [Hebrew].

"Many Hikers in Eilat; Lack of Lodging Spaces." *Davar*, April 7, 1960, 2 [Hebrew].

Marcus, Menachem. *Disappeared in Bhutan: A Searchers' Journey in the Himalayan Mountains*. Jerusalem: Keter, 1997 [Hebrew].

———. "It's Also Possible without the Cult of Signs." *Teva va-Aretz* 254 (March 1993): 42–45 [Hebrew].

———. *The Judean Desert: Landscape Survey and Hiking Routes*. Jerusalem: Nature Reserves Authority, 1984 [Hebrew].

Masa'ot *of Company Gimel*. Palmach Museum Photo Archive, Tel Aviv [Hebrew].

Masterman, E. W. G. "'Ain el-Feshkhah, El-Hajar el-Asbah, and Khurbet Kumran." *Palestine Exploration Fund Quarterly Statement* 34 (1902): 160–65.

———. "Observation of the Dead Sea Levels." *Palestine Exploration Fund Quarterly Statement* 27 (1902): 155–60.

Mazar, Benjamin, Trude Krakauer Dothan, and Immanuel Dunayevsky. *En-Gedi: The First and Second Seasons of Excavations, 1961–1962*. Jerusalem: Department of Antiquities, Ministry of Education and Culture, 1966.

Miller, Judith. "Herzliya Diary 2010." *Tablet*, February 4, 2010. https://www.tabletmag.com/sections/israel-middle-east/articles/herzliya-diary.

Morris, Yaakov. *Masters of the Desert: 6000 Years in the Negev*. New York: G. P. Putnam's Sons, 1961.

"Nabatean Farm Reconstructed at Shivta." *Davar*, June 2, 1959, 11 [Hebrew].

Naor, Mordechai. "Rambling in the Land: The Place of *Tiyulim* in the Framework of Eretz-Israeli Youth Movements." In *Youth Movements: 1920–1960*, edited by Mordechai Naor, 246–56. Jerusalem: Yad Ben-Zvi, 1989 [Hebrew].

Nardi, Noah. *Education in Palestine, 1920–1945*. Washington, DC: Zionist Organization of America, 1945.

Netanyahu, Benjamin. "Address by PM Netanyahu at the Herzliya Conference," *Israeli Ministry of Foreign Affairs*, February 3, 2010. http://mfa.gov.il/MFA/PressRoom/2010/Pages/PM_Netanyahu_Herzliya_Conference_3-Feb-2010.aspx.

"Netanyahu: Ori Dvir Was the Beauty Mark of Israel." *Arutz Sheva*, July 3, 2011. http://www.inn.co.il/News/Flash.aspx/331576 [Hebrew].

Neumann, Boaz. *Land and Desire in Early Zionism*. Waltham, MA: Brandeis University Press, 2011.

"News and Tips: Palestine Guide Leads Travellers [*sic*] into Danger." *The Observer*, April 28, 2002, 4.

Noy, Chaim, and Erik Cohen, "Introduction: Backpacking as a Rite of Passage in Israel." In *Israeli Backpackers: From Tourism to Rite of Passage*, edited by Chaim Noy and Erik Cohen, 1–40. Albany, NY: SUNY Press, 2005.

"On the Unsupervised Hike in the Judean Desert." *Davar*, July 1, 1935, 8 [Hebrew].

"Ori Dvir, 1931–2011." *Society for the Protection of Nature in Israel*, July 3, 2011. http://www.teva.org.il/?CategoryID=279&ArticleID=6488 [Hebrew].

"Path-Marking Initiative Begins on Hiking Paths in the Judean Desert." *Ma'ariv*, April 15, 1959, 4 [Hebrew].

"Pedagogical Poem of Ein Gedi." *Davar*, August 30, 1963, 20 [Hebrew].

Peres, Shimon. *Battling for Peace: A Memoir*. New York: Random House, 1995.

Poliak, Shira. "Palestinian National Trail to Open Tomorrow." *Jerusalem Post*, July 22, 2011, 18.

Public Committee for Trail Marking. "Conclusion of Meeting." Collection of Dany Gaspar, August 1, 1989 [Hebrew].

"Quiet Along Lebanese and Syrian Borders; Thousands of Hikers in Golan Heights Yesterday." *Ma'ariv*, March 5, 1972, 3 [Hebrew].

Rabineau, Shay, Julian Bender, Matt Harms, and David Landis. "Masar Ibrahim/ Abraham Path Waymarking Standards." May 2015, personal collection of author, Vestal, NY.

Reichman, Shalom. "The Evolution of Land Transportation in Palestine." *Jerusalem Studies in Geography* 2 (1971): 55–90.

Reinstein, Ziv. "The Eastern Israel National Trail: The Alternative That Will Go through the Territories." *Walla*, March 23, 2017. https://travel.walla.co.il/item/3051127 [Hebrew].

Reuveni, Aharon. "The Trip Around the Dead Sea in the Summer of 1923," edited by Shimon Rubenstein. Jerusalem, 2007 [Hebrew].

Rinat, Tzafrir. "'The Eastern Israel National Trail': The New Initiative to Bring Hikers across the Green Line." *Haaretz*, October 6, 2016. https://www.haaretz.co.il /magazine/tozeret/.premium-1.3088583 [Hebrew].

Rivlit, Ezra. "Economic Cooperative Established for Development of Dead Sea Shore." *Al ha-Mishmar*, August 17, 1954, 3 [Hebrew].

Robinson, Edward. *Biblical Researches in Palestine, Mount Sinai and Arabia Petraea*, vol. 2. London: John Murray, 1841.

Robinson, Jeffrey C. *The Walk: Notes on a Romantic Image*. Norman, OK: University of Oklahoma, 1989.

Roman, Yadin. "Davar Metzada." *Eretz ve-Teva* 130 (November–December 2010): 62–65 [Hebrew].

———. "The Lure of the Trail." Originally published in *Eretz* 96 (November–December 2004); available online at *Ha-Tzanchanim*, http://202.org.il/Pages/moreshet/petra /roman.php (May 1, 2013).

———. "The Price of Fame." In *Eretz: The Book, 1985–2005*, edited by Yadin Roman, 19–24. Jerusalem: Eretz Group, 2005.

Rozen, Shai. *The Judean Desert: From an Unknown Land to the* Simun Shvilim *Map*. File 35231, Yad Tabenkin Archive, Ramat Ef'al, Israel [Hebrew].

———. *Proposal for Shvil Israel, Center-West*. 1:250,000. Collection of Shai Rozen, 1992 [Hebrew].

Rubin, Rehav. *Portraying the Land: Hebrew Maps of the Land of Israel from Rashi to the Early 20th Century*. Berlin: De Gruyter, 2018.

Sachar, Howard. *A History of Israel: From the Rise of Zionism to Our Time*. New York: Knopf, 1976.

Sayar, M. "'The Crazy People' Have Marked Trails in the Desert." *Ma'ariv*, December 31, 1961, 6 [Hebrew].

Schneider, Howard. "A Spiritual Journey and Then Some." *Washington Post*, June 7, 2009, F1.

Schnitzspahn, Doug. "World's Best Hikes: Epic Trails." *National Geographic*, July 31, 2012. https://www.nationalgeographic.com/adventure/article/worlds-best-grail-trails.

Scholem, Gershom. Gershom Scholem to Franz Rosenzweig, Jerusalem, 1926. In William Cutter, "Ghostly Hebrew, Ghastly Speech: Scholem to Rosenzweig, 1926." *Prooftexts* 10 (1990): 413–33.

Scouting Routes and Journeys of Plugah Gimel, Southern Album. Palmach Museum Photo Archive, Tel Aviv. [Hebrew].

"Second Country-Wide Contest in *Yedi'at ha-Aretz*." *Davar*, May 16, 1963, 6 [Hebrew].

Shachaf, Tal. "Way-Markings—From Dan to Eilat." *Ma'ariv*, March 30, 1987, 21 [Hebrew].

Shaffir, Stav. "The Last Trail on the Way: Farewell to Ori Dvir." *XNet (Yediot Achronot)*, July 4, 2011. http://www.xnet.co.il/articles/0,7340,L-3084711,00.html [Hebrew].

Shafran, Nesia. *The Red Rock: The Forbidden Treks to Petra*." Jerusalem: Yad Yitzhak Ben-Zvi, 2013 [Hebrew].

Shaked, Avraham. "Where Are the Trails Going." In "Tales of the Trails," 38. *Eretz ve-Teva* 75 (September/October 2001): 27–40.

Shalem, Natan. "The Journal of Natan Shalem: The University Expedition to Ein Gedi, 1926." *Ariel* 147–48 (2001): 147–54 [Hebrew].

Shapira, Anita. *Land and Power: The Zionist Resort to Force, 1881–1948*. Oxford University Press, 1992.

Sheetrug, Tzion. "Hillel Birger: Father of Topography in Eretz Israel—Departed." *Mediton* 15 (Sivan 1988), 22 [Hebrew].

———. Interview with Carmela Shantzer, November 5, 2002. *Survey of Israel*. http://www.gis.mapi.gov.il/mapi/gis/moreset_1_new/moreset_1_new/ofer/mis_moreset/makor_mis/zion_shitrug.htm (December 30, 2014). Available via *Internet Archive*, https://web.archive.org/web/20141230095946/http://www.gis.mapi.gov.il/mapi/gis/moreset_1_new/moreset_1_new/ofer/mis_moreset/makor_mis/zion_shitrug.htm (accessed May 3, 2022) [Hebrew].

Shemer, Naomi. "Hopa Hey." Recorded 1961. Track 11 on *Asif*, disc 1. *Musica Israelit*, 2004, compact disc [Hebrew].

Simon, Roi. "Green News Flashes." *Eretz Binyamin* 350 (March 2009); available online at http://www.binyamin.org.il/?CategoryID=614&ArticleID=1487 (May 1, 2013) [Hebrew].

"*Simun Shvilim* in the Golan." *Teva va-Aretz* 4 (1973): 204 [Hebrew].

Singer, Milton. "Pronouns, Persons and the Semiotic Self." In *Semiotics, Self, and Society*, edited by Benjamin Lee and Greg Urban, 229–96. Berlin: Walter de Gruyter, 1989.

"6000 Ascend to Masada During Hanukkah." *Davar*, December 14, 1961, 4 [Hebrew].

Smilansky, Yizhar. "A Land without Wildflowers Will Be a Hotel, Not a Homeland." In *Speaking of Earth: Environmental Speeches That Moved the World*, edited and translated by Alon Tal, 20–24. New Brunswick, NJ: Rutgers University Press, 2006.

Solnit, Rebecca. *Wanderlust: A History of Walking*. New York: Penguin, 2009.

SPNI Golan/Hermon Field School. *Golan and Hermon*. 1:100,000. Tel Aviv: Survey of Israel, 1971 [Hebrew].

"SPNI News." *Teva va-Aretz* (November/December 1976): 140–41 [Hebrew].

Sprinzak, Ehud. *Brother against Brother: Violence and Extremism in Israeli Politics from the Altalena to the Rabin Assassination*. New York: Simon and Schuster, 1999.

Stager, Lawrence E. "Farming in the Judean Desert during the Iron Age." *Bulletin of the American Schools of Oriental Research* 221 (February 1976): 145–58.

"Student and Teacher Disappear on Hike Near Sdom." *Ma'ariv*, April 8, 1959, 1 [Hebrew].

Survey of Israel. *Map of Hikes in the Eilat Region*. 1:50,000. Tel Aviv: Survey of Israel, 1978 [Hebrew].

———. *Map of Waymarking in the Judean Desert*. 1:100,000. Tel Aviv: Survey of Israel, March 1966 [Hebrew].

———. *Waymarking Map of the Eilat Region.* 1:100,000. Tel Aviv: Survey of Israel, March 1966 [Hebrew].

Survey of Israel and Israel Trails Committee. *Eastern Har ha-Negev* Simun Shvilim *Map*, edited by Ori Dvir. 1:50,000. Tel Aviv: Survey of Israel, 1987 [Hebrew].

Survey of Palestine. *Ras Fashkha 19–12.* 1:20,000. Jerusalem: Survey of Palestine, 1942.

———. *Sheet 10: Jerusalem.* 1:100,000. 1st ed. Jerusalem: Survey of Palestine, 1942.

———. *Sheet 10: Jerusalem.* 1:100,000. 2nd ed. Jerusalem: Survey of Palestine, December 1944.

———. *Sheet 13: Dead Sea.* 1:100,000. 2nd ed. Jerusalem: Survey of Palestine, June 1945.

———. *Sheet 16: Jebel Usdum.* 1:100,000. 2nd ed. Jerusalem: Survey of Palestine, June 1945.

"Syrian Minefields Discovered in Golan Heights." *Ma'ariv*, July 19, 1967, 8 [Hebrew].

Tahon, Rafi. *We Circled the Dead Sea on Foot.* Jerusalem: Ariel, 2001 [Hebrew].

Tal, Alon. Introduction to Yizhar Smilansky, "A Land without Wildflowers Will Be a Hotel, Not a Homeland." In *Speaking of Earth: Environmental Speeches That Moved the World*, edited by Alon Tal, 14–20. New Brunswick, NJ: Rutgers University Press, 2006.

———. *Pollution in a Promised Land: An Environmental History of Israel.* Los Angeles, University of California, 2002.

Talmi, Menachem. "Negev Scouts Rescue Lost Hikers in the Desert." *Ma'ariv*, April 1, 1958, 7 [Hebrew].

———. "They Flow to the Bottom of the World." *Ma'ariv*, October 26, 1962, 8 [Hebrew].

Taylor, Di, and Tony Howard. *Walks in Palestine Including the Nativity Trail.* Cumbria, UK: Cicerone, 2001.

Tchernichovsky, Shaul. *Shirim.* Tel Aviv: Schocken, 1950 [Hebrew].

"Television Listings." *Davar*, March 1, 1981, 12 [Hebrew].

Times of Israel Staff. "Arab Muslim Twins Go from Violent Delinquents to Proud Golani Soldiers." *Times of Israel*, May 9, 2020. https://www.timesofisrael.com/arab-muslim-twins-from-east-jerusalem-go-from-delinquents-to-israeli-soldiers/.

Towner, John. "The Grand Tour: A Key Phase in the History of Tourism." *Annals of Tourism Research* XII (1995): 297–33.

Tristram, Henry Baker. *The Land of Israel: A Journal of Travels in Palestine*, 2nd ed. London: Society for Promoting Christian Knowledge, 1866.

Troen, S. Ilan. *Imagining Zion: Dreams, Designs, and Realities in a Century of Jewish Settlement.* New Haven: Yale University Press, 2003.

Tuan, Yi-Fu. "Sacred Space: Explorations of an Idea." In *Dimensions of Human Geography: Essays on Some Familiar and Neglected Themes*, edited by Karl W. Butzer, 84–99. Chicago: University of Chicago, 1978.

Turner, Victor. *The Forest of Symbols: Aspects of Ndembu Ritual.* Ithaca, NY: Cornell University Press, 1967.

"Two New Military Commanders." *Palestine Post*, December 24, 1942, 3.

United Nations. "Resolution 242." In *Israel in the Middle East: Documents and Readings on Society, Politics, and Foreign Relations, Pre-1948 to the Present*, edited by Itamar Rabinovitch and Jehuda Reinharz, 242–43. Waltham, MA: Brandeis University Press, 2008.

United States Central Intelligence Agency. *The World Factbook.* https://www.cia.gov/the-world-factbook/ (accessed May 3, 2022).

Vilnay, Zev. *Guide to Eretz Israel*, 1st ed. Jerusalem: Steimatzky, 1935 [Hebrew].

———. "You Shall Love Your Neighbor As Yourself." In *Sefer Ze'ev Vilnai: Essays on the History, Archaeology, and Lore of the Holy Land, Presented to Ze'ev Vilnai*, edited by Eli Schiller. Jerusalem: Ariel, 1984 [Hebrew].

von Uexküll, Jakob. *Theoretical Biology*. New York: Harcourt and Brace, 1926.

Warren, Charles. "Remarks on a Visit to 'Ain Jidy and the Southern Shores of the Dead Sea in Mid-Summer 1867." *Palestine Exploration Fund Quarterly Statement* 1 (January–March 1869): 143–50.

Weil, Judy. "Jerusalem Calling." *Ynet*, July 27, 2005. http://www.ynetnews.com/articles/0,7340,L-3118810,00.html.

Weintraub, D., M. Lissak, and Y. Azmon. *Moshava, Kibbutz, and Moshav: Patterns of Jewish Rural Settlement and Development in Palestine*. Ithaca, NY: Cornell University Press, 1968.

Weitz, Yehiam. "Introduction." In *Palmach: Sheaves and Sword*, edited by Yehiam Weitz, 9–34. Jerusalem: Ministry of Defense, 2000 [Hebrew].

Wetzler, Brad. "Hiking Through Biblical Backcountry." *New York Times*, June 24, 2012, 9.

Wilkomitz, Simcha Chaim. "A Lecture on the Schools in Our Brothers' Villages in Eretz Israel." In *The Teacher—S. H. Wilkomitz*, edited by L. Y. Riklis. Jerusalem: Teachers' Union of Israel, 1959 [Hebrew].

Williams, John Alexander. *Turning to Nature in Germany: Hiking, Nudism, and Conservation, 1900–1940*. Palo Alto: Stanford University Press, 2007.

Wilson, Charles. "The Dead Sea." *Palestine Exploration Fund Quarterly Statement* (1900): 365–68.

"Woman and Youth from Kibbutz Geva Injured by Mine in Golan Heights." *Ma'ariv*, April 28, 1968, 28 [Hebrew].

World Bank. "Implementation Completion and Results Report on a Small Grant in the Amount of US $3.32 Million to the Abraham Path Initiative (API) for the Abraham Path/Masar Ibrahim: Economic Development across Fragile Communities Project." November 7, 2019. https://documents1.worldbank.org/curated/en/315051586542526533/pdf/West-Bank-and-Gaza-Masar-Ibrahim-Abraham-Path-Economic-Development-Across-Fragile-Communities-Project.pdf.

Yadin, Yigael. *Bar-Kochba: The Rediscovery of the Ancient Hero of the Second Jewish Revolt Against Rome*. New York: Random House, 1971.

"*Yedi'at ha-Aretz* Contest for Students Concludes." *Davar*, July 4, 1962, 3 [Hebrew].

Ze'evi, Rehavam. "The Notebooks of the Reconnaissance Scouts." In "Tales of the Trails," *Eretz* 78 (September/October 2001): 246.

Zerubavel (Vitkin), Ya'akov. "Yizkor," *Ha-Achdut* 11–12 (1912): 29–34 [Hebrew].

Zerubavel, Yael. *Desert in the Promised Land*. Palo Alto: Stanford University Press, 2019.

———. *Recovered Roots: Collective Memory and the Making of Israeli National Tradition*. Chicago: University of Chicago Press, 1995.

INDEX

SHAY RABINEAU is Assistant Professor of Israel Studies and Associate Director of the Center for Israel Studies at Binghamton University. His research is at the intersection of Middle East history, geography, politics, and environment.